What Else Should I Read?

What Else Should I Read?

Guiding Kids to Good Books,
Volume 1

MATT BERMAN

LIBRARIES UNLIMITED, INC.
Englewood, Colorado
1995

*To the person who has made everything possible
for me; Susan Larson, book editor for the New Orleans*
Times Picayune, *who has made that paper a beacon and
a home for lovers of children's literature.*

LIBRARIES UNLIMITED, INC.
P.O. Box 6633
Englewood, CO 80155-6633
1-800-237-6124

Library of Congress Cataloging-in-Publication Data

Berman, Matt.
    What else should I read? : guiding kids to good books,
volume 1 / Matt Berman.
      xxi, 211 p. 22x28 cm.
      Includes index.
      ISBN 1-56308-241-1 (softbound)
      1. Children--United States--Books and reading. 2. Children's
stories, English--Bibliography.
Z1037.B5435   1995
[PR830.C513]
028.1'62--dc20   95-16213
                                                  CIP

Contents

Acknowledgments

Many thanks are due to

Meb Norton, Ginger Gomes, and Maryann Cook, the extraordinary lower school librarians at Metairie Park Country Day School, who have helped with constant advice, encouragement, and occasional editing and by amassing one of the best collections of children's literature anywhere;

the National Endowment for the Humanities, which funded a year of study in children's literature as part of their Teacher/Scholar Program, one of their many exemplary programs for school teachers;

Coleen Salley, professor of children's literature at the University of New Orleans, who introduced me to dozens of authors of great children's books;

the organizers of the Children's Book Festival at the University of Southern Mississippi, the best book conference I know of, where for the past 15 years I have soaked in the thoughts of the best authors and illustrators.

And to my parents, Rick and Toni, who taught me to love to read, and who didn't mind that I never outgrew children's books.

How to Use This Book

Every librarian and teacher has faced the situation in which a child, possibly a reluctant reader (though often not), has read a book, liked it, and asked, "What should I read next? I want another book just like that one." This resource was created as a displayable reference for just such situations. It contains topic webs on 30 great works of children's literature for grades 3 and up. For each topic on each web there is a reproducible bookmark printed with the books on that topic, along with brief descriptions, mostly from the Library of Congress.

Each of the 30 chapters in this book contains the reproducible elements of a book web bulletin board display. The first page of each chapter is the model web. The next page is the reproducible book web center, with the name of the webbed book on it. After that is one or two pages of topics, with the recommended book titles under each heading. Finally, each chapter has the bookmarks themselves, each with a corresponding topic title and the descriptions of recommended books under each topic. To make a bulletin board display, photocopy the elements of a web, enlarging them if you choose; cut them out, and post them on the board, using the model web in the book as a guide. Staple or glue pockets (library card pockets or sealed envelopes cut in half) to the board next to the bookmark topics. Use thread or magic markers to make the lines of the web. Then photocopy the bookmarks for that web, cut them apart, and place each set in the pocket for the corresponding topic.

When children have read and enjoyed one of the webbed books and are looking for something else to read, they can go to the web, think about what aspect of the book particularly appealed to them, pull a copy of the bookmark for that topic out of the pocket, and then go looking for whichever of the books listed sounds interesting. When a pocket runs out of bookmarks, more can be run off (reproduction permission is granted for use in one library or classroom). Many webs can be displayed at once, or they can be rotated regularly. Having children add suggestions to the webs or make their own webs about their own favorite books is a great reading-related activity.

A few notes about the topic lists: Choosing to present this reference work in a format that can be displayed for student use introduced a size constraint. Therefore, there are other topics that you might think of for some of the books and other books that could have been included under each topic. Instead of a limitation, this situation can be an opportunity for students and teachers to collaborate on adding to the webs on their own boards.

Also, because of space, books were not listed under all the topics they could have been within a web. Therefore, it is a good idea to encourage students to look at all of the lists for a given web, not just one or two. Nonfiction books were not included because, while searching through the card catalog is a dismal method for looking up topics in fiction, card catalogs are quite thorough for nonfiction. For the same reason, lists of sequels and other books by the same author were only included when there was space, but for any book it is always a good idea to encourage students to look under the author in the card catalog.

Whenever possible, the books are listed in order from those most like the webbed book to those least like it. This ranking is highly subjective and often a difficult call. Because this book was intended primarily for use by librarians and classrooms, most—but not all—of the books listed were in print at the time of writing. Some of them come in and out of print on publishers' backlists, and all are books that can be found on the shelves of many libraries.

Although only 30 books got their own webs, hundreds were included in the lists. All of the books on a list are, of course, related by their topic, so even if a book doesn't have its own web, similar books can be found in the topic lists in which it appears.

Introduction—The Whole Language Reading Program: A Classroom/Library Collaboration

Literature for children is the response of the creative spirit up and down the ages, a revelation which shows at some point the triumph of the human spirit.

—Anne Carroll Moore

PART 1:
THE WHOLE READING PROGRAM

Philosophy and Goals

The philosophy of the whole language reading program is simple. The primary way that children above second grade become better readers is by reading, not practicing for reading, nor getting ready to read, nor playing reading games, nor doing workbook pages on "reading skills." Reading great literature expands the mind, feeds the imagination, and generates excitement. Intelligent discussion of points of interpretation in a story creates more excitement—intellectual excitement. Reading great literature improves reading skills, writing skills, thinking skills, reasoning, empathizing, and a whole host of other real-life abilities.

The objectives of both teachers and librarians are equally simple. We want all of our students to be able to read at least on-level, intelligently, critically, and with sufficient comprehension, not only to relate the events of the book but also to discuss their implications, characters, motivations, author's intentions, philosophical concepts, uses of language, and anything else of interest. More important, we want all of our students to love reading and to make it a part of their lives, because we believe that the child who has learned to hate reading has been doomed to an impoverished life, not to mention scholastic mediocrity.

Given these objectives and philosophy (which are extensively proven in research; see *The Power of Reading* by Stephen Krashen, 1993), it follows that we must do everything we can to make reading an enjoyable experience. It helps to provide comfortable places to read, to read with and to the children, to amass a large variety of books to choose from, to know children's books well ourselves, and to place few constraints on their choices (although we are always eager to recommend a book when asked).

It also follows that classroom teachers and librarians should work together. Teachers are the ones assigned to teach reading, of course, but librarians can offer expertise in, enthusiasm about, and access to children's literature. They can educate teachers by talking to them about great books, and they can work with teachers to help children learn to love literature. A literature program cannot be complete without the participation of both teachers and librarians. If your school does not have a library or librarian, then it is time to make contact with your local public librarian and to start arranging trips there.

The Program

Before enumerating the components of a complete reading program, which makes for a somewhat frightening list at first, it may help to remind you of what you already know: that reading is the most important subject in the elementary school and that all of the other subjects depend on it, as do the pleasure and success of the child's later life. As such, it justifies more time in class, and more teacher time as well.

Fortunately, it is also more enjoyable for the teacher; it involves work, of course, but it is intellectually stimulating and exciting. A novel-based reading program may take more time, because it involves reading a wide range of books to choose from, plus preparing the books you assign, but that is surely better than correcting another dratted pile of workbooks. It involves the pleasure of reading great literature, work you can do sitting out on the porch or in bed at night. I hope that, in addressing the readers of this book, I am preaching to the choir, but I'll make this categorical statement anyway. Those who don't love children's literature should not be teaching it. If you look on reading these books as drudgery, then you might as well stop reading now, because nothing else I am going to say will be of any use to you.

Teaching reading this way takes faith; when the primary emphasis is on love of reading, all the skills and vocabulary follow, but they are not skills in a vacuum. It is not blind faith, however, for research backs up this faith and shows a high correlation between love of reading and test scores (and hardly any between filling out workbooks and test scores).

A literature-based reading program is multifaceted; it begins, but does not end, with reading groups. Here, then, are some of the parts of "The Whole Reading Program," discussed in more detail below.

1. Discussion groups (covered in part 2)
2. SSR (Sustained Silent Reading)
3. Read aloud
4. Free reading
5. Booktalks
6. Book clubs
7. Reading in content areas
8. Listening center (optional, but nice to have)
9. Reading Day
10. Reading together
11. Reading decorations
12. Reading as reward
13. Read-alouds on field trips
14. Reading-related field trips
15. Author talks
16. Additional elements of your own choosing

1. Discussion groups: All of the children are divided into discussion groups that meet at least once a week to discuss common readings. Groups can discuss points of interpretation, character development, use of language, philosophical issues, and anything else they find interesting. Different types of novels can be read at different times; for instance, in the fall we can read historical fiction related to our history class, in the winter and spring we read paperback novels, and in between we can read selections from the Junior Great Books Program and other short-story collections. All of these books should be chosen because they are books children enjoy that have literary merit. Basal readers need not be used at all. The poetry in basal readers is usually insipid, and the stories are not chosen for their literary merit, so we have to go elsewhere for inspiration. See part 2 for how to do all this.

2. SSR: Every day there should be a silent reading period that lasts about 15 or 20 minutes, in which everyone (even the teacher) reads. The children should be expected to always have with them (both at home and at school) a book to read.

3. Read aloud: Children should be read to every day for 15 or 20 minutes. For children who are not accustomed to this, it takes time to get them used to reading aloud and silent reading, but they will. Give it the time it deserves. The books chosen should have complicated sentence structure, rich vocabulary, detailed description, and good values, and they should make for absorbing reading. Besides this regular reading aloud, it is good to read to the children anything you come across in your own reading that might interest them, such as articles from newspapers or magazines, passages from adult novels, or short stories. For the best and most inspirational book on reading aloud, get Jim Trelease's *The New Read-Aloud Handbook* (1989). Another valuable resource is Sharron McElmeel's *The Latest and Greatest Read-Alouds* (1994). Read them yourself and lend them to the parents of your students. It may be the best thing you ever do for them.

4. Free reading: Although exceptions for longer books can be allowed, generally the expectation that students will read at least one book of their own choosing each week is not unreasonable. Many read more. STUDENTS SHOULD NOT BE REQUIRED TO DO BOOK REPORTS ON THEM! These books are for pleasure. Students can keep lists of the books they read, but these lists should be private, not posted on the bulletin board, or else it becomes a numerical competition. Students should not be tested on free books, but informal discussions are always fun.

5. Booktalks: This is simply a time when you and your students get together and talk about books they have read and enjoyed recently. The children look forward to these sessions, both as a way of sharing new finds and as a way of finding new books to try. The walls of the classroom and library can provide places for children to post recommendations for books that they particularly enjoyed. This is also a good time for teachers and librarians to present booktalks (commercials) for new and interesting books.

6. Book clubs: There are several commercial book clubs available (see list of clubs at the end of this introduction), and they are highly recommended. Ordering books from these clubs serves three useful functions. It gets books into the hands of the children inexpensively, it generates a great deal of excitement about the books, and it gets free books for the classroom and library. Most of these clubs also sell a certain amount of nonbook material, such as sticker collecting albums, and so on. Don't be shy about restricting your children to ordering only real books, if you are so inclined. If you are willing to put in a bit more time, just type up the books, descriptions, and prices, and hand out that list instead of the newsletter the book club sends you.

7. Reading in content areas: The reading your kids do for science, history, and other subjects is also important. While the reading program itself emphasizes fiction, it is also important to make sure your students read plenty of nonfiction, poetry, and news articles.

8. Listening center: A nice luxury, if you can manage it, is a listening center with unabridged audiotapes (including student-made tapes), along with copies of the books so that students can read books that are difficult for them by listening and following along. Sometimes you can also watch movie versions of books your students have read.

9. Reading Day: Once or twice a year it creates a great deal of excitement to have a Reading Day. This is a day when the whole class or school does nothing but reading-related activities. Parents and guests are invited. Activities can include extended SSR (including reading with a friend or parent), read-aloud periods, booktalks, visits from authors, illustrating favorite books, dressing up as characters from books, making dioramas of scenes from books, reading to younger students, reading outside, presenting skits based on scenes from discussion group books, storytelling, and anything else you or the kids can think of. It adds to the atmosphere if all of the furniture is pushed to the side and the students can bring pillows, blankets, sleeping bags, and stuffed animals.

10. Reading together: Reading can be a wonderful social activity. If you are a parent, then you already know the joy of curling up with a child and a good book. Share the joy; invite other adults and older children into your room to read with your students, and let your children read with each other and to the younger children in your school.

11. Reading decorations: Cover the walls of the classroom, hallways, and library with posters, enlarged book illustrations, child-made illustrations, posted book recommendations by children and adults, and other book-related decorations. Many publishers will send posters for the asking, and they are always handing them out at conventions. Be sure to ask visiting illustrators for any sketches they make while talking to the students; most are happy to oblige.

12. Reading as reward: Allow children to read as a standard privilege whenever they have finished their work or done particularly well.

13. Read-alouds on field trips: It is amazing how quickly even the most boisterously excited group of students will settle down when you pull out a book, whether on the bus, at lunch, or in between scheduled visits, or while waiting generally.

14. Reading-related field trips: Take your students to local literary festivals, or if there are none, talk to other teachers and librarians about organizing one.

15. Author talks: Invite authors to your school, or take your students when authors are giving public talks or book signings in town.

16. Anything else you can think of, such as

> reading to younger students
>
> reading to old folks, the blind, at day-care centers, etc.
>
> making book presentations (not reports), projects, dioramas, bookmarks, calendars, etc.
>
> writing and performing plays based on books in school assemblies or on visitors' days
>
> making, or adding to, book webs

You should have many hopes and expectations for the children and their reading. Expect them to read every single night, seven nights a week, 52 weeks a year, for at least 20 minutes (but hope for longer). Reading just before bedtime is a wonderful lifelong habit to develop. Expect them to always have a book with them to be read during reading periods or whenever they have a little free time. Our hopes for them are effectively conveyed by the following passage by Mary Ellen Chase: "I write in tribute to two young parents, who knew well that in opening the wide doors of reading to their children, they were building for them houses not made with hands, dwelling places of the mind, which would always furnish them with food, shelter, and delight. . . . For there is no substitute for books in the life of a child, and the first understanding of the simple and irrefutable truth must come from the early perception of his parents' faith in it. They alone can give him the knowledge just as they alone are responsible for the practice of their faith."

PART 2:
HOW TO ORGANIZE AND RUN A
BOOK DISCUSSION GROUP

Children's Books for Adults

Besides working together on all of the activities in part 1, teachers and librarians should collaborate on the discussion groups as well. While in most cases it will be up to classroom teachers to run the discussion groups, often they have no training in how to select the books to use or in how to discuss them. These are areas where librarians can be of particular help.

The first step is that all of the adults involved must love children's books. This is easy to do. The term *children's literature* itself has become something of a misnomer. The term has come gradually to mean almost all books about children, including books that only a generation ago were thought of as adult fiction. Go to the young adult section of your local bookstore, and you will see *To Kill a Mockingbird*, *The Adventures of Huckleberry Finn*, *A Tree Grows in Brooklyn*, and many others. Children's literature today simply means literature that is accessible to children and is often about children, but which is *for* anyone who loves great literature.

The last decade or so has been a golden age for children's literature. It is the fastest-growing field in publishing, and many of the best of today's authors are working in it. While it's true that there is a great deal of garbage being published as well, there is an incredible quantity of exceptionally high-quality books coming out every month. Because this increase has roughly coincided with a decline in adult novels, the result is that anyone who skips the children's section is often missing most of the best books being published. Children's books have all the elements of so-called adult fiction, but the writing is far more disciplined and less self-indulgent; it is simple, spare, clean, and often intensely lyrical and poetic. For any adult today—teacher, librarian, parent, or none of these—I would recommend that at least half of their reading for pleasure comes from the children's section.

For an adult just starting out, here are a few books to recommend: *The Boy Who Could Make Himself Disappear* by Kin Platt; *The Light in the Forest* by Conrad Richter; *Sarah, Plain and Tall* and *The Facts and Fictions of Minna Pratt* by Patricia MacLachlan; *The Planet of Junior Brown* by Virginia Hamilton; *The Moves Make the Man* by Bruce Brooks; and *Incident at Hawk's Hill* by Allan W. Eckert.

Steps to Leading a Literature Discussion

1. Choosing the books. While librarians can be very important in guiding teachers toward books to read (and of course in guiding students to free-reading books), it is a mistake for librarians to choose books for discussion unless they will be leading the discussion themselves. The discussion leader should choose the book. Aside from the (I hope) obvious fact that the leader must have read the whole book before the first discussion, it should also be a book the leader loves and thinks the kids will love too.

Tastes change, both kids' and teachers', and teachers needs to tune in to that phenomenon, to balance their own excitement (which is very important) with what the current crop of students will probably like. Once a book is chosen, however, don't allow the kids to veto it partway through because they don't like it so far. This encourages them to work at giving a book a chance. If by the end they really don't like it, use that opinion as a basis for discussion and note it for the future.

To begin with, look for an opening hook, an exciting first chapter. While this is not essential, it certainly helps. Probably the most extreme example of this is the first chapter of *A Day No Pigs Would Die* by Robert Newton Peck. Other good examples are *North to Freedom* by Anne Holm, *Maniac Magee* by Jerry Spinelli, *The True Confessions of Charlotte Doyle* by Avi, and *Bel-Air Bambi and the Mall Rats* by Richard Peck.

Next, look for the same things you look for in your read-alouds: complicated sentence structure, rich vocabulary, detailed description, good values, intellectual depth, riveting plots, good characters, powerful emotion, humor, and generally absorbing reading. It is a myth that kids don't like detailed description. They just have good literary taste; they don't like description that is overblown, overused, vague, unnecessary, airy-fairy, or show-offy, or that interferes with, rather than enhances, the movement of the story. And, interestingly enough, while kids like funny stories, it is the powerful ones they love forever. A recent nationwide poll showed that the favorite book among children aged 9-12 was *Where the Red Fern Grows* by Wilson Rawls.

Choose books that push the group's reading level just a bit. If a book is too easy, students will assume you think they are not good readers, or they may not give it a fair chance because they think it is a "baby book." But if it is too hard, they will be lost. A good rule of thumb is that read-alouds should be well above their reading level, group books should be slightly above their level, and free-choice books should be on their level, or even below, if they are chosen because of genuine interest rather than because they were the shortest books on the shelf. All, of course, should match their interest level. Also, choose books that provide lots to think and talk about.

2. Generating questions. There are three types of questions that can be asked during a discussion session. The first is the one we are most familiar with: factual. These are questions with one right answer. They are the logical first step away from the basals for the teacher who has no other training. Go over vocabulary, summarize the plot, ask comprehension questions, and let the kids take turns being the teacher and leading discussion (with preparation). There is nothing wrong with this, and some kids need it more (or more of it) than others. The danger is that it will become the only step, that teachers will get mired in the basal approach to novels and will never progress beyond it. There are two further types of questions that must be used in order to make the best use of novels and have the most enjoyable discussions.

Interpretive questions are open-ended and are questions for which the teacher is genuinely uncertain of the answer. They ask students to give their opinion about the author's meaning, and then to support their opinion with evidence from the text. Do not try to come up with low-level questions; any question of interpretation can start a good discussion. You should have a reasonable certainty that the questions are answerable from the text. Questions should be specific about an important point of interpretation, and they should be clear. Lack of clarity can come from imperfect expression of thoughts, unnecessarily difficult vocabulary, or technical terms.

These questions often start with "why" and sometimes address the author's or character's intentions. Sometimes they are done in clusters of related questions. For example, in *The Wizard of Oz,* a story with which we are all familiar, here are just a few of the questions that might be asked: Why did the Wizard send Dorothy to kill the Witch of the West? Did the author intend for us to believe that the Wizard was really a good man? Why did the Witch of the North give Dorothy the magic shoes without telling her how to use them? Was Dorothy the hero of the story? Why did the author include Toto in the story? and so on. While these questions are all very general, most interpretive questions will deal with a particular word or passage.

Training in the methods of the Interpretive Level has been around for many years in the guise of the Junior Great Books Program, whose terrific training sessions are often organized by librarians for teachers. Unfortunately, the training is tied solely to the Junior Great Books themselves, and many teachers have the impression that the method only works with them. In fact, the Junior Great Books (JGB) are nothing more than collections of short stories and folktales. There is nothing magical or even "great" about them. The method, however, is magical, and the training sessions, strictly controlled by the Great Books Foundation, are first-rate. While I will summarize the method here, I highly recommend the training, which is offered all over the country all year long. More information is included about them at the end of this introduction.

The idea behind the JGB method is simple: Instead of, or in addition to, asking questions on vocabulary and comprehension, the teacher leads discussions on questions of interpretation, in the course of which the children's understanding of plot, vocabulary, character, main idea, and the like is exercised much more fully and in a far more interesting context. This method is called "shared inquiry." The teacher's preparation consists of reading and rereading the selection and thinking up interpretive questions. Much of the training consists of learning to generate good questions; the rest covers techniques for leading discussions.

Any one of these questions can easily launch a discussion that can go on for a whole class period, and the discussions generate so much excitement that often the children will continue them after class is over. The teacher's role in the discussion is primarily to participate in the inquiry, but also to make sure it stays tied to the book, to moderate and probe, to ensure that everyone gets a chance to be involved, and to keep the discussion moving. The children will often need to defend their positions with passages from the book, and it quickly becomes obvious when someone has not read or understood the story. Often factual questions are dealt with as a part of the discussion, but because they are in the context of the extended inquiry into a question for which the teacher does not already have the answer, the children see them as both necessary and interesting. They are seen not as ends in themselves but as important means to understanding the story more deeply. Thus this method, while accomplishing all of the same things as the basalization, also excites the children, enhances thinking skills, and provokes intellectual stimulation and interest in the story and in the ideas.

However, after using the Interpretive Level methods for several years, you may find yourself becoming dissatisfied again, feeling that there is more to be gotten out of the books. Or you may find that the children have a tendency to pull the discussion away from the strictly interpretive into the philosophical. Two of the questions above, for example, are likely to cause this to happen: Was the Wizard really a good man, and who was the real hero of the story? It is difficult to discuss these questions without asking, "What is a good man?" in the first case, or without trying to define heroism in the second. When this happens, it is time to move on to the Philosophical Level.

This third type of question is intended to bring about discussion of the issues the author raises, with the text used as a base to leave and return to. Because you are not dealing with interpreting the text, but rather with issues and ideas raised by the text, the discussion can range freely, and events in the story are used to bolster arguments and give the discussion focus. It often seems likely that thinking about the philosophical issues gets us closer to the author's purpose in writing the book. For instance, it is arguable whether L. Frank Baum intended his young readers to think about whether the Witch of the North was really doing Dorothy a favor, but it seems certain that he intended to shake up their ideas about the nature of intelligence, compassion, and courage.

Often interpretive questions will turn into philosophical ones or will hinge on clarifying a philosophical issue first. Thus, preparation is similar to interpretive method. But in formulating questions, the focus is more general—not what did the author mean, but what is meant by this. Often questions turn on trying to define terms; if you want to know who the author intended as the hero of the story, you first need to try to clarify what you mean by *hero*. Usually the terms you are trying to define will be ones of which the kids are sure (at first) they already know the meaning. Thus, your first job will be to make them unsure, so that they will start to think.

Training for this method has also been around for many years under the auspices of the Institute for the Advancement of Philosophy for Children and their Philosophy for Children Program (see the end of this introduction for more information), and there is a network of teacher-trainers across the country and around the world. Their training is also tied to the books that were specifically written for the program, and that together with their teacher materials comprise an amazingly thorough and effective K-12 thinking skills curriculum. But the primary benefit of their method for the classroom teacher is that the techniques are applicable to all subjects, and the skills the children learn carry over into other areas.

In teaching reading, the method is similar to that of JGB, with the important exception that it is often the children who come up with the questions. They call their method a "community of inquiry." The teacher's preparation consists of becoming familiar with the reading and the philosophical concepts that the children might raise. In the discussion itself, the teacher's role is similar to that in JGB, but rather than keeping the discussion tied to the text, it is allowed to travel wherever investigation of the idea leads the group.

Thus, as the children draw on their experiences to think about the ideas, they integrate all that they have learned in school, at home, and with their friends, and make both the ideas and the books more meaningful by tying them together with all of the other aspects of their lives. And that is precisely what reading, and in a larger sense education, is all about: helping us to make sense of our lives, to think about how we should live them, to try to make of them a coherent whole.

As teachers progress through these three levels, they will see many changes taking place in the classroom, in the children, and in the way the teachers approach other subjects. Dramatically better comprehension is only the beginning, for the children are learning not only to parrot back the plot (a skill that is important too) but also to think and reason about its meaning and about the ideas and issues that the author raises. Understanding becomes an active, not passive, process, and the habit of thinking deeply about ideas carries over into the rest of the curriculum. Along the way, the children are taught the skills necessary to reason effectively, to make inferences, to recognize assumptions, and to detect fallacies. Reading becomes what it should be—not a dull collection of unrelated skills with no relation to anything else, but an integrated, exciting, and intellectually stimulating activity related to the rest of the children's lives and containing the seeds for further thought and investigation.

3. Beginning the discussion. In the first part of the year the teacher should be the discussion leader, but later on, once the students have gotten into the habit of discussing books this way, they can take turns leading the group, with advanced preparation and coaching by the teacher. The group meeting can start by asking if anyone has not done the assignment. If anyone admits this, or if it becomes clear in the discussion, they should leave the group, finish the assignment, and write a summary. Their punishment is that they do not get to participate in the group, a natural and reasonable consequence that is, given the enthusiasm that these discussions usually generate, more onerous than you might think.

Then ask if they have any factual questions. It's best to get these out of the way quickly. Whenever possible, try to have the group answer them, or direct them to read aloud a section to figure it out from context. Then, depending on the level and experience of the group, spend some time summarizing and checking comprehension. With more advanced, experienced groups you can skip this step or blend it into the discussions.

Finally you are ready to move on to the discussion itself. The questions used to begin can be ones you have prepared ahead or ones that the students have asked or prepared, or you can ask the kids to generate questions that you list with the asker's name. You will rarely have time to get to more than one or two in any given session.

4. Leading the discussion. The purpose of forming a community of inquiry is to get at the truth. It is not a rap session or an exercise in values clarification. Not all answers are equally valid or valuable. To earn respect and consideration they must be substantiated and defended from the text and with rational argument. Because the joint purpose of the group is to get at the truth, when a position becomes untenable the students must learn to move on rather than defending it simply to win. The goal is to get the students talking to each other, and eventually to get them proficient at testing ideas, rather than have the discussion centered on you.

The teacher's role in the discussion (see part 2) is primarily fulfilled by asking follow-up questions. There are six main reasons to ask follow-up questions:

   a. To get opinions substantiated

   b. To clarify remarks

   c. To get additional opinions

   d. To overcome lack of response

   e. To keep the discussion on track

   f. To introduce devil's advocate facts and elicit and examine alternatives

Other purposes of follow-ups include explicating remarks, interpreting remarks, seeking consistency, defining terms, searching for assumptions, and detecting fallacies.

5. Ending the discussion. The discussion rarely ends with closure. This is just fine; do not attempt to force it. Instead, you can close by summarizing the points made, summarizing where the discussion has led to so far, and giving a final question to think about for when you continue the discussion next time.

6. Alternatives. There are many other ways to run a novel-based reading group. Here are just a few suggestions:

   a. Instead of starting with a question, pick up on a previous discussion.

   b. Begin with a question you asked them to think about at the end of the last session.

   c. Act out scenes from the book.

   d. Do a writing exercise based on the book, such as writing a short sequel or a poem describing one moment in the story.

   e. Do as Socrates did and have your discussion while strolling around the playground or neighborhood.

   f. Have the students write their responses to the question first, then read them aloud and discuss them.

7. Evaluation. If you work in a school where students must be objectively evaluated and graded, here are some of the ways you can do this. The primary criterion you have for judging students is their participation. Using a seating chart, you can keep track of how often students volunteer, answer questions, or fail to respond, and how they cooperate with other members of the group in probing for the truth, listening to others, and avoiding adversarial relationships. The quality of the answers can be judged on how well the students demonstrate that they read and understood the story, how carefully reasoned their arguments are, and how well the arguments are supported, both by reasoning and by evidence from the text. After discussions students can be asked to answer the questions discussed in writing; you'll be amazed at the quality of their writing after a really good discussion.

Discussion Group Resources

Book Clubs for Children

Each company has several different clubs for readers at different levels.

Scholastic Book Clubs Inc.
P.O. Box 7503
Jefferson City, MO 65102
1-800-724-2424

The Trumpet Clubs
P.O. Box 604
Holmes, PA 19043
1-800-826-0110

Troll Book Clubs
2 Lethbridge Plaza
Mahwah, NJ 07430
1-800-541-1097

The Junior Great Books Program

Established in 1947, the Great Books Foundation provides reading and discussion programs for people of all ages. The Foundation is a totally independent, nonprofit educational organization. It derives its income entirely from the sale of its books, fees for training and educational consultation, grants, and other philanthropic contributions.

The Foundation selects and publishes, in paperback volumes only, great classical and modern works of literature for discussion by adults and children. It also offers courses in interpretive reading and discussion techniques to train volunteers, teachers, and librarians who will be conducting the Junior and Adult Great Books programs.

The Foundation trains approximately 13,000 discussion leaders each year. Its Junior Program for elementary and high school students numbers 350,000 participants in 24,000 groups.

(Dennis and Moldof 1978, v)

The Great Books Foundation
40 East Huron Street
Chicago, IL 60611
312-332-5870

Philosophy for Children

The Institute for the Advancement of Philosophy for Children at Montclair State College was begun in the late 1960s by professor of philosophy Dr. Matthew Lipman. Along with his associate Dr. Ann Margaret Sharp, he created the Philosophy for Children Program as a K-12 course in reasoning, thinking skills, and introductory philosophical concepts. It consists of student books, associated teacher's materials, and various books on methodology and theory.

The student books contain stories, written especially for the program, that are dense in concepts and that serve as springboards for intense, wide-ranging discussions of issues and ideas. The stories also provide a model for a "community of inquiry" and show real-life applications of the thinking and reasoning skills that are taught within the program in a sequential and well-thought-out curriculum. The teacher's materials contain explanations of philosophical ideas and reasoning skills, as well as exercises and discussion plans that can be used if needed to move the discussion along.

The program has found wide acceptance in the United States and elsewhere. It was chosen as a "Meritorious Program" for the National Diffusion Network, and affiliate institutes have been established in many states and countries. The program has been translated into other languages and is in use throughout Europe and Central and South America, as well as parts of Asia and Africa, and Russia has recently begun implementing it. Several magazines and newsletters are published by various affiliate organizations, and the International Council for Philosophical Inquiry with Children (ICPIC) holds a conference each year.

> Institute for the Advancement of Philosophy for Children
> Montclair State College
> Upper Montclair, NJ 07043
> 201-893-4277

REFERENCES

Dennis, Richard P., and Edwin P. Moldof. 1978. *Handbook on Interpretive Reading and Discussion.* Chicago: The Great Books Foundation.

Krashen, Stephen. 1993. *The Power of Reading: Insights from the Research.* Englewood, CO: Libraries Unlimited.

McElmeel, Sharron L. 1994. *The Latest and Greatest Read-Alouds.* Englewood, CO: Libraries Unlimited.

Trelease, Jim. 1989. *The New Read-Aloud Handbook*, 2d ed. New York: Penguin.

Afternoon of the Elves

Janet Taylor Lisle

Kids Who Don't Fit In
The Hundred Dresses
The Winchesters
Stargone John
Maizon at Blue Hill
The Ghost Belonged to Me
There's a Boy in the Girls' Bathroom

Individuality
The Bears' House
Unclaimed Treasures
Luke's Garden and *Gramp*
Someday Angeline
North to Freedom
A Place Apart

Kids Acting as Parents
Ask Me Something Easy
Someone's Mother Is Missing
No Kidding
Where the Lilies Bloom
The Outsiders
The Night Swimmers
Stone Fox

Conformity
The Lemming Condition
The Chocolate War
The Outsiders
The Catcher in the Rye
Bel-Air Bambi and the Mall Rats

Miniature Construction
The Village by the Sea
Tunes for Bears to Dance To
Through the Hidden Door
The Borrowers
The Indian in the Cupboard

Afternoon of the Elves

Janet Taylor Lisle

Friends Parents Don't Like
Hey, Dummy
Onion John
The Adventures of Tom Sawyer
Bridge to Terabithia

Tough and Angry Girls
The Shoeshine Girl
The Great Gilly Hopkins
Dust of the Earth
Winter of Fire
True Grit

Difficult Friends
Jennifer, Hecate, Macbeth, William McKinley, and Me, Elizabeth
The Moves Make the Man
The Planet of Junior Brown
Harper & Moon

Working Outdoors
The Secret Garden
Hazel Rye
The Chalkbox Kid
Lost Magic
Miracles on Maple Hill
J. T.

Afternoon of the Elves

Janet Taylor Lisle

Conformity

The Lemming Condition

The Chocolate War

The Outsiders

The Catcher in the Rye

*Bel-Air Bambi and the
Mall Rats*

Miniature Construction

The Village by the Sea

*Tunes for Bears
to Dance To*

Through the Hidden Door

The Borrowers

*The Indian
in the Cupboard*

Friends Parents Don't Like

Hey, Dummy

Onion John

*The Adventures of
Tom Sawyer*

Bridge to Terabithia

Individuality

The Bears' House

Unclaimed Treasures

Luke's Garden and *Gramp*

Someday Angeline

North to Freedom

A Place Apart

Working Outdoors

The Secret Garden

Hazel Rye

The Chalkbox Kid

Lost Magic

Miracles on Maple Hill

J. T.

Kids Who Don't Fit In

The Hundred Dresses

The Winchesters

Stargone John

Maizon at Blue Hill

The Ghost Belonged to Me

*There's a Boy in the
Girls' Bathroom*

Kids Acting as Parents

Ask Me Something Easy

*Someone's Mother
Is Missing*

No Kidding

Where the Lilies Bloom

The Outsiders

The Night Swimmers

Stone Fox

Tough and Angry Girls

The Shoeshine Girl

The Great Gilly Hopkins

Dust of the Earth

Winter of Fire

True Grit

Difficult Friends

*Jennifer, Hecate, Macbeth,
William McKinley, and
Me, Elizabeth*

The Moves Make the Man

*The Planet of Junior
Brown*

Harper & Moon

Individuality
Afternoon of the Elves

☐ *The Bears' House*
by Marilyn Sachs

Fran Ellen is ostracized by her class because she sucks her thumb and smells bad, but her dreadful home life is a secret she tries to keep from them all.

☐ *Unclaimed Treasures*
by Patricia MacLachlan

Willa, who wants to feel extraordinary, thinks that she's in love with the father of the boy next door until she realizes that her ordinary true love is the boy himself.

☐ *Luke's Garden* and *Gramp*
by Joan Tate

In one short novel, a boy is destroyed because he is different; in the other, a boy finds a way to make his grandfather feel useful again.

☐ *Someday Angeline*
by Louis Sachar

As an eight-year-old genius in the sixth grade, Angeline is not too popular, but she tries to adjust to being different.

☐ *North to Freedom*
by Anne Holm

Having escaped from an Eastern European concentration camp where he has spent his life, a 12-year-old boy struggles to cope with an entirely strange world as he flees northward to freedom in Denmark.

☐ *A Place Apart*
by Paula Fox

Victoria and her mother move to a small village outside of Boston, where she meets a wealthy teenage boy who teaches her a valuable but painful lesson about life.

Friends Parents Don't Like
Afternoon of the Elves

☐ *Hey, Dummy*
by Kin Platt

Despite the opposition of his family and friends, Neil befriends the brain-damaged boy newly arrived in the neighborhood.

☐ *Onion John*
by Joseph Krumgold
1960 Newbery Medal

Andy's friendship with the town odd-jobs man, Onion John, causes a conflict between Andy and his father.

☐ *The Adventures of Tom Sawyer*
by Mark Twain

The adventures and pranks of a mischievous boy growing up in a Mississippi River town in the early 19th century, who impresses his friends and horrifies adults by associating with the son of the town drunk, running away from home, attending his own funeral, witnessing a murder, getting lost in a cave, and finding lost treasure.

☐ *Bridge to Terabithia*
by Katherine Paterson
1978 Newbery Medal

The life of a 10-year-old boy in rural Virginia expands when he becomes friends with a newcomer who subsequently meets an untimely death trying to reach their hideaway, Terabithia, during a storm.

Miniature Construction
Afternoon of the Elves

☐ *The Village by the Sea*
by Paula Fox

When her father enters the hospital to have open-heart surgery, 10-year-old Emma is sent to Peconic Bay to live with her tormented aunt, and finds the experience painful until she meets a friend who suggests making a miniature village in the sand.

☐ *Tunes for Bears to Dance To*
by Robert Cormier

Eleven-year-old Henry escapes his family's problems by watching the woodcarving of Mr. Levine, an elderly Holocaust survivor, but when Henry is manipulated into betraying his friend, he comes to know true evil.

☐ *Through the Hidden Door*
by Rosemary Wells

Two young boys stumble upon the remains of an ancient underground mystery civilization.

☐ *The Borrowers*
by Mary Norton

Miniature people who live in an old country house and borrow things from the humans are forced to emigrate from their home under the clock.

☐ *The Indian in the Cupboard*
by Lynne Reid Banks

A nine-year-old boy receives a plastic Indian, a cupboard, and a little key for his birthday and finds himself involved in adventure when the Indian comes to life in the cupboard and befriends him.
Book 1 of the Indian in the Cupboard series

Conformity
Afternoon of the Elves

☐ *The Lemming Condition*
by Alan Arkin

Bubber, a young lemming, is haunted by doubts about the purpose of the great march westward to the sea, and must choose between conformity and free will.

☐ *The Chocolate War*
by Robert Cormier
PG language

A high school freshman discovers the devastating consequences of refusing to join the school's annual fundraising drive and arousing the wrath of the school bullies.
Sequel: *Beyond the Chocolate War*

☐ *The Outsiders*
by S. E. Hinton

The struggle of three brothers to stay together after their parents' deaths and their quest for identity among the conflicting values of their adolescent society.

☐ *The Catcher in the Rye*
by J. D. Salinger

Unable to conform despite pressure from his family, and knowing he is about to be dropped by his school, Holden Caulfield embarks on a journey of self-discovery and spends three days and nights in New York City.

☐ *Bel-Air Bambi and the Mall Rats*
by Richard Peck

Bambi, Buffie, and Brick, three totally cool siblings from Los Angeles, move with their parents to Hickory Fork, a small town terrorized by a high school gang.

Working Outdoors
Afternoon of the Elves

☐ *The Secret Garden*
by Frances Hodgson Burnett

A boy who has lived as a spoiled invalid regains his health when he and his orphaned cousin restore a once lovely garden.

☐ *Hazel Rye*
by Vera and Bill Cleaver

An 11-year-old girl with no appreciation for land and growing things finds her values beginning to change when she agrees to let an impoverished family live in a small house she owns, in exchange for working in her orange grove.

☐ *The Chalkbox Kid*
by Clyde Robert Bulla

Nine-year-old Gregory's house does not have room for a garden, but he creates a surprising and very different garden in an unusual place.

☐ *Lost Magic*
by Berthe Amoss

In the Middle Ages, orphaned Ceridwen learns the art of herbal healing and gains the protection of the local lord until she is accused of witchcraft.

☐ *Miracles on Maple Hill*
by Virginia Sorensen

1957 Newbery Medal

Ten-year-old Marly and her family move from the city to Grandmother's old Pennsylvania farmhouse, hoping that the outdoor life will restore Father's health.

☐ *J. T.*
by Jane Wagner

J. T. begins to change when he discovers there is more satisfaction in caring for an injured cat than in listening to a stolen transistor radio.

Kids Who Don't Fit In
Afternoon of the Elves

☐ *The Hundred Dresses*
by Eleanor Estes

1945 Newbery Honor Book

In winning a medal she is no longer there to receive, a girl teaches her classmates a lesson.

☐ *The Winchesters*
by James Lincoln Collier

Fourteen-year-old Chris, a poor relation of the wealthy Winchesters, must choose whether to be on the side of management or labor when his classmates' parents go on strike at the Winchester mill.

☐ *Stargone John*
by Ellen Kindt McKenzie

Six-year-old John experiences ridicule and punishment at his one-room schoolhouse, until an old retired teacher reaches out from her blindness.

☐ *Maizon at Blue Hill*
by Jacqueline Woodson

After winning a scholarship to an academically challenging boarding school, Maizon finds herself one of only five blacks there and wonders if she will ever fit in.

Sequel to *Last Summer with Maizon*

☐ *The Ghost Belonged to Me*
by Richard Peck

In 1913 in the Midwest, a quartet of characters share adventures, from exploding steamboats to exorcising a ghost.

☐ *There's a Boy in the Girls' Bathroom*
by Louis Sachar

An unmanageable 11-year-old misfit learns to believe in himself when he gets to know the new school counselor, who is a sort of misfit too.

Kids Acting as Parents
Afternoon of the Elves

☐ *Ask Me Something Easy*
by Natalie Honeycutt

After her father leaves the family, Addie must cope with her increasingly hostile, distant mother, perfect older sister, and sensitive younger twin sisters.

☐ *Someone's Mother Is Missing*
by Harry Mazer

When her emotionally disturbed mother disappears, Lisa searches for her, alternately aided and annoyed by her cousin Sam.

☐ *No Kidding*
by Bruce Brooks

In his 21st-century society, 14-year-old Sam is allowed to decide the fate of his family after his mother is released from an alcohol rehabilitation center.

☐ *Where the Lilies Bloom*
by Vera and Bill Cleaver

A 14-year-old girl struggles to keep her family together after their father dies.

Sequel: *Trial Valley*

☐ *The Outsiders*
by S. E. Hinton

The struggle of three brothers to stay together after their parents' deaths.

☐ *The Night Swimmers*
by Betsy Byars

With their mother dead and their father working nights, Retta tries to be mother to her two younger brothers.

☐ *Stone Fox*
by John R. Gardiner

Little Willie hopes to pay the back taxes on his grandfather's farm with the purse from a dogsled race he enters.

Tough and Angry Girls
Afternoon of the Elves

☐ *The Shoeshine Girl*
by Clyde Robert Bulla

Ten-year-old Sarah Ida gets a job at a shoeshine stand.

☐ *The Great Gilly Hopkins*
by Katherine Paterson

1979 Newbery Honor Book

A foster child schemes against everyone who tries to be friendly.

☐ *Dust of the Earth*
by Vera and Bill Cleaver

Fern and her family face hardships when they move to a farm.

☐ *Winter of Fire*
by Sherryl Jordan

A world destroyed by fire is saved from ice by a young woman.

☐ *True Grit*
by Charles Portis

Mattie Ross tries to capture the outlaws who murdered her father.

Difficult Friends
Afternoon of the Elves

☐ *Jennifer, Hecate, Macbeth, William McKinley, and Me, Elizabeth*
by E. L. Konigsburg
Elizabeth meets Jennifer, who claims to be a witch.

☐ *The Moves Make the Man*
by Bruce Brooks
1985 Newbery Honor Book
A black boy and an emotionally troubled white boy form a precarious friendship.

☐ *The Planet of Junior Brown*
by Virginia Hamilton
1972 Newbery Honor Book
Buddy tries to protect an overweight, emotionally disturbed friend.

☐ *Harper & Moon*
by Ramon Royal Ross
Harper's friendship with Moon, an abused, orphaned boy, is tested by a discovery Harper makes.

Bridge to Terabithia

Katherine Paterson

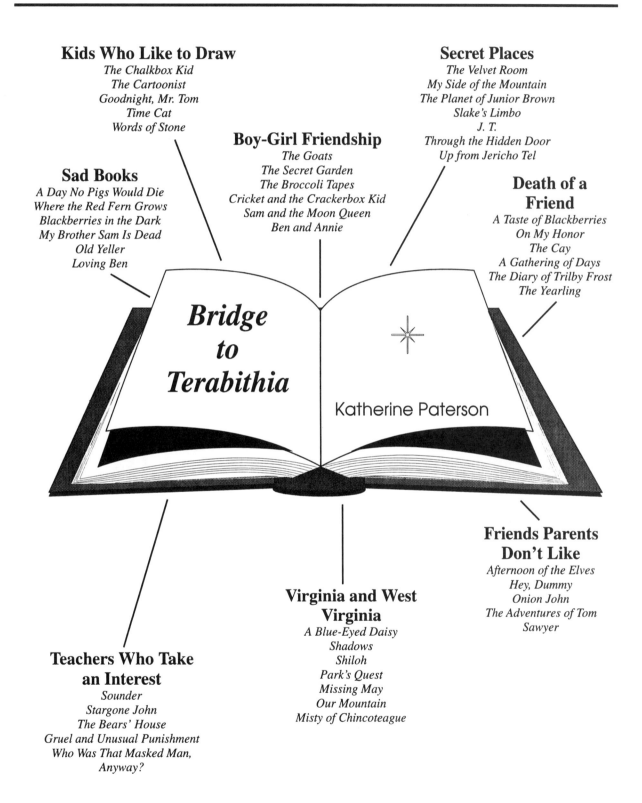

Kids Who Like to Draw
The Chalkbox Kid
The Cartoonist
Goodnight, Mr. Tom
Time Cat
Words of Stone

Secret Places
The Velvet Room
My Side of the Mountain
The Planet of Junior Brown
Slake's Limbo
J. T.
Through the Hidden Door
Up from Jericho Tel

Boy-Girl Friendship
The Goats
The Secret Garden
The Broccoli Tapes
Cricket and the Crackerbox Kid
Sam and the Moon Queen
Ben and Annie

Sad Books
A Day No Pigs Would Die
Where the Red Fern Grows
Blackberries in the Dark
My Brother Sam Is Dead
Old Yeller
Loving Ben

Death of a Friend
A Taste of Blackberries
On My Honor
The Cay
A Gathering of Days
The Diary of Trilby Frost
The Yearling

Friends Parents Don't Like
Afternoon of the Elves
Hey, Dummy
Onion John
The Adventures of Tom Sawyer

Virginia and West Virginia
A Blue-Eyed Daisy
Shadows
Shiloh
Park's Quest
Missing May
Our Mountain
Misty of Chincoteague

Teachers Who Take an Interest
Sounder
Stargone John
The Bears' House
Gruel and Unusual Punishment
Who Was That Masked Man, Anyway?

Bridge to Terabithia

Katherine Paterson

Friends
Parents Don't Like

Afternoon of the Elves

Hey, Dummy

Onion John

*The Adventures of
Tom Sawyer*

Sad Books

A Day No Pigs Would Die

Where the Red Fern Grows

Blackberries in the Dark

My Brother Sam Is Dead

Old Yeller

Loving Ben

Death
of a Friend

A Taste of Blackberries

On My Honor

The Cay

A Gathering of Days

The Diary of Trilby Frost

The Yearling

Boy-Girl
Friendship

The Goats

The Secret Garden

The Broccoli Tapes

*Cricket and
the Crackerbox Kid*

Sam and the Moon Queen

Ben and Annie

Virginia and
West Virginia

A Blue-Eyed Daisy

Shadows

Shiloh

Park's Quest

Missing May

Our Mountain

Misty of Chincoteague

Teachers
Who Take an Interest

Sounder

Stargone John

The Bears' House

*Gruel and Unusual
Punishment*

*Who Was That Masked
Man, Anyway?*

Kids
Who Like to Draw

The Chalkbox Kid

The Cartoonist

Goodnight, Mr. Tom

Time Cat

Words of Stone

Secret Places

The Velvet Room

My Side of the Mountain

*The Planet of Junior
Brown*

Slake's Limbo

J. T.

Through the Hidden Door

Up from Jericho Tel

Boy-Girl Friendship
Bridge to Terabithia

☐*The Goats*
by Brock Cole

A boy and a girl form an uneasy bond that grows into a deep friendship when they decide to run away.

☐*The Secret Garden*
by Frances Hodgson Burnett

A boy who has lived as a spoiled invalid regains his health when he and his orphaned cousin restore a once lovely garden.

☐*The Broccoli Tapes*
by Jan Slepian

During a stay in Hawaii with her family, Sara reports her experiences by tape back to her sixth-grade class in Boston, detailing her adoption of a wild cat, a friendship with a troubled Hawaiian boy, and the death of a beloved grandmother.

☐*Cricket and the Crackerbox Kid*
by Alane Ferguson

Cricket thinks she has finally found a friend in Dominic until they quarrel over ownership of a dog, and their classroom becomes a courtroom to decide who is right.

☐*Sam and the Moon Queen*
by Alison Cragin Herzig and Jane Lawrence Mali

Sympathetic to a homeless girl's plight, Sam tries to help her find food for herself and medical aid for her dog.

☐*Ben and Annie*
by Joan Tate

Ben has a special friendship with his crippled neighbor Annie, which is spoiled by misunderstanding.

Death of a Friend
Bridge to Terabithia

☐*A Taste of Blackberries*
by Doris B. Smith

A young boy recounts his efforts to adjust to the accidental death of his best friend.

☐*On My Honor*
by Marian Dane Bauer
1987 Newbery Honor Book

When his best friend drowns while they are both swimming in a treacherous river that they had promised never to go near, Joel is devastated and terrified at having to tell both sets of parents.

☐*The Cay*
by Theodore Taylor

When their ship is torpedoed by a German submarine, a white boy, blinded by a blow on the head, and an old black man are stranded on a tiny Caribbean island.

Prequel/sequel: *Timothy of the Cay*

☐*A Gathering of Days*
by Joan W. Blos
1980 Newbery Honor Book

The journal of a 14-year-old girl records daily events in her small town, her father's remarriage, and the death of her best friend.

☐*The Diary of Trilby Frost*
by Dianne Glaser

Teenager Trilby Frost records in her diary her growing realization that life continues even though her father, younger brother, and closest friend die.

☐*The Yearling*
by Marjorie Kinnan Rawlings

A young boy living in the backwoods is forced to decide the fate of a fawn he has raised as a pet.

Sad Books
Bridge to Terabithia

☐*A Day No Pigs Would Die*
by Robert Newton Peck

To a 13-year-old Vermont farm boy whose father slaughters pigs for a living, maturity comes early as he learns to do what's got to be done, especially regarding his pet pig who cannot produce a litter.

☐*Where the Red Fern Grows*
by Wilson Rawls

The adventures of a 10-year-old boy and the two dogs he bought with money he had earned.

☐*Blackberries in the Dark*
by Mavis Jukes

Nine-year-old Austin visits his grandmother the summer after his grandfather dies, and together they try to come to terms with their loss.

☐*My Brother Sam Is Dead*
by Christopher and James Lincoln Collier

Recounts the tragedy that strikes the Meeker family during the Revolution when one son joins the rebel forces while the rest of the family tries to stay neutral in a Tory town.

☐*Old Yeller*
by Fred Gipson
1957 Newbery Honor Book

In the late 1860s in the Texas hill country, a big yellow dog and a 14-year-old boy form a close, loving relationship.

☐*Loving Ben*
by Elizabeth Laird

Anna's teen years bring maturity and fulfillment as she experiences the birth and death of a loved hydrocephalic brother, and working with a child with Down's syndrome.

Friends Parents Don't Like
Bridge to Terabithia

☐*Afternoon of the Elves*
by Janet Taylor Lisle
1990 Newbery Honor Book

As Hillary works in the miniature village, allegedly built by elves, in Sara-Kate's backyard, she becomes more and more curious about Sara-Kate's real life inside her big, gloomy house with her mysterious, silent mother.

☐*Hey, Dummy*
by Kin Platt

Despite the opposition of his family and friends, Neil befriends the brain-damaged boy newly arrived in the neighborhood.

☐*Onion John*
by Joseph Krumgold
1960 Newbery Medal

Andy's friendship with the town odd-jobs man, Onion John, causes a conflict between Andy and his father.

☐*The Adventures of Tom Sawyer*
by Mark Twain

The adventures and pranks of a mischievous boy growing up in a Mississippi River town in the early 19th century, who impresses his friends and horrifies adults by associating with the son of the town drunk, running away from home, attending his own funeral, witnessing a murder, getting lost in a cave, and finding lost treasure.

Virginia and West Virginia
Bridge to Terabithia

☐ *A Blue-Eyed Daisy*
by Cynthia Rylant

Relates episodes in the life of 11-year-old Ellie and her family, who live in a coal mining town.

☐ *Shadows*
by Dennis Haseley

Jamie's lonely life with his aunt and uncle changes when Grandpa comes to visit.

☐ *Shiloh*
by Phyllis Reynolds Naylor
1992 Newbery Medal

When he finds a lost beagle, Marty tries to hide it from his family and the dog's real owner, a mean-spirited man known to mistreat his dogs.

☐ *Park's Quest*
by Katherine Paterson

Eleven-year-old Park travels to his grandfather's farm to learn about his father, who died in the Vietnam War.

☐ *Missing May*
by Cynthia Rylant
1993 Newbery Medal

After the death of the beloved aunt who has raised her, 12-year-old Summer and her uncle Ob leave their West Virginia trailer in search of the strength to go on living.

☐ *Our Mountain*
by Ellen Harvey Showell

Two brothers living in the mountains of West Virginia describe their family, home, and favorite pastimes.

☐ *Misty of Chincoteague*
by Marguerite Henry
1948 Newbery Honor Book

Two children's determination to own a Chincoteague pony is greatly increased when the Phantom and her colt are among those rounded up.

Teachers Who Take an Interest
Bridge to Terabithia

☐ *Sounder*
by William H. Armstrong
1970 Newbery Medal

When his sharecropper father is jailed for stealing food for his family, a young black boy grows in courage and understanding with the help of the dog Sounder and learns to read and write.
Sequel: *Sourland*

☐ *Stargone John*
by Ellen Kindt McKenzie

Six-year-old John experiences ridicule and punishment at his one-room schoolhouse, until an old retired teacher reaches out from her blindness.

☐ *The Bears' House*
by Marilyn Sachs

Fran Ellen is ostracized by her class because she sucks her thumb and smells bad, but her dreadful home life is a secret she tries to keep from them all.

☐ *Gruel and Unusual Punishment*
by Jim Arter

Undaunted by his second stint in the seventh grade, Arnold continues to specialize in annoying and antisocial behavior, but becomes uncomfortably aware that the teacher he calls Apeface has taken a special interest in his case.

☐ *Who Was That Masked Man, Anyway?*
by Avi

In the early 1940s, when nearly everyone else is thinking about World War II, sixth-grader Frankie Wattleson gets in trouble at home and at school because of his preoccupation with his favorite radio programs.

Kids Who Like to Draw
Bridge to Terabithia

☐ *The Chalkbox Kid*
by Clyde Robert Bulla

Nine-year-old Gregory's house does not have room for a garden, but he creates a surprising and very different garden in an unusual place.

☐ *The Cartoonist*
by Betsy Byars

Threatened with the loss of his private place in the attic of his crowded home, a young boy determines to keep it at all costs.

☐ *Goodnight, Mr. Tom*
by Michelle Magorian

A battered child learns to embrace life when he is adopted by an old man in the English countryside during World War II.

☐ *Time Cat*
by Lloyd Alexander

Gareth, a cat with miraculous powers, takes his human friend Jason with him when he travels through time to visit countries all over the world during different periods of history.

☐ *Words of Stone*
by Kevin Henkes

Busy trying to deal with his many fears and his troubled feelings for his dead mother, 10-year-old Blaze has his life changed when he meets the boisterous and irresistible Joselle.

Secret Places
Bridge to Terabithia

☐ *The Velvet Room*
by Zilpha Keatley Snyder

Robin finds a haven from the world in the velvet room of the deserted McGurdy mansion.

☐ *My Side of the Mountain*
by Jean Craighead George
1960 Newbery Honor Book

Young Sam Gribley spends a year living by himself in a remote area of the Catskill Mountains.
Sequel: *On the Far Side of the Mountain*

☐ *The Planet of Junior Brown*
by Virginia Hamilton
1972 Newbery Honor Book

Already a leader in New York's underground world of homeless children, Buddy Clark takes on the responsibility of protecting an overweight, emotionally disturbed friend.

☐ *Slake's Limbo*
by Felice Holman

Thirteen-year-old Aremis Slake, hounded by his fears and misfortunes, flees into New York City's subway tunnels.

☐ *J. T.*
by Jane Wagner

J. T. begins to change when he discovers there is more satisfaction in caring for an injured cat than in listening to a stolen transistor radio.

☐ *Through the Hidden Door*
by Rosemary Wells

Two young boys stumble upon the remains of an ancient underground mystery civilization.

☐ *Up from Jericho Tel*
by E. L. Konigsburg

The spirit of a dead actress turns two children invisible and sends them out among a group of colorful street performers to search for a missing necklace.

Call It Courage

Armstrong Sperry

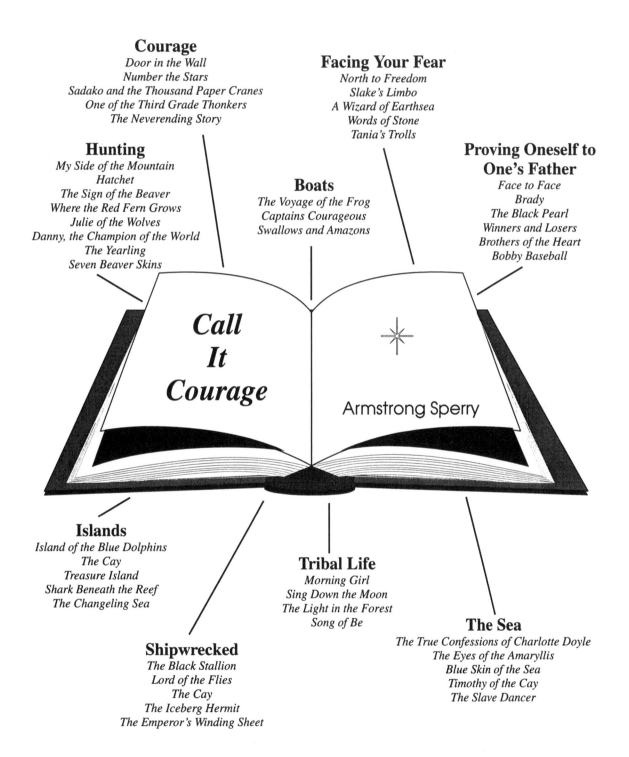

Courage
Door in the Wall
Number the Stars
Sadako and the Thousand Paper Cranes
One of the Third Grade Thonkers
The Neverending Story

Facing Your Fear
North to Freedom
Slake's Limbo
A Wizard of Earthsea
Words of Stone
Tania's Trolls

Hunting
My Side of the Mountain
Hatchet
The Sign of the Beaver
Where the Red Fern Grows
Julie of the Wolves
Danny, the Champion of the World
The Yearling
Seven Beaver Skins

Boats
The Voyage of the Frog
Captains Courageous
Swallows and Amazons

**Proving Oneself to
One's Father**
Face to Face
Brady
The Black Pearl
Winners and Losers
Brothers of the Heart
Bobby Baseball

*Call
It
Courage*

Armstrong Sperry

Islands
Island of the Blue Dolphins
The Cay
Treasure Island
Shark Beneath the Reef
The Changeling Sea

Tribal Life
Morning Girl
Sing Down the Moon
The Light in the Forest
Song of Be

The Sea
The True Confessions of Charlotte Doyle
The Eyes of the Amaryllis
Blue Skin of the Sea
Timothy of the Cay
The Slave Dancer

Shipwrecked
The Black Stallion
Lord of the Flies
The Cay
The Iceberg Hermit
The Emperor's Winding Sheet

13

Call It Courage

Armstrong Sperry

Hunting

My Side of the Mountain

Hatchet

The Sign of the Beaver

Where the Red Fern Grows

Julie of the Wolves

Danny, the Champion of the World

The Yearling

Seven Beaver Skins

Proving Oneself to One's Father

Face to Face

Brady

The Black Pearl

Winners and Losers

Brothers of the Heart

Bobby Baseball

Islands

Island of the Blue Dolphins

The Cay

Treasure Island

Shark Beneath the Reef

The Changeling Sea

Boats

The Voyage of the Frog

Captains Courageous

Swallows and Amazons

Tribal Life

Morning Girl

Sing Down the Moon

The Light in the Forest

Song of Be

Courage

Door in the Wall

Number the Stars

Sadako and the Thousand Paper Cranes

One of the Third Grade Thonkers

The Neverending Story

Facing Your Fear

North to Freedom

Slake's Limbo

A Wizard of Earthsea

Words of Stone

Tania's Trolls

The Sea

The True Confessions of Charlotte Doyle

The Eyes of the Amaryllis

Blue Skin of the Sea

Timothy of the Cay

The Slave Dancer

Shipwrecked

The Black Stallion

Lord of the Flies

The Cay

The Iceberg Hermit

The Emperor's Winding Sheet

Boats
Call It Courage

☐ *The Voyage of the Frog*
by Gary Paulsen

When David goes out on his sailboat to scatter his recently deceased uncle's ashes, he is caught in a storm and must survive many days on his own.

☐ *Captains Courageous*
by Rudyard Kipling

Harvey, the spoiled son of a millionaire, is saved from drowning by a fishing schooner and must share the hard life and labor of the crew.

☐ *Swallows and Amazons*
by Arthur Ransome

Introduces the Walker family, the camp on Wild Cat Island, the able Catboat Swallow, and the two intrepid amazons, Nancy and Peggy.

Many sequels

Islands
Call It Courage

☐ *Island of the Blue Dolphins*
by Scott O'Dell

1961 Newbery Medal

Records the courage and self-reliance of an Indian girl who lived alone for 18 years on an isolated island off the California coast when her tribe emigrated and she was left behind.

☐ *The Cay*
by Theodore Taylor

When the freighter on which they are traveling is torpedoed by a German submarine during World War II, an adolescent white boy, blinded by a blow on the head, and an old black man are stranded on a tiny Caribbean island where the boy acquires a new kind of vision, courage, and love from his old companion.

Prequel/sequel: *Timothy of the Cay*

☐ *Treasure Island*
by Robert Louis Stevenson

While going through the possessions of a deceased guest who owed them money, the mistress of the inn and her son find a treasure map that leads them to a pirate's fortune.

☐ *Shark Beneath the Reef*
by Jean Craighead George

On the island of Coronado, a young Mexican fisherman comes of age as he becomes aware of the politics, corruption, and changes around him.

☐ *The Changeling Sea*
by Patricia McKillip

A floor scrubber and a magician try to help a prince return to his home beneath the sea and help his half-brother, a human trapped in the body of a sea monster, return to the land.

Proving Oneself to One's Father
Call It Courage

☐ *Face to Face*
by Marion Dane Bauer

Picked on at school by bullies, 13-year-old Michael confronts his fears during a trip to Colorado to see his father, who works as a whitewater rafting guide.

☐ *Brady*
by Jean Fritz

A young boy takes part in the pre-Civil War antislavery activities.

☐ *The Black Pearl*
by Scott O'Dell

1968 Newbery Honor Book

In claiming as his own the magnificent black pearl he finds, a 16-year-old youth enrages the sea devil who legend says is its owner.

☐ *Winners and Losers*
by Stephen Hoffius

When a heart condition threatens to curtail his friend Daryl's track career, Curt finds himself the lead contender for the conference championship and the new obsession of Daryl's driven father.

☐ *Brothers of the Heart*
by Joan W. Blos

Fourteen-year-old Shem spends six months in the wilderness alone with a dying Indian woman, who helps him survive and mature to the point where he can return to his family and the difficulties of life as a cripple in a frontier village.

☐ *Bobby Baseball*
by Robert Kimmel Smith

Ten-year-old Bobby is passionate about baseball and convinced that he is a great player. The only problem is to get a chance to prove his skill to his father.

Hunting
Call It Courage

☐ *My Side of the Mountain*
by Jean Craighead George

1960 Newbery Honor Book

Young Sam Gribley spends a year living by himself in a remote area of the Catskill Mountains.

Sequel: *On the Far Side of the Mountain*

☐ *Hatchet*
by Gary Paulsen

1988 Newbery Honor Book

After a plane crash, 13-year-old Brian spends 54 days in the wilderness, learning to survive with only the aid of a hatchet.

☐ *The Sign of the Beaver*
by Elizabeth George Speare

1984 Newbery Honor Book

Left alone to guard the family's wilderness home, a boy is hard-pressed to survive until local Indians teach him their skills.

☐ *Where the Red Fern Grows*
by Wilson Rawls

The adventures of a 10-year-old boy and the two dogs he bought with money he had earned.

☐ *Julie of the Wolves*
by Jean Craighead George

1973 Newbery Honor Book

A 13-year-old Eskimo girl becomes lost and is befriended by a wolf pack.

☐ *Danny, the Champion of the World*
by Roald Dahl

Danny and his poacher father share a special adventure together.

☐ *The Yearling*
by Marjorie Kinnan Rawlings

A young boy living in the Florida backwoods is forced to decide the fate of a fawn he has lovingly raised as a pet.

☐ *Seven Beaver Skins*
by Erick Berry

A story of the Dutch in New Amsterdam.

Tribal Life
Call It Courage

☐ *Morning Girl*
by Michael Dorris

Morning Girl and her younger brother Star Boy take turns describing their life on an island.

☐ *Sing Down the Moon*
by Scott O'Dell

1971 Newbery Honor Book

A young Navajo girl recounts when her tribe was forced to march to Fort Sumner as prisoners of the white soldiers.

☐ *The Light in the Forest*
by Conrad Richter

After being raised as an Indian for 11 years, John Butler is forcibly returned to his white parents.

☐ *Song of Be*
by Lesley Beake

Be, a young Bushman woman, realizes that she and her people must reconcile new personal and political realities with ancient traditions.

Courage
Call It Courage

☐ *Door in the Wall*
by Marguerite de Angeli

1950 Newbery Medal

A crippled boy in 14th-century England proves his courage and earns recognition from the King.

☐ *Number the Stars*
by Lois Lowry

1990 Newbery Medal

In 1943, during the German occupation of Denmark, 10-year-old Annemarie learns how to be brave and courageous when she helps shelter her Jewish friend from the Nazis.

☐ *Sadako and the Thousand Paper Cranes*
by Eleanor Coerr

Hospitalized with the dreaded atom bomb disease, leukemia, a child in Hiroshima races against time to fold 1,000 paper cranes to verify the legend that by doing so a sick person will become healthy.

☐ *One of the Third Grade Thonkers*
by Phyllis Reynolds Naylor

Ashamed of his wimpy younger cousin, eight-year-old Jimmy is determined to keep him out of his special club for rough, tough, and terrible boys, until an accident involving Jimmy's father demonstrates for him the true meaning of courage.

☐ *The Neverending Story*
by Michael Ende

The magical tale of Bastian, a lonely, solitary boy, who steps through the pages of a book into a special kingdom where he learns the true measure of his courage and creates a new world with his wishes.

Facing Your Fear
Call It Courage

☐ *North to Freedom*
by Anne Holm

Having escaped from an Eastern European concentration camp where he has spent his life, a 12-year-old boy struggles to cope with an entirely strange world as he flees northward to freedom in Denmark.

☐ *Slake's Limbo*
by Felice Holman

Thirteen-year-old Aremis Slake, hounded by his fears and misfortunes, flees into New York City's subway tunnels, never again, he believes, to emerge.

☐ *A Wizard of Earthsea*
by Ursula Le Guin

A boy grows to manhood while attempting to subdue the evil he unleashed on the world as an apprentice to the Master Wizard.

Book 1 of the Earthsea series

☐ *Words of Stone*
by Kevin Henkes

Busy trying to deal with his many fears and his troubled feelings for his dead mother, 10-year-old Blaze has his life changed when he meets the boisterous and irresistible Joselle.

☐ *Tania's Trolls*
by Lisa Westberg Peters

A formidable grandmother helps young Tania overcome her stage fright.

The Sea
Call It Courage

☐ *The True Confessions of Charlotte Doyle*
by Avi

1991 Newbery Honor Book

As the lone young lady on a transatlantic voyage in 1832, Charlotte learns that the captain is murderous and the crew rebellious.

☐ *The Eyes of the Amaryllis*
by Natalie Babbitt

When 11-year-old Jenny goes to stay with her widowed grandmother, who lives by the seaside waiting for a sign from her drowned husband, she learns a great deal about the nature of love and the ways of the sea.

☐ *Blue Skin of the Sea*
by Graham Salisbury

Growing up in Hawaii between 1953 and 1966, Sonny tries to come to terms with his feelings for his fisherman father and the vast sea that dominates his life.

☐ *Timothy of the Cay*
by Theodore Taylor

Having survived being blinded and shipwrecked on a tiny Caribbean island with the old black man Timothy, 12-year-old white Phillip is rescued and hopes to regain his sight with an operation. Alternate chapters follow the life of Timothy from his days as a young cabin boy.

Prequel/sequel to *The Cay*.

☐ *The Slave Dancer*
by Paula Fox

1974 Newbery Medal

Kidnapped by the crew of an Africa-bound ship, a 13-year-old boy discovers to his horror that he is on a slaver and his job is to play music for the exercise periods of the human cargo.

Shipwrecked
Call It Courage

☐ *The Black Stallion*
by Walter Farley

A boy is pulled to a desert island by a wild black stallion he has freed during a shipwreck at sea, then is rescued by a southbound freighter. The boy befriends the horse, trains him by night, and rides him in a match race.

Many sequels

☐ *Lord of the Flies*
by William Golding

Stranded on an island, a group of young boys revert to savagery as they struggle to survive.

☐ *The Cay*
by Theodore Taylor

When the freighter on which they are traveling is torpedoed by a German submarine during World War II, an adolescent white boy, blinded by a blow on the head, and an old black man are stranded on a tiny Caribbean island, where the boy acquires a new kind of vision, courage, and love from his old companion.

Prequel/sequel: *Timothy of the Cay*

☐ *The Iceberg Hermit*
by Arthur Roth

Shipwrecked in 1757 on an iceberg in the Arctic seas with only an orphaned polar bear cub for companionship, 17-year-old Allan begins a seemingly hopeless struggle for survival.

☐ *The Emperor's Winding Sheet*
by Jill Paton Walsh

An English boy, shipwrecked, hungry, and lost, finds his way into the court of Constantine, where he is interpreted as a symbol of good luck and, as such, ordered to always be kept near the king.

Charlie and the Chocolate Factory

Roald Dahl

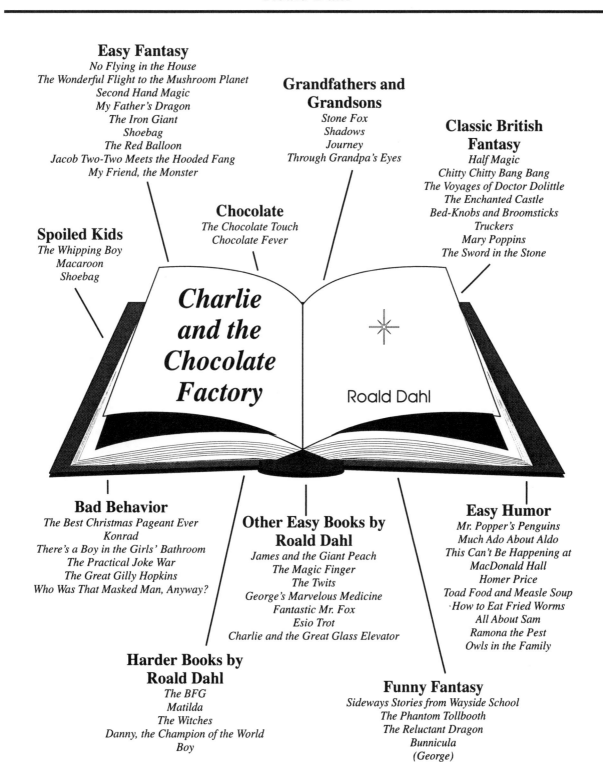

Easy Fantasy
No Flying in the House
The Wonderful Flight to the Mushroom Planet
Second Hand Magic
My Father's Dragon
The Iron Giant
Shoebag
The Red Balloon
Jacob Two-Two Meets the Hooded Fang
My Friend, the Monster

Grandfathers and Grandsons
Stone Fox
Shadows
Journey
Through Grandpa's Eyes

Classic British Fantasy
Half Magic
Chitty Chitty Bang Bang
The Voyages of Doctor Dolittle
The Enchanted Castle
Bed-Knobs and Broomsticks
Truckers
Mary Poppins
The Sword in the Stone

Chocolate
The Chocolate Touch
Chocolate Fever

Spoiled Kids
The Whipping Boy
Macaroon
Shoebag

Bad Behavior
The Best Christmas Pageant Ever
Konrad
There's a Boy in the Girls' Bathroom
The Practical Joke War
The Great Gilly Hopkins
Who Was That Masked Man, Anyway?

Other Easy Books by Roald Dahl
James and the Giant Peach
The Magic Finger
The Twits
George's Marvelous Medicine
Fantastic Mr. Fox
Esio Trot
Charlie and the Great Glass Elevator

Easy Humor
Mr. Popper's Penguins
Much Ado About Aldo
This Can't Be Happening at MacDonald Hall
Homer Price
Toad Food and Measle Soup
·How to Eat Fried Worms
All About Sam
Ramona the Pest
Owls in the Family

Harder Books by Roald Dahl
The BFG
Matilda
The Witches
Danny, the Champion of the World
Boy

Funny Fantasy
Sideways Stories from Wayside School
The Phantom Tollbooth
The Reluctant Dragon
Bunnicula
(George)
The Ghost Belonged to Me

19

Roald Dahl

Charlie and the Chocolate Factory

Other Easy Books by Roald Dahl

James and the Giant Peach

The Magic Finger

The Twits

George's Marvelous Medicine

Fantastic Mr. Fox

Esio Trot

Charlie and the Great Glass Elevator

Chocolate

The Chocolate Touch

Chocolate Fever

Harder Books by Roald Dahl

The BFG

Matilda

The Witches

Danny, the Champion of the World

Boy

Spoiled Kids

The Whipping Boy

Macaroon

Shoebag

Grandfathers and Grandsons

Stone Fox

Shadows

Journey

Through Grandpa's Eyes

Bad Behavior

The Best Christmas Pageant Ever

Konrad

There's a Boy in the Girls' Bathroom

The Practical Joke War

The Great Gilly Hopkins

Who Was That Masked Man, Anyway?

Easy Fantasy

No Flying in the House

The Wonderful Flight to the Mushroom Planet

Second Hand Magic

My Father's Dragon

The Iron Giant

Shoebag

The Red Balloon

Jacob Two-Two Meets the Hooded Fang

My Friend, the Monster

Funny Fantasy

Sideways Stories from Wayside School

The Phantom Tollbooth

The Reluctant Dragon

Bunnicula

(George)

The Ghost Belonged to Me

Classic British Fantasy

Half Magic

Chitty Chitty Bang Bang

The Voyages of Doctor Dolittle

The Enchanted Castle

Bed-Knobs and Broomsticks

Truckers

Mary Poppins

The Sword in the Stone

Easy Humor

Mr. Popper's Penguins

Much Ado About Aldo

*This Can't Be Happening
at MacDonald Hall*

Homer Price

*Toad Food and Measle
Soup*

How to Eat Fried Worms

All About Sam

Ramona the Pest

Owls in the Family

Other Easy Books by Roald Dahl
Charlie and the Chocolate Factory

☐ *James and the Giant Peach*
Wonderful adventures abound after James escapes from his fearful aunts by rolling away inside a giant peach.

☐ *The Magic Finger*
Angered by a neighboring family's sport hunting, an eight-year-old girl turns her magic finger on them.

☐ *The Twits*
The misadventures of two terrible old people who enjoy playing nasty tricks and are finally outwitted by a family of monkeys.

☐ *George's Marvelous Medicine*
George decides that his grumpy, selfish old grandmother must be a witch and concocts some marvelous medicine to take care of her.

☐ *Fantastic Mr. Fox*
Three farmers, each one meaner than the other, try all-out warfare to get rid of the fox and his family.

☐ *Esio Trot*
Shy Mr. Hoppy devises a plan to win the heart of his true love by teaching her a spell to make her tortoise grow bigger.

☐ *Charlie and the Great Glass Elevator*
Willie Wonka and Charlie's family are blasted into space.
Sequel to *Charlie and the Chocolate Factory*

Chocolate
Charlie and the Chocolate Factory

☐ *The Chocolate Touch*
by Patrick Skene Catling
A boy acquires a magical gift that turns everything his lips touch into chocolate.

☐ *Chocolate Fever*
by Robert Kimmel Smith
From eating too much chocolate, Henry breaks out in brown bumps that help him foil some hijackers.

Harder Books by Roald Dahl
Charlie and the Chocolate Factory

☐ *The BFG*
Kidsnatched from her orphanage by a BFG (Big Friendly Giant) who spends his life blowing happy dreams to children, Sophie concocts with him a plan to save the world from nine other man-gobbling cannybul giants.

☐ *Matilda*
Matilda applies her untapped mental powers to rid the school of the evil, child-hating headmistress, Miss Trunchbull, and restore her nice teacher, Miss Honey, to financial security.

☐ *The Witches*
A young boy and his Norwegian grandmother, who is an expert on witches, together foil a witches' plot to destroy the world's children by turning them into mice.

☐ *Danny, the Champion of the World*
Danny describes his relationship with his father, a poacher, and the special adventure they share together.

☐ *Boy*
Presents humorous anecdotes from the author's childhood, including summer vacations in Norway and an English boarding school.

Spoiled Kids
Charlie and the Chocolate Factory

☐ *The Whipping Boy*
by Sid Fleischman
1987 Newbery Medal
A bratty prince and his whipping boy have many adventures when they inadvertently trade places.

☐ *Macaroon*
by Julia Cunningham
A raccoon spends the winter in a disagreeable child's home, but he selects such a nasty, spoiled girl that he can't help trying to reform her.

☐ *Shoebag*
by Mary James
Shoebag, a cockroach who finds himself changed into a boy, changes the lives of those around him.

Grandfathers and Grandsons
Charlie and the Chocolate Factory

☐ *Stone Fox*
by John R. Gardiner

Willie hopes to pay the taxes on his grandfather's farm with the purse from a dogsled race.

☐ *Shadows*
by Dennis Haseley

Jamie's lonely life with his aunt and uncle changes when Grandpa comes to visit.

☐ *Journey*
by Patricia MacLachlan

When their mother abandons them at their grandparents' house, two children feel as if their past has been erased.

☐ *Through Grandpa's Eyes*
by Patricia MacLachlan

A boy learns a different way of seeing from his blind grandfather.

Bad Behavior
Charlie and the Chocolate Factory

☐ *The Best Christmas Pageant Ever*
by Barbara Robinson

The six mean Herdman kids lie, steal, and smoke cigars (even the girls) and then become involved in the community Christmas pageant.

☐ *Konrad*
by Christine Nostlinger

By mistake, an unconventional lady receives a perfectly behaved, factory-made child in the mail. To escape being returned, he must learn normal child behavior.

☐ *There's a Boy in the Girls' Bathroom*
by Louis Sachar

An unmanageable 11-year-old misfit learns to believe in himself when he gets to know the new school counselor, who is a sort of misfit too.

☐ *The Practical Joke War*
by Alane Ferguson

The Dillon children's practical jokes on each other increase to a breaking point where they are finally driven together.

☐ *The Great Gilly Hopkins*
by Katherine Paterson

1979 Newbery Honor Book

An 11-year-old foster child tries to cope with her longings and fears as she schemes against everyone who tries to be friendly.

☐ *Who Was That Masked Man, Anyway?*
by Avi

In the early 1940s, when nearly everyone else is thinking about World War II, sixth-grader Frankie Wattleson gets in trouble at home and at school because of his preoccupation with his favorite radio programs.

Easy Fantasy
Charlie and the Chocolate Factory

☐ *No Flying in the House*
by Betty Brock

A mysterious girl and her miniature talking dog come to live with an old lady.

☐ *The Wonderful Flight to the Mushroom Planet*
by Eleanor Cameron

Two boys build a spaceship that takes them to the planet Basidium.

☐ *Second Hand Magic*
by Ruth Chew

Two children acquire a magic kite.

☐ *My Father's Dragon*
by Ruth Stiles Gannett

1949 Newbery Honor Book

A young boy determines to rescue a baby dragon.

Book 1 of the Dragon series

☐ *The Iron Giant*
by Ted Hughes

The fearsome Iron Giant challenges a huge space monster.

☐ *Shoebag*
by Mary James

A cockroach finds himself changed into a boy.

☐ *The Red Balloon*
by Albert Lamorisse

A young boy finds a red balloon with a mind of its own.

☐ *Jacob Two-Two Meets the Hooded Fang*
by Mordecai Richler

Imprisoned by the Hooded Fang, Jacob Two-Two awaits the aid of the members of Child Power.

☐ *My Friend, the Monster*
by Clyde Robert Bulla

A lonely prince forms a dangerous friendship with a monster.

Funny Fantasy
Charlie and the Chocolate Factory

☐ *Sideways Stories from Wayside School*
by Louis Sachar

Humorous episodes from the classroom on the 30th floor of Wayside School, which was accidentally built sideways, with one classroom on each story.

Sequel: *Wayside School Is Falling Down*

☐ *The Phantom Tollbooth*
by Norton Juster

A journey through a land where Milo learns the importance of words and numbers provides a cure for his boredom.

☐ *The Reluctant Dragon*
by Kenneth Grahame

How can the boy who finds the dragon convince the frightened villagers, and especially St. George the dragonkiller, that there is no call for concern?

☐ *Bunnicula*
by Deborah and James Howe

Chester the cat tries to warn his human family that their foundling baby bunny must be a vampire.

First of a series

☐ *(George)*
by E. L. Konigsburg

When 12-year-old Benjamin refuses to see what is going on in his chemistry lab, the little man who lives inside of him must finally speak out in public.

☐ *The Ghost Belonged to Me*
by Richard Peck

In 1913 in the Midwest, a quartet of characters shares adventures, from exploding steamboats to exorcising a ghost.

Easy Humor
Charlie and the Chocolate Factory

□ *Mr. Popper's Penguins*
by Richard and Florence Atwater
1939 Newbery Honor Book
A large crate containing an Antarctic penguin changes the life of Mr. Popper.

□ *Much Ado About Aldo*
by Johanna Hurwitz
Because of a school project, eight-year-old Aldo decides to give up eating meat.

□ *This Can't Be Happening at MacDonald Hall*
by Gordon Korman
Bruno and Boots seem to be at the bottom of every prank at MacDonald Hall.

□ *Homer Price*
by Robert McCloskey
The adventures of Homer Price, including when his pet skunk captured bandits, and when a donut machine went on the rampage.

□ *Toad Food and Measle Soup*
by Christine McDonnell
Leo survives his mother's experiments with vegetarian cooking.

□ *How to Eat Fried Worms*
by Thomas Rockwell
A boy bets he can eat 15 worms in 15 days.

□ *All About Sam*
by Lois Lowry
The adventures of Sam, starting with his first day as a newborn.

□ *Ramona the Pest*
by Beverly Cleary
Ramona is a little sister who always wants to tag along after the older kids.

□ *Owls in the Family*
by Farley Mowat
A young boy decides to raise two owlets as pets.

Classic British Fantasy
Charlie and the Chocolate Factory

□ *Half Magic*
by Edward Eager
Four children enjoy a series of fantastic adventures by double-wishing on an ancient coin.
This book is British in style, although the author is American.

□ *Chitty Chitty Bang Bang*
by Ian Fleming
An inventor purchases and restores an old car that has magical powers.

□ *The Voyages of Doctor Dolittle*
by Hugh Lofting
1923 Newbery Medal
The adventures of a doctor who understands animals' language.

□ *The Enchanted Castle*
by E. Nesbit
Four children find a magic garden and wake a princess from a 100-year sleep, only to have her made invisible by a magic ring.

□ *Bed-Knobs and Broomsticks*
by Mary Norton
With the powers they acquire from a witch, three children go on a number of exciting and gruesome trips.

□ *Truckers*
by Terry Pratchett
The nomes look to Masklin, a newly arrived "outsider," to lead them to a safe haven.
Book 1 of the Bromeliad

□ *Mary Poppins*
by P. L. Travers
The Bankses' magical new nanny introduces the Banks children to some strange people and experiences.
Several sequels

□ *The Sword in the Stone*
by T. H. White
Arthur becomes a wiser person and a worthy king as a result of Merlin's lessons.

Chitty Chitty Bang Bang

Ian Fleming

Easy Fantasies
The Wonderful Flight to the Mushroom Planet
The Chocolate Touch
Charlie and the Chocolate Factory
James and the Giant Peach
My Father's Dragon
The Iron Giant
Jacob Two-Two Meets the Hooded Fang

Magical Objects
Penelope's Pendant
The Eyes of Kid Midas
The Magic Skateboard
Cart and Cwidder
Second Hand Magic
Travel Far, Pay No Fare

Eccentrics
Konrad
The Facts and Fictions of Minna Pratt
Unclaimed Treasures
Nekomah Creek
Portrait of Ivan
Arthur for the Very First Time
A Likely Place
The Ghost Belonged to Me

Kidnapping
The BFG
The Case of the Baker Street Irregular
The Famous Stanley Kidnapping Case
Tuck Everlasting
Father's Arcane Daughter
Song of the Gargoyle

Chitty Chitty Bang Bang

Ian Fleming

Kids Who Stop the Bad Guys
(George)
The Battle for the Castle
The Witches
The Wolves of Willoughby Chase
Momo
Brady
Circle of Fire
Treasure Island

Outlaws
The Whipping Boy
Ronia the Robber's Daughter
Oh, Those Harper Girls
Emil and the Detectives
Chocolate Fever
Wild Jack

Magical Journeys
The Phantom Tollbooth
Bed-Knobs and Broomsticks
Time Cat
Peter Pan
The Nutcracker
Mary Poppins
The Lives of Christopher Chant

Classic British Fantasy
Half Magic
The Voyages of Doctor Dolittle
The Enchanted Castle
Truckers
The Sword in the Stone
The Box of Delights: When the Wolves Were Running

Chitty Chitty Bang Bang

Ian Fleming

Eccentrics

Konrad

The Facts and Fictions of Minna Pratt

Unclaimed Treasures

Nekomah Creek

Portrait of Ivan

Arthur for the Very First Time

A Likely Place

The Ghost Belonged to Me

Kidnapping

The BFG

The Case of the Baker Street Irregular

The Famous Stanley Kidnapping Case

Tuck Everlasting

Father's Arcane Daughter

Song of the Gargoyle

Kids Who Stop the Bad Guys

(George)

The Battle for the Castle

The Witches

The Wolves of Willoughby Chase

Momo

Brady

Circle of Fire

Treasure Island

Outlaws

The Whipping Boy

Ronia the Robber's Daughter

Oh, Those Harper Girls

Emil and the Detectives

Chocolate Fever

Wild Jack

Magical Journeys

The Phantom Tollbooth

Bed-Knobs and Broomsticks

Time Cat

Peter Pan

The Nutcracker

Mary Poppins

The Lives of Christopher Chant

Easy Fantasy

The Wonderful Flight to the Mushroom Planet

The Chocolate Touch

Charlie and the Chocolate Factory

James and the Giant Peach

My Father's Dragon

The Iron Giant

Jacob Two-Two Meets the Hooded Fang

Classic British Fantasy

Half Magic

The Voyages of Doctor Dolittle

The Enchanted Castle

Truckers

The Sword in the Stone

The Box of Delights: When the Wolves Were Running

Magical Objects

Penelope's Pendant

The Eyes of Kid Midas

The Magic Skateboard

Cart and Cwidder

Second Hand Magic

Travel Far, Pay No Fare

Outlaws
Chitty Chitty Bang Bang

The Whipping Boy
by Sid Fleischman

1987 Newbery Medal

A bratty prince and his whipping boy have many adventures when they inadvertently trade places after becoming involved with dangerous outlaws.

Ronia the Robber's Daughter
by Astrid Lindgren

Ronia, who lives with her father and his band of robbers in a castle in the woods, causes trouble when she befriends the son of a rival robber chieftain.

Oh, Those Harper Girls
by Kathleen Karr

In west Texas in 1869, Lily and her five older sisters participate in a series of misguided schemes to save their father's ranch.

Emil and the Detectives
by Erich Kastner

A German boy and his friends use their ingenuity to catch a thief.

Chocolate Fever
by Robert Kimmel Smith

From eating too much chocolate, Henry breaks out in brown bumps that help him foil some hijackers and teach him a valuable lesson about self-indulgence.

Wild Jack
by John Christopher

In 23rd-century England, young Clive Anderson, unjustly imprisoned in an attempt to mold him into a docile member of society, escapes to the Outlands and is befriended by Wild Jack's outlaw band.

Book 1 of a trilogy

Kids Who Stop the Bad Guys
Chitty Chitty Bang Bang

(George)
by E. L. Konigsburg

When 12-year-old Benjamin refuses to see what is going on in his chemistry lab, the little man who lives inside of him must finally speak out in public.

The Battle for the Castle
by Elizabeth Winthrop

Twelve-year-old William uses a magic token to return to the medieval land of Sir Simon, which is now menaced by a skeleton ship.

Sequel to *Castle in the Attic*

The Witches
by Roald Dahl

A young boy and his grandmother foil a witches' plot to destroy the world's children.

The Wolves of Willoughby Chase
by Joan Aiken

Surrounded by villains, brave Bonnie and gentle cousin Sylvia conquer all obstacles.

Book 1 of the Wolves of Willoughby Chase series

Momo
by Michael Ende

Momo discovers a plot by the men in gray to steal everybody's time.

Brady
by Jean Fritz

A young boy takes part in the pre-Civil War antislavery activities.

Circle of Fire
by William Hooks

Eleven-year-old Harrison overhears a bigot planning a Ku Klux Klan raid on a band of Irish tinkers.

Treasure Island
by Robert Louis Stevenson

A boy finds a treasure map that leads him to a pirate's fortune.

Kidnapping
Chitty Chitty Bang Bang

The BFG
by Roald Dahl

Kidsnatched from her orphanage by a BFG (Big Friendly Giant), Sophie concocts with him a plan to save the world from other man-gobbling giants.

The Case of the Baker Street Irregular
by Robert Newman

Brought to London under mysterious circumstances by his tutor, a young boy seeks the help of Sherlock Holmes when his tutor is kidnapped and he himself is threatened with the same fate.

The Famous Stanley Kidnapping Case
by Zilpha Keatley Snyder

Kidnappers in Italy have their hands full when the captive American children advise them on running a better kidnapping and on proper nutrition.

Tuck Everlasting
by Natalie Babbitt

A 10-year-old girl and a malicious stranger now share the Tucks' secret about a spring whose water prevents one from growing older.

Father's Arcane Daughter
by E. L. Konigsburg

Kidnapped 17 years ago, a man's daughter by a former marriage appears at his new home in Pittsburgh and affects the entire family.

Song of the Gargoyle
by Zilpha Keatley Snyder

When mysterious men in black abduct his father, 13-year-old Tymmon flees into the forest, where he acquires a strange animal companion and plots to rescue his father.

Eccentrics
Chitty Chitty Bang Bang

Konrad
by Christine Nostlinger

By mistake, an unconventional lady receives a perfectly behaved, factory-made child in the mail.

The Facts and Fictions of Minna Pratt
by Patricia MacLachlan

An 11-year-old cellist learns about life from her eccentric family, her first boyfriend, and Mozart.

Unclaimed Treasures
by Patricia MacLachlan

Willa thinks that she's in love with the father of the boy next door.

Nekomah Creek
by Linda Crew

Unwanted attention from a counselor and a bully at school makes Robby self-conscious about how his unconventional family might look to outsiders.

Portrait of Ivan
by Paula Fox

An 11-year-old boy gains new understanding of himself and his father after a trip with unusual people.

Arthur for the Very First Time
by Patricia MacLachlan

Arthur spends a summer with his unconventional aunt and uncle.

A Likely Place
by Paula Fox

A little boy who can't ever seem to please his parents spends a week with a kooky baby-sitter.

The Ghost Belonged to Me
by Richard Peck

In 1913 a quartet of characters must exorcise a ghost.

Magical Objects
Chitty Chitty Bang Bang

📖 *Penelope's Pendant*
by Douglas Hill

Eleven-year-old Penelope finds a slightly damaged pendant on the beach and discovers that it gives her the power to move herself and other objects through space.

📖 *The Eyes of Kid Midas*
by Neal Shusterman

Kevin is entranced when he finds a pair of sunglasses that turn his desires into reality, but then things start to get out of control.

📖 *The Magic Skateboard*
by Enid Richemont

On his way home from school in London just before Christmas, Danny meets a strange-looking woman who transforms his skateboard into a kind of flying carpet that allows him to visit any place he imagines.

📖 *Cart and Cwidder*
by Diana Wynne Jones

When their father, a traveling minstrel, is killed, three children involved in rebellion and intrigue inherit a lute-like cwidder with more than musical powers.

📖 *Second Hand Magic*
by Ruth Chew

Two children acquire a magic kite and, with some secondhand items from a nearby store, enjoy a series of adventures.

📖 *Travel Far, Pay No Fare*
by Anne Lindbergh

When 12-year-old Owen finds that his nine-year-old cousin has a magic bookmark, he joins her when she enters different stories in hopes of finding a way to prevent their parents' upcoming marriage.

Classic British Fantasy
Chitty Chitty Bang Bang

📖 *Half Magic*
by Edward Eager

Four children enjoy a series of fantastic adventures by double-wishing on an ancient coin.

This book is British in style, although the author is American.

📖 *The Voyages of Doctor Dolittle*
by Hugh Lofting
1923 Newbery Medal

The adventures of a kind-hearted doctor, who is fond of animals and understands their language, as he travels to Africa with some of his favorite pets to cure the monkeys of a terrible sickness.

📖 *The Enchanted Castle*
by E. Nesbit

Four children find a magic garden and wake a princess from a 100-year sleep, only to have her made invisible by a magic ring.

📖 *Truckers*
by Terry Pratchett

The nomes look to Masklin, a newly arrived "outsider," to lead them to a safe haven.

Book 1 of the Bromeliad

📖 *The Sword in the Stone*
by T. H. White

Arthur becomes a wiser person and a worthy king as a result of Merlin's lessons.

📖 *The Box of Delights: When the Wolves Were Running*
by John Masefield

Kay finds himself involved in a fantastic adventure when he becomes guardian of the mysterious Box of Delights.

Easy Fantasy
Chitty Chitty Bang Bang

📖 *The Wonderful Flight to the Mushroom Planet*
by Eleanor Cameron

Two boys build a spaceship that takes them to the planet Basidium.

Book 1 of the Mushroom Planet series

📖 *The Chocolate Touch*
by Patrick Skene Catling

A boy acquires a magical gift that turns everything his lips touch into chocolate.

📖 *Charlie and the Chocolate Factory*
by Roald Dahl

Five children discover entry tickets into Mr. Willy Wonka's mysterious chocolate factory.

Sequel: *Charlie and the Great Glass Elevator*

📖 *James and the Giant Peach*
by Roald Dahl

Wonderful adventures abound after James escapes from his fearful aunts by rolling away inside a giant peach.

📖 *My Father's Dragon*
by Ruth Stiles Gannett
1949 Newbery Honor Book

A young boy determines to rescue a poor baby dragon.

Book 1 of the Dragon series

📖 *The Iron Giant*
by Ted Hughes

The fearsome Iron Giant becomes a hero when he challenges a huge space monster.

📖 *Jacob Two-Two Meets the Hooded Fang*
by Mordecai Richler

Unjustly imprisoned by the Hooded Fang, Jacob Two-Two awaits the aid of the members of Child Power to free him.

Magical Journeys
Chitty Chitty Bang Bang

📖 *The Phantom Tollbooth*
by Norton Juster

A journey through a land where he learns the importance of words and numbers provides a cure for Milo's boredom.

📖 *Bed-Knobs and Broomsticks*
by Mary Norton

With the powers they acquire from a witch, three children go on a number of exciting and gruesome trips.

📖 *Time Cat*
by Lloyd Alexander

Gareth, a cat with miraculous powers, takes his human friend Jason with him when he travels through time.

📖 *Peter Pan*
by J. M. Barrie

Peter Pan teaches Wendy and her brothers to fly to Neverland, where they have some exciting adventures with Indians and pirates.

📖 *The Nutcracker*
by E. T. A. Hoffman

After hearing how her toy nutcracker got his ugly face, a little girl helps break the spell.

📖 *Mary Poppins*
by P. L. Travers

The Bankses' magical new nanny introduces the Banks children to some strange people and experiences.

Several sequels

📖 *The Lives of Christopher Chant*
by Diana Wynne Jones

Young Christopher Chant, training to become the next head controller of magic in the world, becomes a key figure in a battle with renegade sorcerers.

Circle of Gold

Candy Dawson Boyd

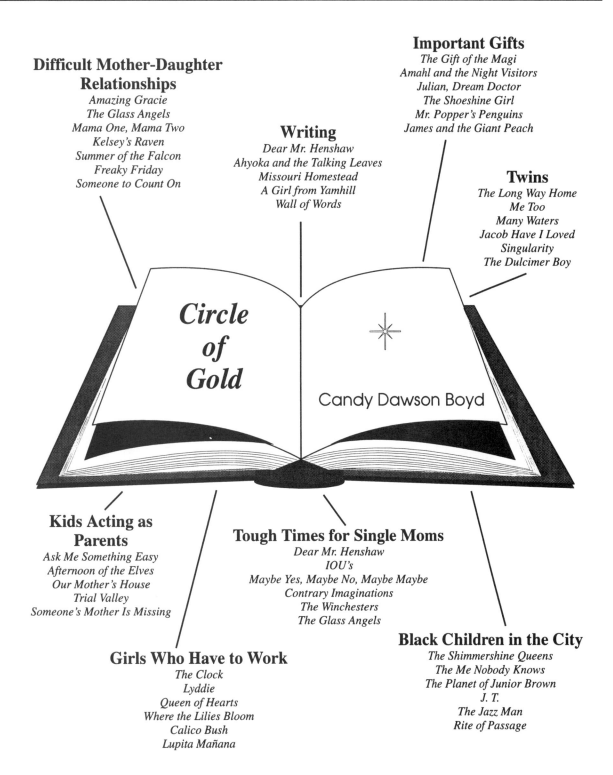

Important Gifts
The Gift of the Magi
Amahl and the Night Visitors
Julian, Dream Doctor
The Shoeshine Girl
Mr. Popper's Penguins
James and the Giant Peach

Difficult Mother-Daughter Relationships
Amazing Gracie
The Glass Angels
Mama One, Mama Two
Kelsey's Raven
Summer of the Falcon
Freaky Friday
Someone to Count On

Writing
Dear Mr. Henshaw
Ahyoka and the Talking Leaves
Missouri Homestead
A Girl from Yamhill
Wall of Words

Twins
The Long Way Home
Me Too
Many Waters
Jacob Have I Loved
Singularity
The Dulcimer Boy

Kids Acting as Parents
Ask Me Something Easy
Afternoon of the Elves
Our Mother's House
Trial Valley
Someone's Mother Is Missing

Tough Times for Single Moms
Dear Mr. Henshaw
IOU's
Maybe Yes, Maybe No, Maybe Maybe
Contrary Imaginations
The Winchesters
The Glass Angels

Black Children in the City
The Shimmershine Queens
The Me Nobody Knows
The Planet of Junior Brown
J. T.
The Jazz Man
Rite of Passage

Girls Who Have to Work
The Clock
Lyddie
Queen of Hearts
Where the Lilies Bloom
Calico Bush
Lupita Mañana

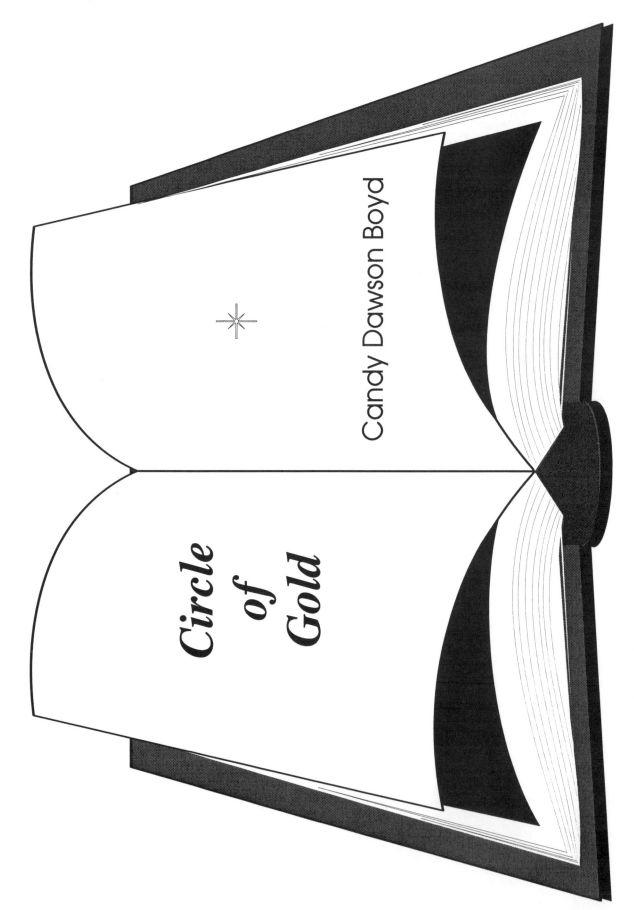

Candy Dawson Boyd

Circle
of
Gold

Difficult Mother-Daughter Relationships

Amazing Gracie
The Glass Angels
Mama One, Mama Two
Kelsey's Raven
Summer of the Falcon
Freaky Friday
Someone to Count On

Important Gifts

The Gift of the Magi

Amahl and the Night Visitors

Julian, Dream Doctor

The Shoeshine Girl

Mr. Popper's Penguins

James and the Giant Peach

Writing

Dear Mr. Henshaw

Ahyoka and the Talking Leaves

Missouri Homestead

A Girl from Yamhill

Wall of Words

Twins

The Long Way Home

Me Too

Many Waters

Jacob Have I Loved

Singularity

The Dulcimer Boy

Girls Who Have to Work

The Clock

Lyddie

Queen of Hearts

Where the Lilies Bloom

Calico Bush

Lupita Mañana

Tough Times for Single Moms

Dear Mr. Henshaw

IOU's

Maybe Yes, Maybe No, Maybe Maybe

Contrary Imaginations

The Winchesters

The Glass Angels

Kids Acting as Parents

Ask Me Something Easy

Afternoon of the Elves

Our Mother's House

Trial Valley

Someone's Mother Is Missing

Black Children in the City

The Shimmershine Queens

The Me Nobody Knows

The Planet of Junior Brown

J. T.

The Jazz Man

Rite of Passage

Difficult Mother-Daughter Relationships
Circle of Gold

☐ *Amazing Gracie*
by A. E. Cannon

A high school girl has a lot to deal with when her mother, who suffers from depression, remarries; a new brother is acquired; and the family moves to Salt Lake City.

☐ *The Glass Angels*
by Susan Hill

Even though times are hard, Tilly looks forward to spending Christmas with her mother, until illness and an accident threaten her plans.

☐ *Mama One, Mama Two*
by Patricia MacLachlan

A young child lives with a foster family until her own mother is well enough to care for her.

☐ *Kelsey's Raven*
by Sylvia Peck

The discovery of a raven in the chimney of her New York apartment proves to be a harbinger of change in Kelsey's life.

☐ *Summer of the Falcon*
by Jean Craighead George

As June trainees her hawk, she chafes at her mother's insistence that she assume the responsibilities of her own increasing age.

☐ *Freaky Friday*
by Mary Rodgers

A 13-year-old girl gains more sympathetic understanding of her mother when she has to spend a day in her mother's body.

☐ *Someone to Count On*
by Patricia Hermes

When 11-year-old Sam visits her grandfather's ranch, she finds a new life very different from the one she has known with her vagabond mother.

Important Gifts
Circle of Gold

☐ *The Gift of the Magi*
by O. Henry

A husband and wife sacrifice treasured possessions to get each other presents for Christmas.

☐ *Amahl and the Night Visitors*
by Giancarlo Menotti

Relates how a crippled young shepherd comes to accompany the three kings on their way to pay homage to the newborn Jesus.

☐ *Julian, Dream Doctor*
by Ann Cameron

Julian and Huey try to find the perfect birthday gift for Dad with amusing results.
Sequel to *The Stories Julian Tells*

☐ *The Shoeshine Girl*
by Clyde Robert Bulla

Determined to earn some money, 10-year-old Sarah Ida gets a job at a shoeshine stand and learns a great many things besides shining shoes.

☐ *Mr. Popper's Penguins*
by Richard and Florence Atwater
1939 Newbery Honor Book

The unexpected delivery of a large crate containing an Antarctic penguin changes the life and fortunes of Mr. Popper, a house painter obsessed by dreams of the polar regions.

☐ *James and the Giant Peach*
by Roald Dahl

Wonderful adventures abound after James escapes from his fearful aunts by rolling away inside a giant peach.

Writing
Circle of Gold

☐ *Dear Mr. Henshaw*
by Beverly Cleary
1984 Newbery Medal

In his letters to his favorite author, 10-year-old Leigh reveals his problems in coping with his parents' divorce, being the new boy in school, and generally finding his own place in the world.
Sequel: *Strider*

☐ *Ahyoka and the Talking Leaves*
by Peter and Connie Roop

Ahyoka helps her father Sequoyah in his quest to create a system of writing for his people.

☐ *Missouri Homestead*
by T. L. Tedrow

In 1884, when Laura, Manly, and their daughter Rose come from South Dakota to Mansfield, Missouri, looking for a better life, Laura's outspoken articles against a local timberman cause some problems.
Book 1 of The Days of Laura Ingalls Wilder series

☐ *A Girl from Yamhill*
by Beverly Cleary

Follows Cleary from her childhood years in Oregon through high school and into young adulthood, highlighting her family life and her growing interest in writing.

☐ *Wall of Words*
by Tim Kennemore

Kate waits for her father, who has left home to write a novel, to return, while her sister suffers from a phobia about school.

Twins
Circle of Gold

☐ *The Long Way Home*
by Barbara Cohen

Sally's relationship with an elderly bus driver who recites Shakespeare stories helps her cope with the problems of her mother's cancer and being separated from her twin sister at summer camp.

☐ *Me Too*
by Vera and Bill Cleaver

Hoping to expunge neighborhood prejudice and to do something everyone else has failed to do, a 12-year-old desperately tries to teach her retarded twin.

☐ *Many Waters*
by Madeleine L'Engle

The 15-year-old Murry twins, Sandy and Dennys, are accidentally sent back to a strange Biblical time period in which a man named Noah is building a boat.

☐ *Jacob Have I Loved*
by Katherine Paterson
1981 Newbery Medal

Feeling deprived all her life of schooling, friends, mother, and even her name by her twin sister, Louise finally begins to find her identity.

☐ *Singularity*
by William Sleator

Sixteen-year-old twins Harry and Barry stumble across a gateway to another universe, where distortion in time and space causes a dramatic change in their competitive relationship.

☐ *The Dulcimer Boy*
by Tor Seidler

Twin brothers are abandoned on their uncle's doorstep in turn-of-the-century New England with nothing but a silver-stringed dulcimer.

Girls Who Have to Work
Circle of Gold

☐ *The Clock*
by James Lincoln Collier and Christopher Collier

In 1810 in Connecticut, trapped in a grueling job in the local textile mill to help pay her father's debts, 15-year-old Annie becomes the victim of the cruel overseer and plots revenge against him.

☐ *Lyddie*
by Katherine Paterson

Impoverished Vermont farm girl Lyddie Worthen is determined to gain her independence by becoming a factory worker in Lowell, Massachusetts, in the 1840s.

☐ *Queen of Hearts*
by Vera and Bill Cleaver

Although there is no love lost between them, 12-year-old Wilma is her willful and peppery grandmother's choice for a companion.

☐ *Where the Lilies Bloom*
by Vera and Bill Cleaver

In the Great Smoky Mountains, a 14-year-old girl struggles to keep her family together after their father dies.

☐ *Calico Bush*
by Rachel Field
1932 Newbery Honor Book

In 1742, Marguerite left France with her grandmother and uncle to seek a home in America. A year later, 13-year-old Marguerite is alone in the world and an indentured servant on her way to Maine.

☐ *Lupita Mañana*
by Patricia Beatty

To help her poverty-stricken family, 13-year-old Lupita enters California as an illegal alien and starts to work while constantly on the watch for "la migra."

Tough Times for Single Moms
Circle of Gold

☐ *Dear Mr. Henshaw*
by Beverly Cleary
1984 Newbery Medal

In his letters to his favorite author, 10-year-old Leigh reveals his problems in coping with his parents' divorce and being the new boy in school.
Sequel: Strider

☐ *IOU's*
by Ouida Sebestyen

Thirteen-year-old Stowe Garrett is caught between the loyalty and love he feels for his mother and a yearning to break free and experiment with life.

☐ *Maybe Yes, Maybe No, Maybe Maybe*
by Susan Patron

When her hardworking mother decides to move, eight-year-old PK uses her imagination and storytelling to help her older and younger sisters adjust.

☐ *Contrary Imaginations*
by Larry Callen

When their mother can't decide where to dispose of their father's ashes, three children take matters into their own hands.

☐ *The Winchesters*
by James Lincoln Collier

Fourteen-year-old Chris, a poor relation of the wealthy Winchesters, must choose sides when his classmates' parents go on strike at the Winchester mill.

☐ *The Glass Angels*
by Susan Hill

Even though times are hard, Tilly looks forward to spending Christmas with her mother in their small attic apartment, until illness and an accident threaten her plans.

Kids Acting as Parents
Circle of Gold

☐ *Ask Me Something Easy*
by Natalie Honeycutt

After her father leaves the family, Addie must cope with her increasingly hostile, distant mother, perfect older sister, and sensitive younger twin sisters.

☐ *Afternoon of the Elves*
by Janet Taylor Lisle
1990 Newbery Honor Book

As Hillary works in the miniature village, allegedly built by elves, in Sara-Kate's backyard, she becomes more and more curious about Sara-Kate's real life inside her big, gloomy house with her mysterious, silent mother.

☐ *Our Mother's House*
by Julian Gloag

A group of children tries to survive and keep the death of their parents a secret.

☐ *Trial Valley*
by Vera and Bill Cleaver

The Luther children, who have raised themselves since their father's death, find an abandoned boy near their home.
Sequel: Where the Lilies Bloom

☐ *Someone's Mother Is Missing*
by Harry Mazer

When her emotionally disturbed mother disappears from their home, Lisa searches for her, alternately aided and annoyed by her cousin Sam.

Black Children in the City
Circle of Gold

☐ *The Shimmershine Queens*
by Camille Yarbrough

Two fifth-graders try to lift themselves and their classmates out of a less-than-beautiful urban present by encouraging dreams and the desire to achieve them.

☐ *The Me Nobody Knows*
Stephen M. Joseph, ed.

Poems by children of the ghetto.

☐ *The Planet of Junior Brown*
by Virginia Hamilton
1972 Newbery Medal

Already a leader in New York's underground world of homeless children, eighth-grader Buddy Clark takes on the responsibility of protecting the overweight, emotionally disturbed friend with whom he has been playing hooky.

☐ *J. T.*
by Jane Wagner

J. T. begins to change when he discovers there is more satisfaction in caring for an injured cat than in listening to a stolen transistor radio.

☐ *The Jazz Man*
by Mary Hays Weik
1967 Newbery Honor Book

Zeke spends a lot of time watching his neighbor, a jazz pianist, out the window, until Zeke is abandoned by his parents.

☐ *Rite of Passage*
by Richard Wright
PG language

When 15-year-old Johnny Gibbs is told that he is really a foster child, he runs off into the streets of Harlem and meets up with a gang that wants him to participate in a mugging.

Dear Mr. Henshaw

Beverly Cleary

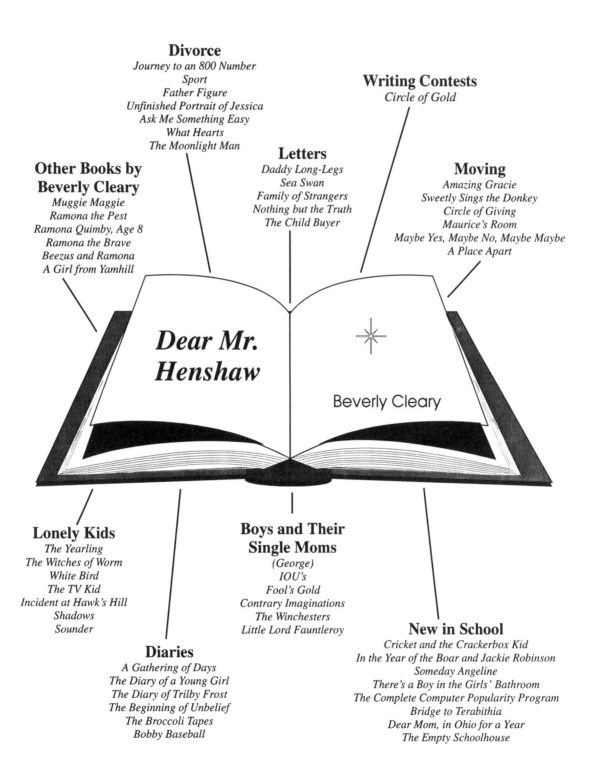

Divorce
Journey to an 800 Number
Sport
Father Figure
Unfinished Portrait of Jessica
Ask Me Something Easy
What Hearts
The Moonlight Man

Writing Contests
Circle of Gold

**Other Books by
Beverly Cleary**
Muggie Maggie
Ramona the Pest
Ramona Quimby, Age 8
Ramona the Brave
Beezus and Ramona
A Girl from Yamhill

Letters
Daddy Long-Legs
Sea Swan
Family of Strangers
Nothing but the Truth
The Child Buyer

Moving
Amazing Gracie
Sweetly Sings the Donkey
Circle of Giving
Maurice's Room
Maybe Yes, Maybe No, Maybe Maybe
A Place Apart

Dear Mr. Henshaw

Beverly Cleary

Lonely Kids
The Yearling
The Witches of Worm
White Bird
The TV Kid
Incident at Hawk's Hill
Shadows
Sounder

**Boys and Their
Single Moms**
(George)
IOU's
Fool's Gold
Contrary Imaginations
The Winchesters
Little Lord Fauntleroy

Diaries
A Gathering of Days
The Diary of a Young Girl
The Diary of Trilby Frost
The Beginning of Unbelief
The Broccoli Tapes
Bobby Baseball

New in School
Cricket and the Crackerbox Kid
In the Year of the Boar and Jackie Robinson
Someday Angeline
There's a Boy in the Girls' Bathroom
The Complete Computer Popularity Program
Bridge to Terabithia
Dear Mom, in Ohio for a Year
The Empty Schoolhouse

Beverly Cleary

Dear Mr. Henshaw

From *What Else Should I Read?* © 1995. Libraries Unlimited. (800) 237-6124.

Divorce

Journey to an 800 Number

Sport

Father Figure

Unfinished Portrait of Jessica

Ask Me Something Easy

What Hearts

The Moonlight Man

Diaries

A Gathering of Days

The Diary of a Young Girl

The Diary of Trilby Frost

The Beginning of Unbelief

The Broccoli Tapes

Bobby Baseball

Other Books by Beverly Cleary

Muggie Maggie

Ramona the Pest

Ramona Quimby, Age 8

Ramona the Brave

Beezus and Ramona

A Girl from Yamhill

Writing Contests

Circle of Gold

New in School

Cricket and the Crackerbox Kid

In the Year of the Boar and Jackie Robinson

Someday Angeline

There's a Boy in the Girls' Bathroom

The Complete Computer Popularity Program

Bridge to Terabithia

Dear Mom, in Ohio for a Year

The Empty Schoolhouse

Letters

Daddy Long-Legs

Sea Swan

Family of Strangers

Nothing but the Truth

The Child Buyer

Boys and Their Single Moms

(George)

IOU's

Fool's Gold

Contrary Imaginations

The Winchesters

Little Lord Fauntleroy

Moving

Amazing Gracie

Sweetly Sings the Donkey

Circle of Giving

Maurice's Room

Maybe Yes, Maybe No, Maybe Maybe

A Place Apart

Lonely Kids

The Yearling

The Witches of Worm

White Bird

The TV Kid

Incident at Hawk's Hill

Shadows

Sounder

Divorce
Dear Mr. Henshaw

Journey to an 800 Number
by E. L. Konigsburg

Bo learns from the unusual characters he meets when he is sent to live with his father after his mother decides to remarry.

Sport
by Louise Fitzhugh

Eleven-year-old Sport lives happily with his absentminded father, but his ruthless mother suddenly wants custody of him.

Father Figure
by Richard Peck

After Jim has been a father figure for years, he and his younger brother are reunited with their divorced father.

Unfinished Portrait of Jessica
by Richard Peck

A trip to Mexico to visit the divorced vagabond father whom she idolizes cures 14-year-old Jessica of certain illusions.

Ask Me Something Easy
by Natalie Honeycutt

After her father leaves the family, Addie must cope with her increasingly hostile mother, perfect older sister, and sensitive younger twin sisters.

What Hearts
by Bruce Brooks

1993 Newbery Honor Book

After his mother divorces his father and remarries, Asa's sharp intellect helps him deal with his new world.

The Moonlight Man
by Paula Fox

Fifteen-year-old Catherine and her father take their first joint vacation and finally get to know each other.

Diaries
Dear Mr. Henshaw

A Gathering of Days
by Joan W. Blos

1980 Newbery Medal

The journal of a 14-year-old girl records her father's remarriage and the death of her friend.

The Diary of a Young Girl
by Anne Frank

The journal of a Jewish girl in her early teens describes both the joys and the torments of daily life throughout the two years spent hiding with her family from the Nazis.

The Diary of Trilby Frost
by Dianne Glaser

Teenager Trilby Frost records in her diary her growing realization that life continues even though her father, younger brother, and closest friend die.

The Beginning of Unbelief
by Robin Jones

While keeping a journal to record some upheavals in his life, 15-year-old Hal creates within its pages a science fiction story starring his alter ego, Zach.

The Broccoli Tapes
by Jan Slepian

During a stay in Hawaii with her family, Sara reports her experiences by tape back to her sixth-grade class in Boston, detailing her adoption of a wild cat, a friendship with a troubled Hawaiian boy, and the death of a beloved grandmother.

Bobby Baseball
by Robert Kimmel Smith

Ten-year-old Bobby is passionate about baseball and convinced that he is a great player. The only problem is to get a chance to prove his skill.

Other Books by Beverly Cleary
Dear Mr. Henshaw

Muggie Maggie
Maggie resists learning cursive writing in the third grade, until she discovers that knowing how to read and write cursive promises to open up an entirely new world of knowledge for her.

Ramona the Pest
Ramona is a little sister who always wants to tag along after Beezus and the older kids.

Ramona Quimby, Age 8
1982 Newbery Honor Book

The further adventures of the Quimby family as Ramona enters the third grade.

Ramona the Brave
Six-year-old Ramona tries to cope with an unsympathetic first-grade teacher.

Beezus and Ramona
Four-year-old Ramona has an imagination that makes her a menace to everyone around her, particularly her older sister Beezus.

A Girl from Yamhill
Follows Beverly Cleary from her childhood years in Oregon through high school and into young adulthood, highlighting her family life and her growing interest in writing.

Writing Contests
Dear Mr. Henshaw

Circle of Gold
by Candy Dawson Boyd

Mattie is determined to get her mother a beautiful gold pin for Mother's Day, even though she has not saved enough money and has just lost her job.

Moving
Dear Mr. Henshaw

☐ *Amazing Gracie*
by A. E. Cannon

A high school girl has a lot to deal with when her mother, who suffers from depression, remarries; a new brother is acquired; and the family moves to Salt Lake City.

☐ *Sweetly Sings the Donkey*
by Vera Cleaver

When 14-year-old Lily and her family move to Florida, it falls to her to keep her family together and start a new life.

☐ *Circle of Giving*
by Ellen Howard

When Marguerite moves to Los Angeles she suddenly becomes shy and withdrawn until a girl with cerebral palsy moves in across the street.

☐ *Maurice's Room*
by Paula Fox

Eight-year-old Maurice's struggle to protect his bedroom full of treasured junk from unsympathetic parents undergoes a transformation when the family moves to the country.

☐ *Maybe Yes, Maybe No, Maybe Maybe*
by Susan Patron

When her hardworking mother decides to move, eight-year-old PK uses her imagination and storytelling to help her older and younger sisters adjust.

☐ *A Place Apart*
by Paula Fox

Shortly after her father's death, Victoria and her mother move to a small village where Victoria meets a wealthy teenage boy who teaches her a valuable but painful lesson about life.

Boys and Their Single Moms
Dear Mr. Henshaw

☐ *(George)*
by E. L. Konigsburg

When 12-year-old Benjamin refuses to see what is going on in his chemistry lab, the little man who lives inside of him must finally speak out in public for the safety of all concerned.

☐ *IOU's*
by Ouida Sebestyen

Thirteen-year-old Stowe Garrett is caught between the loyalty and love he feels for his mother and a yearning to break free and experiment with life.

☐ *Fool's Gold*
by Zilpha Keatley Snyder

Reluctant to admit that he suffers from claustrophobia, Rudy tries to find a way to distract his friends from exploring an abandoned gold mine.

☐ *Contrary Imaginations*
by Larry Callen

When their mother can't decide where to dispose of their father's ashes, three children take matters into their own hands.

☐ *The Winchesters*
by James Lincoln Collier

Fourteen-year-old Chris, a poor relation of the wealthy Winchesters, must choose whether to be on the side of management or labor when his classmates' parents go on strike at the Winchester mill in response to a wage cut.

☐ *Little Lord Fauntleroy*
by Frances Hodgson Burnett

A Brooklyn boy discovers that he is the heir to an earldom and a fortune, and goes to live with his bad-tempered, selfish, and cantankerous grandfather.

Letters
Dear Mr. Henshaw

☐ *Daddy Long-Legs*
by Jean Webster

A 17-year-old orphan is sent to a posh northeastern college for women by an anonymous benefactor. All she must do is write to the man she nicknames Daddy Long-Legs and tell him of her progress.

☐ *Sea Swan*
by Kathryn Lasky

At the age of 75, Elzibah Swan decides to take up swimming, a pastime that enriches her life and one that she shares through letters with her young grandchildren.

☐ *Family of Strangers*
by Susan Beth Pfeffer

PG language

Through letters and essays, emotionally disturbed, 16-year-old Abby chronicles her growing desperation in a family consisting of parents who seem devoid of love, one older sister bent on self-destruction, and another older sister who has always seemed perfect.

☐ *Nothing but the Truth*
by Avi

1992 Newbery Honor Book

A ninth-grader's suspension for singing "The Star Spangled Banner" during homeroom becomes a national news story.

☐ *The Child Buyer*
by John Hersey

A novel in the form of hearings before the Standing Committee on Education, Welfare & Public Morality of a certain State Senate, investigating the conspiracy of Mr. Wissey Jones, with others, to purchase a male child.

New in School
Dear Mr. Henshaw

☐ *Cricket and the Crackerbox Kid*
by Alane Ferguson

Cricket thinks she has finally found a friend in Dominic until they quarrel over ownership of a dog.

☐ *In the Year of the Boar and Jackie Robinson*
by Betty Bao Lord

In 1947, a Chinese child becomes Americanized by her love for baseball.

☐ *Someday Angeline*
by Louis Sachar

As an eight-year-old genius in the sixth grade, Angeline is not too popular.

☐ *There's a Boy in the Girls' Bathroom*
by Louis Sachar

An unmanageable 11-year-old misfit learns to believe in himself when he gets to know the new school counselor.

☐ *The Complete Computer Popularity Program*
by Todd Strasser

New to town, seventh-grader Tony worries that he'll never have a social life.

☐ *Bridge to Terabithia*
by Katherine Paterson

1978 Newbery Medal

The life of a 10-year-old boy in rural Virginia expands when he becomes friends with a newcomer.

☐ *Dear Mom, in Ohio for a Year*
by Cynthia Stowe

When she is sent to stay with relatives, Cassie must adjust to a new school.

☐ *The Empty Schoolhouse*
by Natalie Savage Carlson

Older sister Emma tells the story of the year when Lullah went to school with the white children.

Lonely Kids
Dear Mr. Henshaw

☐ *The Yearling*
by Marjorie Kinnan Rawlings

A young boy living in the Florida backwoods is forced to decide the fate of a fawn he has lovingly raised as a pet.

☐ *The Witches of Worm*
by Zilpha Keatley Snyder

1973 Newbery Honor Book

A lonely 12-year-old is convinced that her cat is possessed by a witch and is responsible for her own strange behavior.

☐ *White Bird*
by Clyde Robert Bulla

A lonely boy is found and reared by a hermit in the wilderness.

☐ *The TV Kid*
by Betsy Byars

To escape failure, boredom, and loneliness, a young boy plunges with all his imagination into the world of television.

☐ *Incident at Hawk's Hill*
by Allan W. Eckert

1972 Newbery Honor Book

A shy, lonely six-year-old wanders into the Canadian prairie and spends a summer under the protection of a badger.

☐ *Shadows*
by Dennis Haseley

Jamie's lonely life with his aunt and uncle changes when Grandpa comes to visit and teaches him to make shadow pictures.

☐ *Sounder*
by William H. Armstrong

1970 Newbery Medal

When his sharecropper father is jailed for stealing food for his family, a young black boy grows in courage and understanding with the help of the dog Sounder and learns to read and write.

Sequel: *Sourland*

From the Mixed-Up Files of Mrs. Basil E. Frankweiler

E. L. Konigsburg

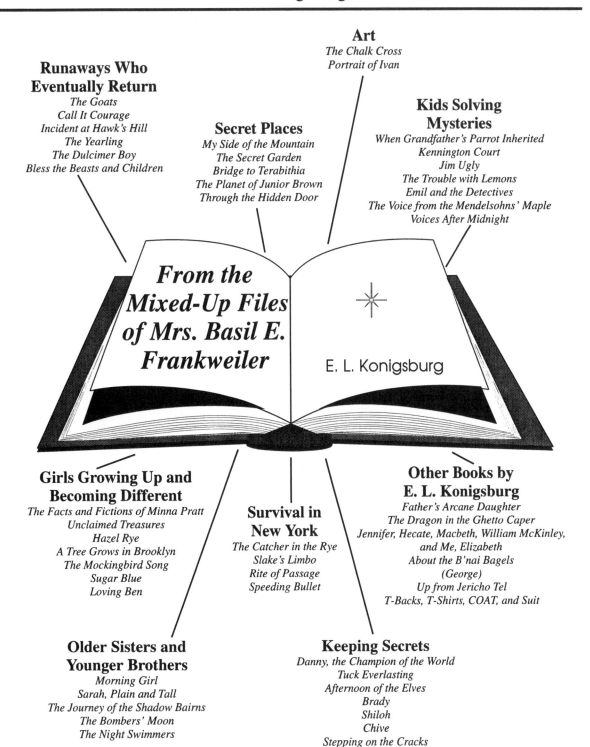

Art
The Chalk Cross
Portrait of Ivan

**Runaways Who
Eventually Return**
The Goats
Call It Courage
Incident at Hawk's Hill
The Yearling
The Dulcimer Boy
Bless the Beasts and Children

Secret Places
My Side of the Mountain
The Secret Garden
Bridge to Terabithia
The Planet of Junior Brown
Through the Hidden Door

**Kids Solving
Mysteries**
When Grandfather's Parrot Inherited
Kennington Court
Jim Ugly
The Trouble with Lemons
Emil and the Detectives
The Voice from the Mendelsohns' Maple
Voices After Midnight

*From the
Mixed-Up Files
of Mrs. Basil E.
Frankweiler*

E. L. Konigsburg

**Girls Growing Up and
Becoming Different**
The Facts and Fictions of Minna Pratt
Unclaimed Treasures
Hazel Rye
A Tree Grows in Brooklyn
The Mockingbird Song
Sugar Blue
Loving Ben

**Survival in
New York**
The Catcher in the Rye
Slake's Limbo
Rite of Passage
Speeding Bullet

**Other Books by
E. L. Konigsburg**
Father's Arcane Daughter
The Dragon in the Ghetto Caper
*Jennifer, Hecate, Macbeth, William McKinley,
and Me, Elizabeth*
About the B'nai Bagels
(George)
Up from Jericho Tel
T-Backs, T-Shirts, COAT, and Suit

**Older Sisters and
Younger Brothers**
Morning Girl
Sarah, Plain and Tall
The Journey of the Shadow Bairns
The Bombers' Moon
The Night Swimmers

Keeping Secrets
Danny, the Champion of the World
Tuck Everlasting
Afternoon of the Elves
Brady
Shiloh
Chive
Stepping on the Cracks

E. L. Konigsburg

From the Mixed-Up Files of Mrs. Basil E. Frankweiler

Other Books by E. L. Konigsburg

Father's Arcane Daughter

The Dragon in the Ghetto Caper

Jennifer, Hecate, Macbeth, William McKinley, and Me, Elizabeth

About the B'nai Bagels (George)

Up from Jericho Tel

T-Backs, T-Shirts, COAT, and Suit

Runaways Who Eventually Return

The Goats

Call It Courage

Incident at Hawk's Hill

The Yearling

The Dulcimer Boy

Bless the Beasts and Children

Survival in New York

The Catcher in the Rye

Slake's Limbo

Rite of Passage

Speeding Bullet

Art

The Chalk Cross

Portrait of Ivan

Older Sisters and Younger Brothers

Morning Girl

Sarah, Plain and Tall

The Journey of the Shadow Bairns

The Bombers' Moon

The Night Swimmers

Secret Places

My Side of the Mountain

The Secret Garden

Bridge to Terabithia

The Planet of Junior Brown

Through the Hidden Door

Keeping Secrets

Danny, the Champion of the World

Tuck Everlasting

Afternoon of the Elves

Brady

Shiloh

Chive

Stepping on the Cracks

Girls Growing Up and Becoming Different

The Facts and Fictions of Minna Pratt

Unclaimed Treasures

Hazel Rye

A Tree Grows in Brooklyn

The Mockingbird Song

Sugar Blue

Loving Ben

Kids Solving Mysteries

When Grandfather's Parrot Inherited Kennington Court

Jim Ugly

The Trouble with Lemons

Emil and the Detectives

The Voice from the Mendelsohns' Maple

Voices After Midnight

Art
From the Mixed-Up Files of Mrs. Basil E. Frankweiler

☐ *The Chalk Cross*
by Berthe Amoss

A young girl living in 19th-century New Orleans struggles between her growing familiarity with voodoo and the precepts of the church.

☐ *Portrait of Ivan*
by Paula Fox

An 11-year-old boy gains new understanding of himself and his father after a trip to Florida with unusual people.

Survival in New York
From the Mixed-Up Files of Mrs. Basil E. Frankweiler

☐ *The Catcher in the Rye*
by J. D. Salinger

Unable to conform despite pressure from his family, and knowing he is about to be dropped by his school, Holden Caulfield embarks on a journey of self-discovery and spends three days and nights in New York City.

☐ *Slake's Limbo*
by Felice Holman

Thirteen-year-old Aremis Slake, hounded by his fears and misfortunes, flees into New York City's subway tunnels, never again, he believes, to emerge.

☐ *Rite of Passage*
by Richard Wright
PG language

When 15-year-old Johnny Gibbs is told that he is really a foster child, he runs off into the streets of Harlem and meets up with a gang.

☐ *Speeding Bullet*
by Neal Shusterman

After becoming famous and getting the attention of the daughter of a wealthy New York City developer following his rescue of a little girl from a speeding subway train, Nick looks for other people to rescue.

Runaways Who Eventually Return
From the Mixed-Up Files of Mrs. Basil E. Frankweiler

☐ *The Goats*
by Brock Cole

Stripped and marooned on a small island by their fellow campers, a boy and a girl form an uneasy bond that grows into a deep friendship when they decide to run away and disappear without a trace.

☐ *Call It Courage*
by Armstrong Sperry
1941 Newbery Medal

Based on a Polynesian legend, this is the story of a youth, the son of a Polynesian chief whose people worship courage. Though the youth is afraid of the sea, he sets out alone in his canoe to conquer his fear and prove his courage to himself and his tribe.

☐ *Incident at Hawk's Hill*
by Allan W. Eckert
1972 Newbery Honor Book

A shy, lonely six-year-old wanders into the Canadian prairie and spends a summer under the protection of a badger.

☐ *The Yearling*
by Marjorie Kinnan Rawlings

A young boy living in the Florida backwoods is forced to decide the fate of a fawn he has lovingly raised as a pet.

☐ *The Dulcimer Boy*
by Tor Seidler

Twin brothers are abandoned on their uncle's doorstep in turn-of-the-century New England with nothing but a silver-stringed dulcimer.

☐ *Bless the Beasts and Children*
by Glendon Swarthout

While at camp, a group of disturbed boys searches for a way to improve their lives.

Other Books by E. L. Konigsburg
From the Mixed-Up Files of Mrs. Basil E. Frankweiler

☐ *Father's Arcane Daughter*

Kidnapped 17 years ago, a man's daughter by a former marriage appears at his new home in Pittsburgh and affects the entire family.

☐ *The Dragon in the Ghetto Caper*

Determined to be a famous detective, Andy goes to the ghetto, where he encounters crime for the first time.

☐ *Jennifer, Hecate, Macbeth, William McKinley, and Me, Elizabeth*

Elizabeth is very lonely until she meets Jennifer, who claims to be a witch.

☐ *About the B'nai Bagels*

Mark Setzer tells about his troubles in general, and in particular his misfortunes on the Little League team managed by his mother and coached by his brother.

☐ *(George)*

When 12-year-old Benjamin refuses to see what is going on in his chemistry lab, the little man who lives inside of him must finally speak out in public for the safety of all concerned.

☐ *Up from Jericho Tel*

The spirit of a dead actress turns two children invisible and sends them out among a group of street performers to search for a missing necklace.

☐ *T-Backs, T-Shirts, COAT, and Suit*

Twelve-year-old Chloe and her aunt become involved in a controversy surrounding the wearing of T-back bathing suits.

Girls Growing Up and Becoming Different
From the Mixed-Up Files of Mrs. Basil E. Frankweiler

☐ *The Facts and Fictions of Minna Pratt*
by Patricia MacLachlan

An 11-year-old cellist learns about life from her eccentric family, her first boyfriend, and Mozart.

☐ *Unclaimed Treasures*
by Patricia MacLachlan

Willa, who wants to feel extraordinary, thinks that she's in love with the father of the boy next door.

☐ *Hazel Rye*
by Vera and Bill Cleaver

An 11-year-old girl agrees to let an impoverished family live in a small house she owns, in exchange for working in her orange grove.

☐ *A Tree Grows in Brooklyn*
by Betty Smith

Young Francie Nolan experiences the problems of growing up in a Brooklyn, New York, slum.

☐ *The Mockingbird Song*
by Berthe Amoss

Unable to get along with her new stepmother, 11-year-old Lindy goes to live with the elderly lady next door.

☐ *Sugar Blue*
by Vera and Bill Cleaver

Unenthusiastic when her four-year-old niece comes for a prolonged visit, 11-year-old Amy finds her relationship with the small girl changing her view of herself and life in general.

☐ *Loving Ben*
by Elizabeth Laird

Anna experiences the birth and death of a loving, hydrocephalic brother and works with a child with Down's syndrome.

Keeping Secrets
From the Mixed-Up Files of Mrs. Basil E. Frankweiler

☐ *Danny, the Champion of the World*
by Roald Dahl

Danny and his poacher father share an adventure.

☐ *Tuck Everlasting*
by Natalie Babbitt

A 10-year-old girl and a malicious stranger now share the Tucks' secret about a spring whose water prevents one from growing older.

☐ *Afternoon of the Elves*
by Janet Taylor Lisle

1990 Newbery Honor Book

As Hillary works in the miniature village in Sara-Kate's backyard, she becomes curious about Sara-Kate's life inside her gloomy house with her mysterious, silent mother.

☐ *Brady*
by Jean Fritz

A young boy takes part in the pre-Civil War antislavery activities.

☐ *Shiloh*
by Phyllis Reynolds Naylor

1992 Newbery Medal

When he finds a lost beagle, Marty tries to hide it from the dog's owner, a man known to mistreat his dogs.

☐ *Chive*
by Shelley A. Barre

Eleven-year-old Chive, homeless because his parents have lost their farm, strikes up an unusual friendship with 11-year-old Terry and competes with him in a skateboard competition.

☐ *Stepping on the Cracks*
by Mary Downing Hahn

Eleven-year-old Margaret gets a new view of the school bully when she finds him hiding his brother, an army deserter.

Secret Places
From the Mixed-Up Files of Mrs. Basil E. Frankweiler

☐ *My Side of the Mountain*
by Jean Craighead George

1960 Newbery Honor Book

Young Sam Gribley leaves New York City and spends a year living by himself in a remote area of the Catskill Mountains.

Sequel: *On the Far Side of the Mountain*

☐ *The Secret Garden*
by Frances Hodgson Burnett

A boy who has lived as a spoiled invalid regains his health when he and his orphaned cousin restore a once lovely garden.

☐ *Bridge to Terabithia*
by Katherine Paterson

1978 Newbery Medal

The life of a 10-year-old boy in rural Virginia expands when he becomes friends with a newcomer who subsequently meets an untimely death trying to reach their hideaway, Terabithia, during a storm.

☐ *The Planet of Junior Brown*
by Virginia Hamilton

1972 Newbery Honor Book

Already a leader in New York's underground world of homeless children, eighth-grader Buddy Clark takes on the responsibility of protecting the overweight, emotionally disturbed friend with whom he has been playing hooky all semester.

☐ *Through the Hidden Door*
by Rosemary Wells

Two young boys stumble upon the remains of an ancient underground mystery civilization.

Older Sisters and Younger Brothers
From the Mixed-Up Files of Mrs. Basil E. Frankweiler

☐ *Morning Girl*
by Michael Dorris

Morning Girl, who loves the day, and her younger brother Star Boy, who loves the night, take turns describing their life on an island in pre-Colombian America; in Morning Girl's last narrative, she witnesses the arrival of the first Europeans in her world.

☐ *Sarah, Plain and Tall*
by Patricia MacLachlan

1986 Newbery Medal

When their father invites a mail-order bride to come live with them in their prairie home, Caleb and Anna are captivated by their new mother and hope that she will stay.

☐ *The Journey of the Shadow Bairns*
by Margaret J. Anderson

When her parents die suddenly, leaving only a little money and a one-way passage to Canada, a young Scottish girl decides she and her four-year-old brother will pursue family plans to relocate.

☐ *The Bombers' Moon*
by Betty Vander Els

In the summer of 1942, an American missionary family living in China is separated when the two children are evacuated to India with their school class to escape the Japanese invasion.

☐ *The Night Swimmers*
by Betsy Byars

With their mother dead and their father working nights, Retta tries to be mother to her two younger brothers.

Kids Solving Mysteries
From the Mixed-Up Files of Mrs. Basil E. Frankweiler

☐ *When Grandfather's Parrot Inherited Kennington Court*
by Linda Allen

Appalled that Grandfather left his inheritance to his parrot, the relatives seek to break the will; but young Miranda, who is caring for the parrot, makes a discovery that settles everything.

☐ *Jim Ugly*
by Sid Fleischman

The adventures of 12-year-old Jake and Jim Ugly, his father's part-mongrel, part-wolf dog, as they travel through the Old West trying to find out what really happened to Jake's actor father.

☐ *The Trouble with Lemons*
by Daniel Hayes

Tyler and Lymie, eighth-grade misfits, discover a dead body in a quarry and work to uncover the mystery behind it.

☐ *Emil and the Detectives*
by Erich Kastner

A German boy and his friends use their ingenuity to catch a thief.

☐ *The Voice from the Mendelsohns' Maple*
by Mary C. Ryan

Penny meets an elderly, practically naked woman in a tree and soon finds herself embroiled in a mystery involving the Beacon Manor Senior Citizen's Residence.

☐ *Voices After Midnight*
by Richard Peck

Chad and Luke uncover a mystery involving the former tenants of the house when the two brothers slip back in time to 1888.

A Gathering of Days

Joan W. Blos

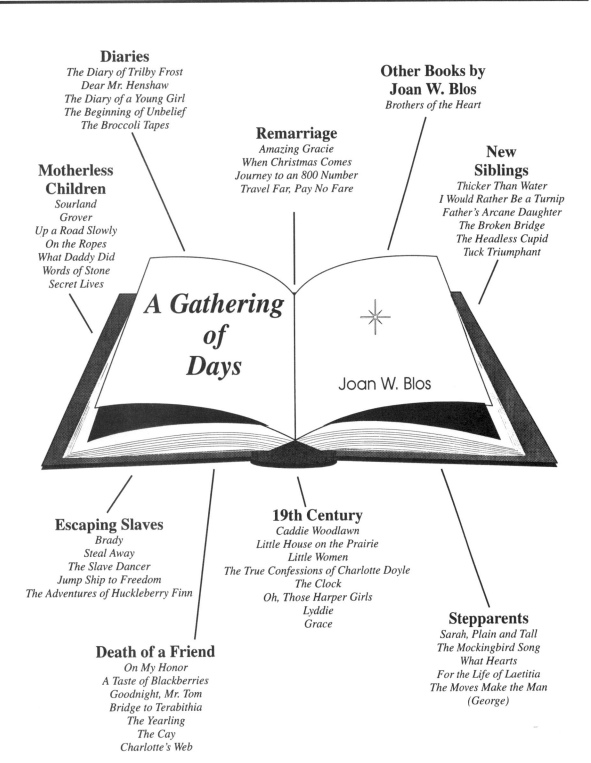

Diaries
The Diary of Trilby Frost
Dear Mr. Henshaw
The Diary of a Young Girl
The Beginning of Unbelief
The Broccoli Tapes

**Other Books by
Joan W. Blos**
Brothers of the Heart

Remarriage
Amazing Gracie
When Christmas Comes
Journey to an 800 Number
Travel Far, Pay No Fare

**New
Siblings**
Thicker Than Water
I Would Rather Be a Turnip
Father's Arcane Daughter
The Broken Bridge
The Headless Cupid
Tuck Triumphant

**Motherless
Children**
Sourland
Grover
Up a Road Slowly
On the Ropes
What Daddy Did
Words of Stone
Secret Lives

*A Gathering
of
Days*

Joan W. Blos

Escaping Slaves
Brady
Steal Away
The Slave Dancer
Jump Ship to Freedom
The Adventures of Huckleberry Finn

19th Century
Caddie Woodlawn
Little House on the Prairie
Little Women
The True Confessions of Charlotte Doyle
The Clock
Oh, Those Harper Girls
Lyddie
Grace

Death of a Friend
On My Honor
A Taste of Blackberries
Goodnight, Mr. Tom
Bridge to Terabithia
The Yearling
The Cay
Charlotte's Web

Stepparents
Sarah, Plain and Tall
The Mockingbird Song
What Hearts
For the Life of Laetitia
The Moves Make the Man
(George)

A

Gathering

of

Days

Joan W. Blos

Diaries

The Diary of Trilby Frost

Dear Mr. Henshaw

*The Diary
of a Young Girl*

*The Beginning of
Unbelief*

The Broccoli Tapes

Motherless Children

Sourland

Grover

Up a Road Slowly

On the Ropes

What Daddy Did

Words of Stone

Secret Lives

Stepparents

Sarah, Plain and Tall

The Mockingbird Song

What Hearts

For the Life of Laetitia

*The Moves Make
the Man*

(George)

Remarriage

Amazing Gracie

When Christmas Comes

*Journey to an
800 Number*

Travel Far, Pay No Fare

Other Books by Joan W. Blos

Brothers of the Heart

Escaping Slaves

Brady

Steal Away

The Slave Dancer

Jump Ship to Freedom

*The Adventures
of Huckleberry Finn*

New Siblings

Thicker Than Water

*I Would Rather Be
a Turnip*

Father's Arcane Daughter

The Broken Bridge

The Headless Cupid

Tuck Triumphant

Death of a Friend

On My Honor

A Taste of Blackberries

Goodnight, Mr. Tom

Bridge to Terabithia

The Yearling

The Cay

Charlotte's Web

19th Century

Caddie Woodlawn

Little House on the Prairie

Little Women

*The True Confessions of
Charlotte Doyle*

The Clock

Oh, Those Harper Girls

Lyddie

Grace

Diaries
A Gathering of Days

The Diary of Trilby Frost
by Dianne Glaser

Growing up in rural Tennessee at the turn of the century, teenager Trilby Frost records in her diary her growing realization that life continues even though her father, younger brother, and closest friend die.

Dear Mr. Henshaw
by Beverly Cleary
1984 Newbery Medal

In his letters to his favorite author, 10-year-old Leigh reveals his problems in coping with his parents' divorce and being the new boy in school.
Sequel: *Strider*

The Diary of a Young Girl
by Anne Frank

The journal of a Jewish girl in her early teens describes both the joys and the torments of daily life throughout the two years spent hiding with her family during the Nazi occupation of Holland.

The Beginning of Unbelief
by Robin Jones

While keeping a journal to record some upheavals in his life, 15-year-old Hal creates within its pages a science fiction story starring his alter ego, Zach.

The Broccoli Tapes
by Jan Slepian

During a stay of several months in Hawaii with her family, Sara reports her experiences by tape back to her sixth-grade class in Boston, detailing her adoption of a wild cat, a friendship with a troubled Hawaiian boy, and the death of a beloved grandmother.

Motherless Children
A Gathering of Days

Sourland
by William H. Armstrong

For three motherless children, the quiet black man who is teacher and friend fills a lonely void.
Sequel to *Sounder*

Grover
by Vera and Bill Cleaver

A 10-year-old boy adjusts to the changes in his life after his mother dies.

Up a Road Slowly
by Irene Hunt
1967 Newbery Medal

After the death of her mother, Julie is sent to live with her aunt and uncle.

On the Ropes
by Otto R. Salassi

On the death of their mother, Squint and Julie's father moves back home with a troupe of wrestlers.

What Daddy Did
by Neal Shusterman

A 14-year-old learns that his father is to be released from prison after serving time for killing the boy's mother.

Words of Stone
by Kevin Henkes

Trying to deal with his dead mother, 10-year-old Blaze has his life changed when he meets the boisterous Joselle.

Secret Lives
by Berthe Amoss

Living with her straitlaced aunts in New Orleans, 13-year-old Addie unravels the mystery of her dead mother's past.

Stepparents
A Gathering of Days

Sarah, Plain and Tall
by Patricia MacLachlan
1986 Newbery Medal

When their father invites a mail-order bride to come live with them in their prairie home, Caleb and Anna are captivated by their new mother and hope that she will stay.

The Mockingbird Song
by Berthe Amoss

Unable to get along with her new stepmother, 11-year-old Lindy goes to live with the elderly lady next door.

What Hearts
by Bruce Brooks
1993 Newbery Honor Book

After his mother divorces his father and remarries, Asa's sharp intellect and capacity for forgiveness help him deal with the instabilities of his new world.

For the Life of Laetitia
by Merle Hodge

As the first in her family to go to secondary school, 12-year-old Lacey struggles with a variety of problems, including a cruel teacher and a difficult home life with her father and stepmother.

The Moves Make the Man
by Bruce Brooks
1985 Newbery Honor Book

A black boy and an emotionally troubled white boy in North Carolina form a precarious friendship.

(George)
by E. L. Konigsburg

When 12-year-old Benjamin refuses to see what is going on in his chemistry lab, the little man who lives inside of him must finally speak out in public for the safety of all concerned.

Remarriage
A Gathering of Days

Amazing Gracie
by A. E. Cannon

A high school girl has a lot to deal with when her mother, who suffers from depression, remarries; a new brother is acquired; and the family moves to Salt Lake City.

When Christmas Comes
by Elizabeth Starr Hill

With Christmas approaching, Callie is drawn into a confrontation about the meaning of family when her father decides to remarry.

Journey to an 800 Number
by E. L. Konigsburg

Bo learns about kindness, love, loyalty, appearances, and pretense from the unusual characters he meets when he is sent to live with his father after his mother decides to remarry.

Travel Far, Pay No Fare
by Anne Lindbergh

Twelve-year-old Owen and his nine-year-old cousin use a magic bookmark to enter different stories, trying to find a way to prevent their parents from marrying.

Death of a Friend
A Gathering of Days

☐ *On My Honor*
by Marian Dane Bauer
1987 Newbery Honor Book
When his best friend drowns while they are both swimming in a river that they had promised never to go near, Joel is terrified at having to tell both sets of parents.

☐ *A Taste of Blackberries*
by Doris B. Smith
A young boy recounts his efforts to adjust to the death of his best friend.

☐ *Goodnight, Mr. Tom*
by Michelle Magorian
A battered child learns to embrace life when he is adopted by an old man during World War II.

☐ *Bridge to Terabithia*
by Katherine Paterson
1978 Newbery Medal
The life of a 10-year-old boy expands when he becomes friends with a newcomer.

☐ *The Yearling*
by Marjorie Kinnan Rawlings
A young boy living in the Florida backwoods is forced to decide the fate of a fawn he has lovingly raised as a pet.

☐ *The Cay*
by Theodore Taylor
When their ship is torpedoed by a German submarine, a white boy, blinded by a blow on the head, and an old black man are stranded on a tiny island.
Prequel/sequel: *Timothy of the Cay*

☐ *Charlotte's Web*
by E. B. White
1953 Newbery Honor Book
Wilbur the pig is desolate when he discovers that he is destined to be dinner, until his spider friend Charlotte decides to help him.

New Siblings
A Gathering of Days

☐ *Thicker Than Water*
by Penelope Farmer
When Will comes to live with his cousin Becky and her family after his mother's death, he is haunted by the ghost of a child coal miner.

☐ *I Would Rather Be a Turnip*
by Vera and Bill Cleaver
When her illegitimate nephew comes to live with her, a girl has to deal with the hostility of her small-town neighbors.

☐ *Father's Arcane Daughter*
by E. L. Konigsburg
Kidnapped 17 years ago, a man's daughter by a former marriage appears at his new home in Pittsburgh and affects the entire family.

☐ *The Broken Bridge*
by Philip Pullman
Sixteen-year-old Ginny, the mixed-race artist daughter of an English father and a Haitian mother, learns that she has a half-brother from her father's earlier marriage and that her own mother may still be alive.

☐ *The Headless Cupid*
by Zilpha Keatley Snyder
1972 Newbery Honor Book
Life is never quite the same again for 11-year-old David after the arrival of his stepsister, a student of the occult.

☐ *Tuck Triumphant*
by Theodore Taylor
Fourteen-year-old Helen and her blind dog Friar Tuck face some challenges when they discover that the Korean boy they have adopted is deaf.
Sequel to *The Trouble with Tuck*

Escaping Slaves
A Gathering of Days

☐ *Brady*
by Jean Fritz
A young Pennsylvania boy takes part in the pre-Civil War antislavery activities.

☐ *Steal Away*
by Jennifer Armstrong
In 1855 two 13-year-old girls, one white and one black, run away from a southern farm and make the difficult journey north to freedom, living to recount their story 41 years later to two similar young girls.

☐ *The Slave Dancer*
by Paula Fox
1974 Newbery Medal
Kidnapped by the crew of an Africa-bound ship, a 13-year-old boy discovers to his horror that he is on a slaver and his job is to play music for the exercise periods of the human cargo.

☐ *Jump Ship to Freedom*
by James Lincoln Collier and Christopher Collier
In 1787 a 14-year-old slave, anxious to buy freedom for himself and his mother, escapes from his dishonest master and tries to find help in cashing the soldier's notes received by his father for fighting in the Revolution.

☐ *The Adventures of Huckleberry Finn*
by Mark Twain
A 19th-century boy from a Mississippi River town recounts his adventures as he travels down the river with a runaway slave on a raft, encountering a family involved in a feud, two scoundrels pretending to be royalty, and Tom Sawyer's aunt (who mistakes him for Tom).

Other Books by Joan W. Blos
A Gathering of Days

☐ *Brothers of the Heart*
Fourteen-year-old Shem spends six months in the Michigan wilderness alone with a dying Indian woman, who helps him not only to survive but also to mature to the point where he can return to his family and the difficulties of life as a cripple in a frontier village.

19th Century
A Gathering of Days

☐ *Caddie Woodlawn*
by Carol Ryrie Brink

1936 Newbery Medal

The adventures of an 11-year-old tomboy growing up on the frontier.

☐ *Little House on the Prairie*
by Laura Ingalls Wilder

A family travels from Wisconsin to the prairie, where they build a home and fight a prairie fire.

Many sequels

☐ *Little Women*
by Louisa May Alcott

The classic story of the sentimental and humorous adventures of the four March sisters.

☐ *The True Confessions of Charlotte Doyle*
by Avi

1991 Newbery Honor Book

As the ship's lone passenger, Charlotte learns that the captain is murderous and the crew rebellious.

☐ *The Clock*
by James Lincoln Collier and Christopher Collier

Trapped in a grueling job in the mill, 15-year-old Annie becomes the victim of the cruel overseer and plots revenge.

☐ *Oh, Those Harper Girls*
by Kathleen Karr

In west Texas in 1869, Lily and her five sisters participate in a series of misguided schemes to save their father's ranch.

☐ *Lyddie*
by Katherine Paterson

Lyddie is determined to become a factory worker.

☐ *Grace*
by Jill Paton Walsh

After helping her father rescue the survivors of a shipwreck, Grace finds herself fashioned into a national hero.

The Goats

Brock Cole

Camps
Bless the Beasts and Children
The Long Way Home

Boy-Girl Friendship
Bridge to Terabithia
Words of Stone
The Secret Garden
Sam and the Moon Queen
The Broccoli Tapes
Cricket and the Crackerbox Kid

Runaways
Slake's Limbo
Come to the Edge
*From the Mixed-Up Files of
Mrs. Basil E. Frankweiler*
The Yearling
Maniac Magee
The Dulcimer Boy
My Side of the Mountain

**Serious
Consequences
of Bullying**
Face to Face
The Chocolate War
Stepping on the Cracks

The Goats

Brock Cole

Stealing
J. T.
Sounder
My Crooked Family
The Great Gilly Hopkins
Rite of Passage
Poor Badger

**Kids Who Don't
Fit In**
The Hundred Dresses
Afternoon of the Elves
Stargone John
The Bears' House
There's a Boy in the Girls' Bathroom
The Winchesters

Survival
Call It Courage
Incident at Hawk's Hill
Lost on a Mountain in Maine
Julie of the Wolves
Lord of the Flies
The Wild Children
Save Queen of Sheba
Hatchet
The Cay
The Black Stallion
Soaring Eagle
Island of the Blue Dolphins

Dangerous Journeys
Grab Hands and Run
The Journey of the Shadow Bairns
Steal Away
The Adventures of Huckleberry Finn
North to Freedom
The Flight of the Doves

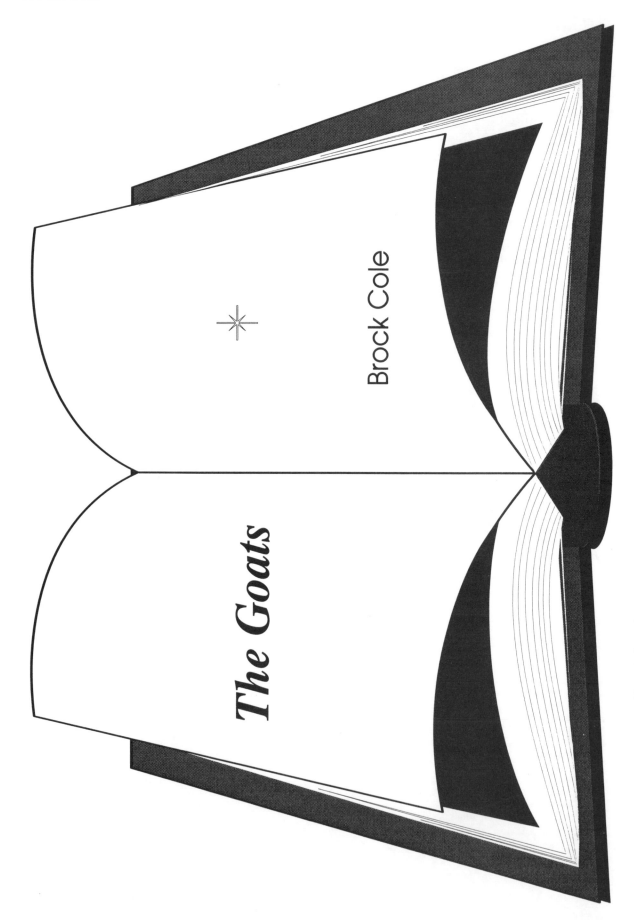

The Goats

Brock Cole

Camps

Bless the Beasts and Children

The Long Way Home

Serious Consequences of Bullying

Face to Face

The Chocolate War

Stepping on the Cracks

Boy-Girl Friendship

Bridge to Terabithia

Words of Stone

The Secret Garden

Sam and the Moon Queen

The Broccoli Tapes

Cricket and the Crackerbox Kid

Kids Who Don't Fit In

The Hundred Dresses

Afternoon of the Elves

Stargone John

The Bears' House

There's a Boy in the Girls' Bathroom

The Winchesters

Stealing

J. T.

Sounder

My Crooked Family

The Great Gilly Hopkins

Rite of Passage

Poor Badger

Runaways

Slake's Limbo

Come to the Edge

From the Mixed-Up Files of Mrs. Basil E. Frankweiler

The Yearling

Maniac Magee

The Dulcimer Boy

My Side of the Mountain

Dangerous Journeys

Grab Hands and Run

The Journey of the Shadow Bairns

Steal Away

The Adventures of Huckleberry Finn

North to Freedom

The Flight of the Doves

Survival

Call It Courage

Incident at Hawk's Hill

Lost on a Mountain in Maine

Julie of the Wolves

Lord of the Flies

The Wild Children

Save Queen of Sheba

Hatchet

The Cay

The Black Stallion

Soaring Eagle

Island of the Blue Dolphins

Kids Who Don't Fit In
The Goats

□ *The Hundred Dresses*
by Eleanor Estes

1945 Newbery Honor Book

In winning a medal she is no longer there to receive, a tight-lipped little Polish girl teaches her classmates a lesson.

□ *Afternoon of the Elves*
by Janet Taylor Lisle

1990 Newbery Honor Book

As Hillary works in the miniature village in Sara-Kate's backyard, she becomes more and more curious about Sara-Kate's real life inside her big, gloomy house with her mysterious, silent mother.

□ *Stargone John*
by Ellen Kindt McKenzie

Six-year-old John experiences ridicule and punishment at his school, until an old retired teacher reaches out from her blindness to share with him the world of reading and writing.

□ *The Bears' House*
by Marilyn Sachs

Fran Ellen is ostracized by her class because she sucks her thumb and smells bad, but she keeps her dreadful home life a secret.

□ *There's a Boy in the Girls' Bathroom*
by Louis Sachar

An unmanageable 11-year-old misfit learns to believe in himself when he gets to know the new school counselor, who is a sort of misfit too.

□ *The Winchesters*
by James Lincoln Collier

Fourteen-year-old Chris, a poor relation of the wealthy Winchesters, must choose whether to be on the side of management or labor when his classmates' parents go on strike at the Winchester mill.

Boy-Girl Friendship
The Goats

□ *Bridge to Terabithia*
by Katherine Paterson

1978 Newbery Medal

The life of a 10-year-old boy in rural Virginia expands when he becomes friends with a newcomer.

□ *Words of Stone*
by Kevin Henkes

Ten-year-old Blaze has his life changed when he meets the boisterous and irresistible Joselle.

□ *The Secret Garden*
by Frances Hodgson Burnett

A boy who has lived as a spoiled invalid regains his health when he and his orphaned cousin restore a once lovely garden.

□ *Sam and the Moon Queen*
by Alison Cragin Herzig and Jane Lawrence Mali

Sympathetic to a homeless girl's plight, Sam tries to help her find food for herself and medical aid for her dog.

□ *The Broccoli Tapes*
by Jan Slepian

During a stay in Hawaii with her family, Sara reports her experiences by tape back to her sixth-grade class in Boston, detailing her adoption of a wild cat, a friendship with a troubled Hawaiian boy, and the death of a beloved grandmother.

□ *Cricket and the Crackerbox Kid*
by Alane Ferguson

Pampered, 11-year-old rich kid Cricket thinks she has finally found a friend in Dominic, until they quarrel over ownership of a dog, and their classroom becomes a courtroom to decide who is right.

Serious Consequences of Bullying
The Goats

□ *Face to Face*
by Marion Dane Bauer

Picked on at school by bullies, 13-year-old Michael confronts his fears during a trip to Colorado to see his father, who works as a whitewater rafting guide and who Michael has not seen in eight years.

□ *The Chocolate War*
by Robert Cormier

PG language

A high school freshman discovers the devastating consequences of refusing to join the school's annual fundraising drive and arousing the wrath of the school bullies.

Sequel: *Beyond the Chocolate War*

□ *Stepping on the Cracks*
by Mary Downing Hahn

In 1944, while her brother is overseas fighting in World War II, 11-year-old Margaret gets a new view of the school bully Gordy when she finds him hiding his own brother, an army deserter, and decides to help him.

Camps
The Goats

□ *Bless the Beasts and Children*
by Glendon Swarthout

While at Box Canyon Boys Camp, a group of disturbed boys searches for a way to improve their lives.

□ *The Long Way Home*
by Barbara Cohen

Sally's relationship with an elderly bus driver who recites Shakespeare stories helps her cope with the problems of her mother's cancer and being separated from her twin sister at summer camp.

Survival
The Goats

☐ *Call It Courage*
by Armstrong Sperry
1941 Newbery Medal

☐ *Incident at Hawk's Hill*
by Allan W. Eckert
1972 Newbery Honor Book
A shy, lonely six-year-old spends a summer under the protection of a badger.

☐ *Lost on a Mountain in Maine*
by Donn Fendler as told to Joseph B. Egan
A 12-year-old describes his nine-day struggle to survive in the mountains of Maine in 1939.

☐ *Julie of the Wolves*
by Jean Craighead George
1973 Newbery Medal

☐ *Lord of the Flies*
by William Golding
Stranded on an island, young boys revert to savagery as they struggle to survive.

☐ *The Wild Children*
by Felice Holman
Alex falls in with a gang of other desperate homeless children.

☐ *Save Queen of Sheba*
by Louise Moeri
After surviving a Sioux Indian raid, a brother and sister set out to find the rest of the settlers.

☐ *Hatchet*
by Gary Paulsen
1988 Newbery Honor Book
After a plane crash, 13-year-old Brian spends 54 days in the wilderness, learning to survive with only the aid of a hatchet.

☐ *The Cay*
by Theodore Taylor
Prequel/sequel: *Timothy of the Cay*

☐ *The Black Stallion*
by Walter Farley
A boy befriends a horse, trains him by night, and rides him in a match race.
Many sequels

☐ *Soaring Eagle*
by Mary Peace Finley
Julio, a 13-year-old boy in 1845, finds friendship and a clue to his identity while living with the Cheyenne.

☐ *Island of the Blue Dolphins*
by Scott O'Dell
1961 Newbery Medal

Dangerous Journeys
The Goats

☐ *Grab Hands and Run*
by Frances Temple
After his father disappears, 12-year-old Felipe, his mother, and his younger sister set out to make their way from El Salvador to Canada.

☐ *The Journey of the Shadow Bairns*
by Margaret J. Anderson
When her parents die suddenly, leaving only a one-way passage to Canada, a Scottish girl decides she and her four-year-old brother will pursue family plans to relocate.

☐ *Steal Away*
by Jennifer Armstrong
In 1855 two 13-year-old girls, one white and one black, run away from a southern farm and make the difficult journey north to freedom.

☐ *The Adventures of Huckleberry Finn*
by Mark Twain
A 19th-century boy from a Mississippi River town recounts his adventures as he travels down the river with a runaway slave on a raft.

☐ *North to Freedom*
by Anne Holm
Having escaped from an Eastern European concentration camp where he has spent his life, a 12-year-old boy struggles to cope with an entirely strange world as he flees northward.

☐ *The Flight of the Doves*
by Walter Macken
A 12-year-old English boy and his seven-year-old sister run away from their abusive stepfather and set out to reach their grandmother in Ireland.

Runaways
The Goats

☐ *Slake's Limbo*
by Felice Holman
Thirteen-year-old Aremis Slake, hounded by his fears and misfortunes, flees into New York City's subway tunnels.

☐ *Come to the Edge*
by Julia Cunningham
After he is befriended by a sign painter, a confused runaway finds trust and a purpose for living.

☐ *From the Mixed-Up Files of Mrs. Basil E. Frankweiler*
by E. L. Konigsburg
1968 Newbery Medal
Two children run away from their home and live in New York's Metropolitan Museum of Art.

☐ *The Yearling*
by Marjorie Kinnan Rawlings
A young boy living in the Florida backwoods is forced to decide the fate of a fawn he has raised as a pet.

☐ *Maniac Magee*
by Jerry Spinelli
1991 Newbery Medal
After his parents die, Jeffrey Lionel Magee's life becomes legendary, as he accomplishes athletic and other feats.

☐ *The Dulcimer Boy*
by Tor Seidler
Twin brothers are abandoned on their uncle's doorstep with nothing but a silver-stringed dulcimer.

☐ *My Side of the Mountain*
by Jean Craighead George
1960 Newbery Honor Book
Sam Gribley leaves New York City and spends a year living by himself in a remote area of the Catskill Mountains.
Sequel: *On the Far Side of the Mountain*

Stealing
The Goats

☐ *J. T.*
by Jane Wagner
J. T. discovers more satisfaction in caring for an injured cat than in listening to a stolen transistor radio.

☐ *Sounder*
by William H. Armstrong
1970 Newbery Medal
When his sharecropper father is jailed for stealing food for his family, a young black boy grows in courage and understanding with the help of the dog Sounder and learns to read and write.
Sequel: *Sourland*

☐ *My Crooked Family*
by James Lincoln Collier
Living with irresponsible parents in a seedy part of a big city in 1910, 13-year-old Roger falls in with a gang of murderous burglars and discovers an unpleasant secret about his father.

☐ *The Great Gilly Hopkins*
by Katherine Paterson
1979 Newbery Honor Book
An 11-year-old foster child tries to cope with her longings and fears as she schemes against everyone who tries to be friendly.

☐ *Rite of Passage*
by Richard Wright
PG language
Fifteen-year-old Johnny Gibbs runs off into the streets of Harlem and meets up with a gang that wants him to participate in a mugging.

☐ *Poor Badger*
by K. M. Peyton
Having become passionately devoted to a pony who is being mistreated by his owner, nine-year-old Ros decides to steal him in the night.

Goodnight, Mr. Tom
Michelle Magorian

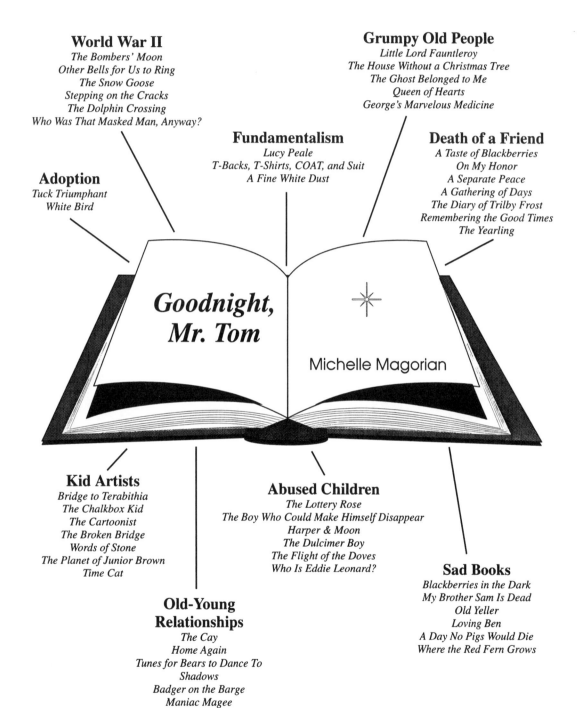

World War II
The Bombers' Moon
Other Bells for Us to Ring
The Snow Goose
Stepping on the Cracks
The Dolphin Crossing
Who Was That Masked Man, Anyway?

Grumpy Old People
Little Lord Fauntleroy
The House Without a Christmas Tree
The Ghost Belonged to Me
Queen of Hearts
George's Marvelous Medicine

Fundamentalism
Lucy Peale
T-Backs, T-Shirts, COAT, and Suit
A Fine White Dust

Death of a Friend
A Taste of Blackberries
On My Honor
A Separate Peace
A Gathering of Days
The Diary of Trilby Frost
Remembering the Good Times
The Yearling

Adoption
Tuck Triumphant
White Bird

Kid Artists
Bridge to Terabithia
The Chalkbox Kid
The Cartoonist
The Broken Bridge
Words of Stone
The Planet of Junior Brown
Time Cat

Abused Children
The Lottery Rose
The Boy Who Could Make Himself Disappear
Harper & Moon
The Dulcimer Boy
The Flight of the Doves
Who Is Eddie Leonard?

Sad Books
Blackberries in the Dark
My Brother Sam Is Dead
Old Yeller
Loving Ben
A Day No Pigs Would Die
Where the Red Fern Grows

Old-Young Relationships
The Cay
Home Again
Tunes for Bears to Dance To
Shadows
Badger on the Barge
Maniac Magee

Michelle Magorian

Goodnight, Mr. Tom

World War II

The Bombers' Moon

Other Bells for Us to Ring

The Snow Goose

Stepping on the Cracks

The Dolphin Crossing

Who Was That Masked Man, Anyway?

Fundamentalism

Lucy Peale

T-Backs, T-Shirts, COAT, and Suit

A Fine White Dust

Adoption

Tuck Triumphant

White Bird

Abused Children

The Lottery Rose

The Boy Who Could Make Himself Disappear

Harper & Moon

The Dulcimer Boy

The Flight of the Doves

Who Is Eddie Leonard?

Death of a Friend

A Taste of Blackberries

On My Honor

A Separate Peace

A Gathering of Days

The Diary of Trilby Frost

Remembering the Good Times

The Yearling

Kid Artists

Bridge to Terabithia

The Chalkbox Kid

The Cartoonist

The Broken Bridge

Words of Stone

The Planet of Junior Brown

Time Cat

Old-Young Relationships

The Cay

Home Again

Tunes for Bears to Dance To

Shadows

Badger on the Barge

Maniac Magee

Grumpy Old People

Little Lord Fauntleroy

The House Without a Christmas Tree

The Ghost Belonged to Me

Queen of Hearts

George's Marvelous Medicine

Sad Books

Blackberries in the Dark

My Brother Sam Is Dead

Old Yeller

Loving Ben

A Day No Pigs Would Die

Where the Red Fern Grows

World War II
Goodnight, Mr. Tom

☐ *The Bombers' Moon*
by Betty Vander Els

An American missionary family living in China is separated when the two children are evacuated to India with their school class to escape the Japanese invasion.

☐ *Other Bells for Us to Ring*
by Robert Cormier

When her father is transferred to an army camp during World War II, Darcy feels isolated in her French-Canadian neighborhood until she meets the vivacious Kathleen Mary O'Hara and learns about Catholicism.

☐ *The Snow Goose*
by Paul Gallico

Against the backdrop of World War II, a friendship develops between a lonely crippled artist living alone in a lighthouse and a village girl, who together minister to an injured snow goose.

☐ *Stepping on the Cracks*
by Mary Downing Hahn

Eleven-year-old Margaret gets a new view of the school bully Gordy when she finds him hiding his brother, an army deserter.

☐ *The Dolphin Crossing*
by Jill Paton Walsh

In wartime England, two boys, too young to fight, take part in the evacuation from Dunkirk.

☐ *Who Was That Masked Man, Anyway?*
by Avi

In the early 1940s, sixth-grader Frankie Wattleson gets in trouble at home and at school because of his preoccupation with his favorite radio programs.

Fundamentalism
Goodnight, Mr. Tom

☐ *Lucy Peale*
by Colby Rodowsky

PG sex

Failing to get sympathy from her strict fundamentalist father when a rape leaves her pregnant, Lucy flees her home on Maryland's Eastern Shore and attempts to find self-reliance in nearby Ocean City.

☐ *T-Backs, T-Shirts, COAT, and Suit*
by E. L. Konigsburg

Spending the summer in Florida with her stepfather's sister, who operates a "meals-on-wheels" van, 12-year-old Chloe and her aunt become involved in a controversy surrounding the wearing of T-back bathing suits.

☐ *A Fine White Dust*
by Cynthia Rylant

1987 Newbery Honor Book

The visit of the traveling Preacher Man to a small North Carolina town gives new impetus to 13-year-old Peter's struggle to reconcile his own deeply felt religious belief with the beliefs and nonbeliefs of his family and friends.

Adoption
Goodnight, Mr. Tom

☐ *Tuck Triumphant*
by Theodore Taylor

Fourteen-year-old Helen, her blind dog Friar Tuck, and her family face some dramatic challenges when they discover that the Korean boy they have adopted is deaf.

Sequel to *The Trouble with Tuck*

☐ *White Bird*
by Clyde Robert Bulla

A lonely boy is found and reared by a hermit in the wilderness of the Tennessee mountains in the 1880s.

Abused Children
Goodnight, Mr. Tom

☐ *The Lottery Rose*
by Irene Hunt

A young victim of child abuse gradually overcomes his fears and suspicions when placed in a home with other boys.

☐ *The Boy Who Could Make Himself Disappear*
by Kin Platt

A 12-year-old boy with a speech defect gradually withdraws into schizophrenia after moving to live with his mother following the divorce of his harsh and detached parents.

☐ *Harper & Moon*
by Ramon Royal Ross

Although 12-year-old Harper has always liked Moon, an abused, orphaned, older boy, their friendship is tested by a discovery Harper makes when Moon joins the army in 1943.

☐ *The Dulcimer Boy*
by Tor Seidler

Twin brothers are abandoned on their uncle's doorstep in turn-of-the-century New England with nothing but a silver-stringed dulcimer.

☐ *The Flight of the Doves*
by Walter Macken

A 12-year-old English boy and his seven-year-old sister run away from their abusive stepfather and set out to reach their grandmother in western Ireland.

☐ *Who Is Eddie Leonard?*
by Harry Mazer

A 14-year-old boy who was raised by an abusive old woman, and who has always had questions about his parents, sees a picture of a missing child and sets out to discover if he is that child.

Death of a Friend
Goodnight, Mr. Tom

▢ *A Taste of Blackberries*
by Doris B. Smith

A young boy recounts his efforts to adjust to the accidental death of his best friend.

▢ *On My Honor*
by Marian Dane Bauer

1987 Newbery Honor Book

When his best friend drowns while they are both swimming in a treacherous river that they had promised never to go near, Joel is devastated and terrified at having to tell both sets of parents.

▢ *A Separate Peace*
by John Knowles

Gene and Finny's friendship is marred by Finny's crippling fall.

▢ *A Gathering of Days*
by Joan W. Blos

1980 Newbery Medal

The journal of a 14-year-old girl records daily events in her small town, her father's remarriage, and the death of her best friend.

▢ *The Diary of Trilby Frost*
by Dianne Glaser

Teenager Trilby Frost records in her diary her growing realization that life continues even though her father, younger brother, and closest friend die.

▢ *Remembering the Good Times*
by Richard Peck

Trav, Kate, and Buck's special friendship may not be enough to save Trav as he pressures himself relentlessly to succeed.

▢ *The Yearling*
by Marjorie Kinnan Rawlings

A young boy living in the backwoods is forced to decide the fate of a fawn he has raised as a pet.

Kid Artists
Goodnight, Mr. Tom

▢ *Bridge to Terabithia*
by Katherine Paterson

1978 Newbery Medal

The life of a 10-year-old boy expands when he becomes friends with a newcomer.

▢ *The Chalkbox Kid*
by Clyde Robert Bulla

Nine-year-old Gregory creates a surprising and very different garden in an unusual place.

▢ *The Cartoonist*
by Betsy Byars

Threatened with the loss of his private place in the attic of his crowded home, a young boy determines to keep it at all costs.

▢ *The Broken Bridge*
by Philip Pullman

Sixteen-year-old Ginny, the artist daughter of an English father and a Haitian mother, learns that her mother may still be alive.

▢ *Words of Stone*
by Kevin Henkes

Busy trying to deal with his troubled feelings for his dead mother, 10-year-old Blaze has his life changed when he meets the boisterous and irresistible Joselle.

▢ *The Planet of Junior Brown*
by Virginia Hamilton

1972 Newbery Honor Book

Buddy Clark takes on the responsibility of protecting his overweight, emotionally disturbed friend.

▢ *Time Cat*
by Lloyd Alexander

Gareth, a cat with miraculous powers, takes his human friend Jason with him when he travels through time.

Old-Young Relationships
Goodnight, Mr. Tom

▢ *The Cay*
by Theodore Taylor

When their ship is torpedoed by a German submarine, a white boy, blinded by a blow on the head, and an old black man are stranded on a tiny Caribbean island.

Prequel/sequel: *Timothy of the Cay*

▢ *Home Again*
by R. Wright Campbell

Hugh Badoum remembers a day when he and his grandfather entered their pigeon in a race and his grandfather had a stroke.

Previously titled *Where Pigeons Go to Die*

▢ *Tunes for Bears to Dance To*
by Robert Cormier

Eleven-year-old Henry escapes his family's problems by watching the woodcarving of Mr. Levine, an elderly Holocaust survivor, but when Henry is manipulated into betraying his friend, he comes to know true evil.

▢ *Shadows*
by Dennis Haseley

Jamie's lonely life with his aunt and uncle changes when Grandpa comes to visit.

▢ *Badger on the Barge*
by Janni Howker

A collection of five short stories exploring complex relationships and rare understandings among the young and old.

▢ *Maniac Magee*
by Jerry Spinelli

1991 Newbery Medal

After his parents die, Jeffrey Lionel Magee's life becomes legendary, as he accomplishes athletic and other feats that awe his contemporaries.

Grumpy Old People
Goodnight, Mr. Tom

▢ *Little Lord Fauntleroy*
by Frances Hodgson Burnett

A Brooklyn boy discovers that he is the heir to an earldom and a fortune, and goes to live with his bad-tempered, selfish, and cantankerous grandfather.

▢ *The House Without a Christmas Tree*
by Gail Rock

In 1946 a 10-year-old girl tries to understand and overcome her stern father's objections to having a Christmas tree in the house.

Sequel: *The Thanksgiving Treasure*

▢ *The Ghost Belonged to Me*
by Richard Peck

In 1913 in the Midwest, a quartet of characters share adventures, from exploding steamboats to exorcising a ghost.

▢ *Queen of Hearts*
by Vera and Bill Cleaver

Although there is no love lost between them, 12-year-old Wilma is her willful and peppery grandmother's choice for a companion.

▢ *George's Marvelous Medicine*
by Roald Dahl

George decides that his grumpy, selfish old grandmother must be a witch and concocts some marvelous medicine to take care of her.

Sad Books
Goodnight, Mr. Tom

☐ *Blackberries in the Dark*
   by Mavis Jukes

Nine-year-old Austin visits his grandmother the summer after his grandfather dies, and together they try to come to terms with their loss.

☐ *My Brother Sam Is Dead*
   by Christopher and
   James Lincoln Collier

Recounts the tragedy that strikes the Meeker family during the Revolution, when one son joins the rebel forces while the rest of the family tries to stay neutral in a Tory town.

☐ *Old Yeller*
   by Fred Gipson
   1957 Newbery Honor Book

In the late 1860s in the Texas hill country, a big yellow dog and a 14-year-old boy form a close, loving relationship.

☐ *Loving Ben*
   by Elizabeth Laird

Anna's teen years bring maturity and fulfillment as she experiences the birth and death of a loved hydrocephalic brother and works with a child with Down's syndrome.

☐ *A Day No Pigs Would Die*
   by Robert Newton Peck

To a 13-year-old Vermont farm boy whose father slaughters pigs for a living, maturity comes early as he learns to do what's got to be done, especially regarding his pet pig, who cannot produce a litter.

☐ *Where the Red Fern Grows*
   by Wilson Rawls

The adventures of a 10-year-old boy and the two dogs he bought with money he had earned.

The Indian in the Cupboard

Lynne Reid Banks

Tiny People
The Return of the Twelves
The Castle in the Attic
The Borrowers
The Littles
Truckers
The Adventures of Treehorn
The Box of Delights: When the
Wolves Were Running

Time Travel
The Chalk Cross
Charlotte Sometimes
Many Waters
Tom's Midnight Garden
Voices After Midnight
Uptime, Downtime
George Washington's Socks
The Devil's Arithmetic
A Dig in Time

Magical Objects
Travel Far, Pay No Fare
Penelope's Pendant
Half Magic
Second Hand Magic
The Gilded Cat
The Magic Skateboard
The Chocolate Touch

**People from the Past in
Modern Times**
Switching Well
The Dreadful Future of
Blossom Culp
The Princess in the Pigpen

Sequels
The Return of the Indian
The Secret of the Indian
The Mystery of the Cupboard

The Indian in the Cupboard

Lynne Reid Banks

Fantasy Series
The Book of Three
The Children of Green Knowe
The Dark Is Rising
A Wizard of Earthsea
The Magician's Nephew
My Father's Dragon
The Wonderful Wizard of Oz

**Toys That Come
to Life**
Lady Daisy
The Oracle Doll

**Miniature
Villages**
Afternoon of the Elves
The Village by the Sea
Through the Hidden Door
Tunes for Bears to Dance To

**Taking Responsibility
for Others**
King Matt the First
The Planet of Junior Brown
Quest for a Maid
Circle of Fire
The Summer of the Swans
Shiloh
Stepping on the Cracks

**Humorous but
Hair-Raising Fantasy**
The Eyes of Kid Midas
The Boggart
George's Marvelous Medicine
Aunt Maria
The Power of Three

The Indian
in the
Cupboard

Lynne Reid Banks

Tiny People

The Return of the Twelves

The Castle in the Attic

The Borrowers

The Littles

Truckers

The Adventures of Treehorn

The Box of Delights: When the Wolves Were Running

Humorous but Hair-Raising Fantasy

The Eyes of Kid Midas

The Boggart

George's Marvelous Medicine

Aunt Maria

The Power of Three

People from the Past in Modern Times

Switching Well

The Dreadful Future of Blossom Culp

The Princess in the Pigpen

Toys That Come to Life

Lady Daisy

The Oracle Doll

Fantasy Series

The Book of Three

The Children of Green Knowe

The Dark Is Rising

A Wizard of Earthsea

The Magician's Nephew

My Father's Dragon

The Wonderful Wizard of Oz

Miniature Villages

Afternoon of the Elves

The Village by the Sea

Through the Hidden Door

Tunes for Bears to Dance To

Sequels

The Return of the Indian

The Secret of the Indian

The Mystery of the Cupboard

Time Travel

The Chalk Cross

Charlotte Sometimes

Many Waters

Tom's Midnight Garden

Voices After Midnight

Uptime, Downtime

George Washington's Socks

The Devil's Arithmetic

A Dig in Time

Taking Responsibility for Others

King Matt the First

The Planet of Junior Brown

Quest for a Maid

Circle of Fire

The Summer of the Swans

Shiloh

Stepping on the Cracks

Magical Objects

Travel Far, Pay No Fare

Penelope's Pendant

Half Magic

Second Hand Magic

The Gilded Cat

The Magic Skateboard

The Chocolate Touch

Tiny People
The Indian in the Cupboard

☐ *The Return of the Twelves*
by Pauline Clarke

Max finds 12 old wooden soldiers in the attic of his home and discovers they are alive.

☐ *The Castle in the Attic*
by Elizabeth Winthrop

A gift of a toy castle introduces William to an adventure involving magic and a personal quest.
Sequel: *The Battle for the Castle*

☐ *The Borrowers*
by Mary Norton

Miniature people live in an old country house by borrowing things from the humans.

Many sequels

☐ *The Littles*
by John Peterson

When the Bigs go on a vacation, the Littles must contend with a family from the city who move in.

Many sequels

☐ *Truckers*
by Terry Pratchett

When the department store where they live goes out of business, the other nomes look to Masklin, a newly arrived "outsider," to lead them to a safe haven.

Book 1 of the Bromeliad

☐ *The Adventures of Treehorn*
by Florence Parry Heide

Nobody seems to notice when Treehorn starts to shrink.

☐ *The Box of Delights: When the Wolves Were Running*
by John Masefield

Kay finds himself involved in an adventure when he becomes guardian of the mysterious Box of Delights.

Humorous but Hair-Raising Fantasy
The Indian in the Cupboard

☐ *The Eyes of Kid Midas*
by Neal Shusterman

Kevin is entranced when he finds a pair of sunglasses that turn his desires into reality, but then things start to get out of control.

☐ *The Boggart*
by Susan Cooper

After visiting the castle in Scotland that her family has inherited and returning home to Canada, 12-year-old Emily finds that she has accidentally brought back with her a boggart, an invisible and mischievous spirit with a fondness for practical jokes.

☐ *George's Marvelous Medicine*
by Roald Dahl

George decides that his grumpy, selfish old grandmother must be a witch and concocts some marvelous medicine to take care of her.

☐ *Aunt Maria*
by Diana Wynne Jones

While visiting and caring for Great-Aunt Maria, Mig and Chris discover that their "helpless" relative has frightening powers.

☐ *The Power of Three*
by Diana Wynne Jones

The curse on Orban spreads bad luck to the rest of the Otmounders, the Giants, and the Dorig until three Otmounder children are born with Gifts.

People from the Past in Modern Times
The Indian in the Cupboard

☐ *Switching Well*
by Peni R. Griffin

Two 12-year-old girls, Ada in 1891 and Amber in 1991, switch places through a magic well and try desperately to return to their own times.

☐ *The Dreadful Future of Blossom Culp*
by Richard Peck

Blossom, not the most popular member of her freshman class in 1914, travels ahead 70 years and returns in time to make Halloween a memorable night for her classmates and teachers.

☐ *The Princess in the Pigpen*
by Jane Resh Thomas

Elizabeth, a duke's daughter sick with fever, travels through time from Elizabethan England to a farm in modern Iowa, where she has difficulty convincing anyone of the truth of her story.

Toys That Come to Life
The Indian in the Cupboard

☐ *Lady Daisy*
by Dick King-Smith

Nine-year-old Ned faces a lot of teasing when he decides to keep a Victorian doll that speaks only to him.

☐ *The Oracle Doll*
by Catherine Dexter

When they become the guardians of a talking doll that is actually the reincarnated Oracle of Delphi, three youngsters discover how difficult their task will be.

Time Travel
The Indian in the Cupboard

□ *The Chalk Cross*
by Berthe Amoss
A girl living in New Orleans keeps slipping back to a time of voodoo.

□ *Charlotte Sometimes*
by Penelope Farmer
During Charlotte's first night at boarding school, she slips back in time.

□ *Many Waters*
by Madeleine L'Engle
Fifteen-year-old twins Sandy and Dennys are sent back to the time of Noah.

□ *Tom's Midnight Garden*
by Philippa Pearce
Tom discovers a midnight garden and a mysterious orphan.

□ *Voices After Midnight*
by Richard Peck
Brothers Chad and Luke uncover a mystery when they slip back in time to 1888.

□ *Uptime, Downtime*
by John Peel
When siblings Karyn and Mike discover that they can travel through time, they encounter other time travelers.

□ *George Washington's Socks*
by Elvira Woodruff
Five children find themselves back in the time of Washington and learn the realities of war.

□ *The Devil's Arithmetic*
by Jane Yolen
Hanna travels back to a small Jewish village in Nazi-occupied Poland.

□ *A Dig in Time*
by Peni R. Griffin
A brother and sister dig up artifacts and discover how to use them to travel back through time.

Sequels
The Indian in the Cupboard

□ *The Return of the Indian*
Omri decides to bring Little Bear back, only to find that he is close to death and in need of help.

□ *The Secret of the Indian*
Omri and Patrick find themselves in need of a friend's toy plastic doctors to save wounded people from the Old West that the cupboard enables them to enter.

□ *The Mystery of the Cupboard*
Omri finds many secrets revealed to him when he accidentally discovers the link between the house and the magic cupboard.

Miniature Villages
The Indian in the Cupboard

□ *Afternoon of the Elves*
by Janet Taylor Lisle
1990 Newbery Honor Book
As Hillary works in the miniature village, allegedly built by elves, in Sara-Kate's backyard, she becomes curious about Sara-Kate's mysterious life.

□ *The Village by the Sea*
by Paula Fox
Ten-year-old Emma is sent to live with her tormented aunt, where she meets a friend who suggests making a miniature village in the sand.

□ *Through the Hidden Door*
by Rosemary Wells
Two young boys stumble upon the remains of an ancient underground mystery civilization.

□ *Tunes for Bears to Dance To*
by Robert Cormier
Eleven-year-old Henry likes to watch the woodcarving of an elderly Holocaust survivor, until he is manipulated into betraying his friend.

Fantasy Series
The Indian in the Cupboard

□ *The Book of Three*
by Lloyd Alexander
Taran sets out with the warrior Gwydion to save his country from evil.
Book 1 of the Chronicles of Prydain

□ *The Children of Green Knowe*
by L. M. Boston
Tolly becomes friends with children who lived in the 17th century.
Book 1 of the Green Knowe series

□ *The Dark Is Rising*
by Susan Cooper
On his 11th birthday Will discovers that he is destined to seek the magical Signs that will enable the Old Ones to triumph over the evil forces of the Dark.
Book 2 of the Dark Is Rising series

□ *A Wizard of Earthsea*
by Ursula Le Guin
An apprentice wizard attempts to subdue the evil he unleashed on the world.
Book 1 of the Earthsea series

□ *The Magician's Nephew*
by C. S. Lewis
Two children are sent away by a magician to a place where they witness how Aslan creates Narnia.
Book 6 of the Chronicles of Narnia

□ *My Father's Dragon*
by Ruth Stiles Gannett
1949 Newbery Honor Book
A young boy rescues a baby dragon who is being held captive by wild animals.
Book 1 of the Dragon series

□ *The Wonderful Wizard of Oz*
by L. Frank Baum
Dorothy must seek out the great wizard of Oz in order to return to Kansas.
First of the many Oz books

Taking Responsibility for Others
The Indian in the Cupboard

☐ *King Matt the First*
by Janusz Korczak

A child king introduces reforms to give children the same rights as adults.

☐ *The Planet of Junior Brown*
by Virginia Hamilton

1972 Newbery Honor Book

A leader in New York's underground world of homeless children tries to protect an emotionally disturbed boy.

☐ *Quest for a Maid*
by Frances Mary Hendry

Meg realizes she must protect the young Norwegian princess who has been chosen as rightful heir to the Scottish throne from those, including Meg's sorceress sister, who plot the princess's death.

☐ *Circle of Fire*
by William Hooks

Eleven-year-old Harrison overhears a local bigot planning a Ku Klux Klan raid on a band of Irish tinkers camped nearby.

☐ *The Summer of the Swans*
by Betsy Byars

1971 Newbery Medal

A teenage girl gains new insight into herself and her family when her mentally retarded brother gets lost.

☐ *Shiloh*
by Phyllis Reynolds Naylor

1992 Newbery Medal

Marty tries to hide a lost beagle from his family and the dog's real owner, a mean-spirited man known to mistreat his dogs.

☐ *Stepping on the Cracks*
by Mary Downing Hahn

Eleven-year-old Margaret gets a new view of the school bully when she finds him hiding his brother, a World War II army deserter.

Magical Objects
The Indian in the Cupboard

☐ *Travel Far, Pay No Fare*
by Anne Lindbergh

When 12-year-old Owen finds that his nine-year-old cousin has a magic bookmark, he joins her when she enters different stories.

☐ *Penelope's Pendant*
by Douglas Hill

Eleven-year-old Penelope finds a slightly damaged pendant on the beach that gives her the power to move herself and other objects through space.

☐ *Half Magic*
by Edward Eager

Four children enjoy a series of fantastic adventures by double-wishing on an ancient coin.

☐ *Second Hand Magic*
by Ruth Chew

Two children acquire a magic kite and, with some secondhand items from a nearby store, enjoy a series of adventures.

☐ *The Gilded Cat*
by Catherine Dexter

Twelve-year-old Maggie buys a mummified cat at a yard sale and is drawn into a frightening world of ancient Egyptian magic.

☐ *The Magic Skateboard*
by Enid Richemont

Danny meets a strange-looking woman who transforms his skateboard into a kind of flying carpet that allows him to visit any place he imagines.

☐ *The Chocolate Touch*
by Patrick Skene Catling

A boy acquires a magical gift that turns everything his lips touch into chocolate.

Julie of the Wolves

Jean Craighead George

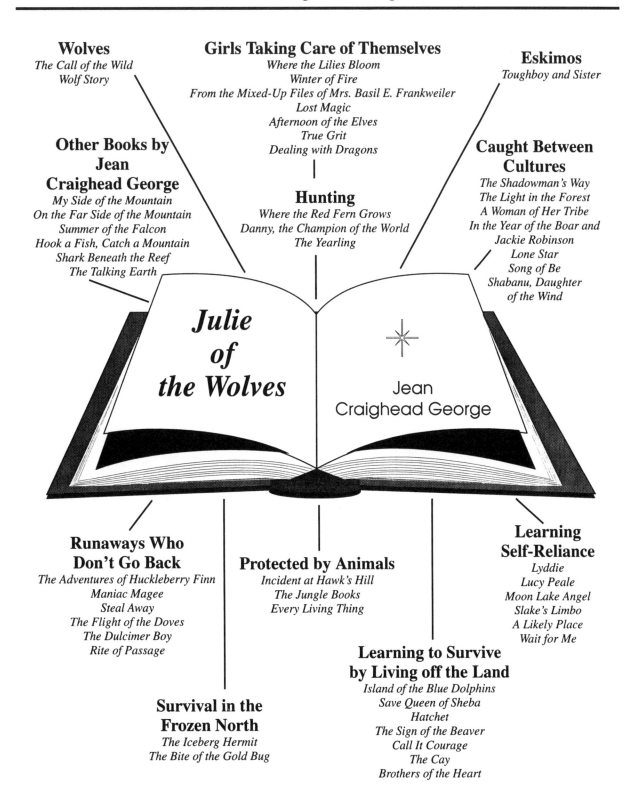

Wolves
The Call of the Wild
Wolf Story

Girls Taking Care of Themselves
Where the Lilies Bloom
Winter of Fire
From the Mixed-Up Files of Mrs. Basil E. Frankweiler
Lost Magic
Afternoon of the Elves
True Grit
Dealing with Dragons

Eskimos
Toughboy and Sister

Other Books by Jean Craighead George
My Side of the Mountain
On the Far Side of the Mountain
Summer of the Falcon
Hook a Fish, Catch a Mountain
Shark Beneath the Reef
The Talking Earth

Hunting
Where the Red Fern Grows
Danny, the Champion of the World
The Yearling

Caught Between Cultures
The Shadowman's Way
The Light in the Forest
A Woman of Her Tribe
In the Year of the Boar and Jackie Robinson
Lone Star
Song of Be
Shabanu, Daughter of the Wind

Julie of the Wolves

Jean Craighead George

Runaways Who Don't Go Back
The Adventures of Huckleberry Finn
Maniac Magee
Steal Away
The Flight of the Doves
The Dulcimer Boy
Rite of Passage

Protected by Animals
Incident at Hawk's Hill
The Jungle Books
Every Living Thing

Learning Self-Reliance
Lyddie
Lucy Peale
Moon Lake Angel
Slake's Limbo
A Likely Place
Wait for Me

Learning to Survive by Living off the Land
Island of the Blue Dolphins
Save Queen of Sheba
Hatchet
The Sign of the Beaver
Call It Courage
The Cay
Brothers of the Heart

Survival in the Frozen North
The Iceberg Hermit
The Bite of the Gold Bug

Julie of the Wolves

of

the Wolves

Jean
Craighead George

Other Books by Jean Craighead George

My Side of the Mountain

On the Far Side of the Mountain

Summer of the Falcon

Hook a Fish, Catch a Mountain

Shark Beneath the Reef

The Talking Earth

Wolves

The Call of the Wild

Wolf Story

Eskimos

Toughboy and Sister

Protected by Animals

Incident at Hawk's Hill

The Jungle Books

Every Living Thing

Survival in the Frozen North

The Iceberg Hermit

The Bite of the Gold Bug

Hunting

Where the Red Fern Grows

Danny, the Champion of the World

The Yearling

Caught Between Cultures

The Shadowman's Way

The Light in the Forest

A Woman of Her Tribe

In the Year of the Boar and Jackie Robinson

Lone Star

Song of Be

Shabanu, Daughter of the Wind

Learning Self-Reliance

Lyddie

Lucy Peale

Moon Lake Angel

Slake's Limbo

A Likely Place

Wait for Me

Runaways Who Don't Go Back

The Adventures of Huckleberry Finn

Maniac Magee

Steal Away

The Flight of the Doves

The Dulcimer Boy

Rite of Passage

**Learning to Survive
by Living off the Land**

*Island of the Blue
Dolphins*

Save Queen of Sheba

Hatchet

The Sign of the Beaver

Call It Courage

The Cay

Brothers of the Heart

**Girls Taking
Care of Themselves**

Where the Lilies Bloom
Winter of Fire

*From the Mixed-Up Files
of Mrs. Basil E.
Frankweiler*

Lost Magic
Afternoon of the Elves
True Grit
Dealing with Dragons

Protected by Animals
Julie of the Wolves

📖 *Incident at Hawk's Hill*
by Allan W. Eckert
1972 Newbery Honor Book

A shy, lonely six-year-old wanders into the Canadian prairie and spends a summer under the protection of a badger.

📖 *The Jungle Books*
by Rudyard Kipling

The adventures of Mowgli, a man-child reared by the jungle wolf packs and educated by wild animals. Also includes other stories set in India.

📖 *Every Living Thing*
by Cynthia Rylant

Twelve short stories in which animals change people's lives for the better.

Eskimos
Julie of the Wolves

📖 *Toughboy and Sister*
by Kirkpatrick Hill

The death of their drunken father strands 11-year-old Toughboy and his younger sister at a remote fishing cabin in the Yukon, where they spend a summer trying to cope with dwindling food supplies and hostile wildlife.

Wolves
Julie of the Wolves

📖 *The Call of the Wild*
by Jack London

The savage frontier rouses primeval instincts in the dog Buck, who is stolen from his home and pressed into service as a sled dog in the Klondike. He becomes the leader of a wolf pack.

📖 *Wolf Story*
by William McCleery

A young father tells his five-year-old son humorous variations on the theme of a hen escaping the clutches of a wily wolf.

Other Books by Jean Craighead George
Julie of the Wolves

📖 *My Side of the Mountain*
1960 Newbery Honor Book

Young Sam Gribley leaves New York City and spends a year living by himself in a remote area of the Catskill Mountains.
Sequel: *On the Far Side of the Mountain*

📖 *On the Far Side of the Mountain*

Sam's peaceful existence in his wilderness home is disrupted when his sister runs away and his pet falcon is confiscated by a conservation officer.
Sequel to *My Side of the Mountain*

📖 *Summer of the Falcon*

As June Pritchard trains her sparrowhawk Zander to prepare for his adult life, she chafes at her mother's insistence that she assume the responsibilities of her own increasing age.

📖 *Hook a Fish, Catch a Mountain*

A girl and her cousin become ecological detectives when the girl catches a fish thought to be extinct in that river.

📖 *Shark Beneath the Reef*

On the island of Coronado, a young Mexican fisherman comes of age as he becomes aware of the politics, corruption, and changes around him.

📖 *The Talking Earth*

Billie Wind ventures out alone into the Florida Everglades to test the legends of her Indian ancestors and learns the importance of listening to the earth's vital messages.

Learning Self-Reliance
Julie of the Wolves

📖*Lyddie*
by Katherine Paterson

Impoverished Vermont farm girl Lyddie Worthen is determined to gain her independence by becoming a factory worker in the 1840s.

📖*Lucy Peale*
by Colby Rodowsky

PG sex

Failing to get sympathy from her strict fundamentalist father when a rape leaves her pregnant, Lucy flees her home on Maryland's Eastern Shore and attempts to find self-reliance in nearby Ocean City.

📖*Moon Lake Angel*
by Vera and Bill Cleaver

Kitty, whose mother does not want to deal with a child, stays with Aunt Petal and eventually learns to accept her mother's weaknesses.

📖*Slake's Limbo*
by Felice Holman

Thirteen-year-old Aremis Slake, hounded by his fears and misfortunes, flees into New York City's subway tunnels, never again, he believes, to emerge.

📖*A Likely Place*
by Paula Fox

A little boy who can't spell or ever seem to please his parents spends a week with a kooky baby-sitter and makes a special friend.

📖*Wait for Me*
by Susan Shreve

As she begins fifth grade, Molly feels left behind by her older sisters and brother and neglected by her former best friends.

Caught Between Cultures
Julie of the Wolves

📖*The Shadowman's Way*
by Paul Pitts

Nelson Sam always managed to stay out of trouble on the reservation—until now.

📖*The Light in the Forest*
by Conrad Richter

After being raised as an Indian for 11 years, John Butler is forcibly returned to his white parents.

📖*A Woman of Her Tribe*
by Margaret A. Robinson

Fifteen-year-old Annette, whose dead father was a Nootka Indian, tries to decide which cultural heritage she should pursue.

📖*In the Year of the Boar and Jackie Robinson*
by Betty Bao Lord

In 1947, a Chinese child in Brooklyn becomes Americanized at school and by her love for baseball.

📖*Lone Star*
by Barbara Barrie

In 1944, a young Jewish girl adopts a new lifestyle that alienates her Orthodox grandfather.

📖*Song of Be*
by Lesley Beake

A young Bushman woman realizes that she and her people must reconcile new realities with ancient traditions.

📖*Shabanu, Daughter of the Wind*
by Suzanne Fisher Staples

1990 Newbery Honor Book

When 11-year-old Shabanu, the daughter of a nomad in the Cholistan Desert, is pledged in marriage to an older man, she must either accept the decision or risk the consequences of defying her father's wishes.

Hunting
Julie of the Wolves

📖*Where the Red Fern Grows*
by Wilson Rawls

The adventures of a 10-year-old boy and the two dogs he bought with money he had earned.

📖*Danny, the Champion of the World*
by Roald Dahl

Danny describes his relationship with his father, a poacher, and the special adventure they share together.

📖*The Yearling*
by Marjorie Kinnan Rawlings

A young boy living in the Florida backwoods is forced to decide the fate of a fawn he has lovingly raised as a pet.

Survival in the Frozen North
Julie of the Wolves

📖*The Iceberg Hermit*
by Arthur Roth

Shipwrecked in 1757 on an iceberg in the Arctic seas with only an orphaned polar bear cub for companionship, 17-year-old Allan begins a seemingly hopeless struggle for survival.

📖*The Bite of the Gold Bug*
by Barthe DeClements

Bucky and his father, prospecting for gold in 1898, must overcome storms, dangerous mountain trails, and wilderness predators before confronting the final challenge of human treachery.

Girls Taking Care of Themselves
Julie of the Wolves

☐ *Where the Lilies Bloom*
by Vera and Bill Cleaver

A 14-year-old girl struggles to keep her family together after their father dies.
Sequel: *Trial Valley*

☐ *Winter of Fire*
by Sherryl Jordan

A world destroyed by fire is saved from ice by a charismatic young woman who has powers beyond those of any human being.

☐ *From the Mixed-Up Files of Mrs. Basil E. Frankweiler*
by E. L. Konigsburg

1968 Newbery Medal

Two suburban children run away to the Metropolitan Museum of Art.

☐ *Lost Magic*
by Berthe Amoss

In the Middle Ages, orphaned Ceridwen learns the art of herbal healing until she is accused of witchcraft.

☐ *Afternoon of the Elves*
by Janet Taylor Lisle

1990 Newbery Honor Book

As Hillary works in the miniature village in Sara-Kate's backyard, she becomes curious about Sara-Kate's real life inside her big, gloomy house with her mysterious, silent mother.

☐ *True Grit*
by Charles Portis

Fourteen-year-old Mattie Ross convinces one-eyed Marshall Rooster Cogburn to help her capture the outlaws who murdered her father.

☐ *Dealing with Dragons*
by Patricia C. Wrede

A princess goes off to live with a group of dragons and becomes involved in fighting against wizards.

Learning to Survive by Living off the Land
Julie of the Wolves

☐ *Island of the Blue Dolphins*
by Scott O'Dell

1960 Newbery Medal

An Indian girl lives alone for 18 years on an isolated island.

☐ *Save Queen of Sheba*
by Louise Moeri

After miraculously surviving a Sioux Indian raid, a brother and sister set out with few provisions to find the rest of the settlers.

☐ *Hatchet*
by Gary Paulsen

1988 Newbery Honor Book

After a plane crash, 13-year-old Brian spends 54 days in the wilderness, learning to survive with only the aid of a hatchet.

☐ *The Sign of the Beaver*
by Elizabeth George Speare

1984 Newbery Honor Book

Left alone to guard the family's wilderness home, a boy is hard-pressed to survive until local Indians teach him their skills.

☐ *Call It Courage*
by Armstrong Sperry

1941 Newbery Medal

Though he is afraid of the sea, the son of a Polynesian chief whose people worship courage sets out alone in his canoe.

☐ *The Cay*
by Theodore Taylor

A white boy, blinded by a blow on the head, and an old black man are stranded on a tiny Caribbean island.
Prequel/sequel: *Timothy of the Cay*

☐ *Brothers of the Heart*
by Joan W. Blos

Fourteen-year-old Shem spends six months in the wilderness alone with a dying Indian woman.

Runaways Who Don't Go Back
Julie of the Wolves

☐ *The Adventures of Huckleberry Finn*
by Mark Twain

A 19th-century boy from a Mississippi River town recounts his adventures as he travels down the river with a runaway slave on a raft, encountering a family involved in a feud, two scoundrels pretending to be royalty, and Tom Sawyer's aunt (who mistakes him for Tom).

☐ *Maniac Magee*
by Jerry Spinelli

1991 Newbery Medal

After his parents die, Jeffrey Lionel Magee's life becomes legendary, as he accomplishes athletic and other feats.

☐ *Steal Away*
by Jennifer Armstrong

In 1855 two 13-year-old girls, one white and one black, run away from a southern farm and make the difficult journey north to freedom.

☐ *The Flight of the Doves*
by Walter Macken

A 12-year-old English boy and his seven-year-old sister run away from their abusive stepfather and set out to reach their grandmother in western Ireland.

☐ *The Dulcimer Boy*
by Tor Seidler

Twin brothers are abandoned on their uncle's doorstep.

☐ *Rite of Passage*
by Richard Wright

PG language

When 15-year-old Johnny Gibbs runs off into the streets of Harlem, he meets up with a gang that wants him to participate in a mugging.

King Matt the First

Janusz Korczak

Taking on Adult Responsibilities
The Giver
The Shoeshine Girl
Stepping on the Cracks
The Planet of Junior Brown
Across Five Aprils
Chive

Kings
The King's Falcon
The Emperor's Winding Sheet

When Kids Are in Charge
Lord of the Flies
The Chocolate War
The Outsiders
Bel-Air Bambi and the Mall Rats
No Kidding

The Reality of War
George Washington's Socks
My Brother Sam Is Dead
AK
The Shining Company
April Morning

Real-Life Education
Ender's Game
Hazel Rye
The Magic Grandfather

King Matt the First

Janusz Korczak

Good Intentions Go Awry
Maniac Magee
Shiloh
Ben and Annie
The Neverending Story
Finding Buck McHenry

Unforeseen Consequences
Nothing but the Truth
On My Honor
T-Backs, T-Shirts, COAT, and Suit
Brady
The Shadow Club

Scheming Enemies
Lost Magic
Quest for a Maid
Black Hearts in Battersea
The Wolves of Willoughby Chase
Tunes for Bears to Dance To
Escape to Witch Mountain
Treasure Island

Rights
North to Freedom
The Pushcart War
Words by Heart
The Child Buyer

King Matt
the
First

Janusz Korczak

Taking on Adult Responsibilities

The Giver

The Shoeshine Girl

Stepping on the Cracks

The Planet of Junior Brown

Across Five Aprils

Chive

The Reality of War

George Washington's Socks

My Brother Sam Is Dead

AK

The Shining Company

April Morning

Good Intentions Go Awry

Maniac Magee

Shiloh

Ben and Annie

The Neverending Story

Finding Buck McHenry

Scheming Enemies

Lost Magic

Quest for a Maid

Black Hearts in Battersea

The Wolves of Willoughby Chase

Tunes for Bears to Dance To

Escape to Witch Mountain

Treasure Island

When Kids Are in Charge

Lord of the Flies

The Chocolate War

The Outsiders

Bel-Air Bambi and the Mall Rats

No Kidding

Unforeseen Consequences

Nothing but the Truth

On My Honor

T-Backs, T-Shirts, COAT, and Suit

Brady

The Shadow Club

Kings

The King's Falcon

The Emperor's Winding Sheet

Real-Life Education

Ender's Game

Hazel Rye

The Magic Grandfather

Rights

North to Freedom

The Pushcart War

Words by Heart

The Child Buyer

Taking on Adult Responsibilities
King Matt the First

☐ *The Giver*
by Lois Lowry
1994 Newbery Medal

Jonas becomes the receiver of memories shared by only one other in his community and discovers the terrible truth about the society in which he lives.

☐ *The Shoeshine Girl*
by Clyde Robert Bulla

Ten-year-old Sarah Ida gets a job at a shoeshine stand and learns a great many things besides shining shoes.

☐ *Stepping on the Cracks*
by Mary Downing Hahn

Eleven-year-old Margaret gets a new view of the school bully Gordy when she finds him hiding his brother, an army deserter.

☐ *The Planet of Junior Brown*
by Virginia Hamilton
1972 Newbery Honor Book

Already a leader in New York's underground world of homeless children, Buddy Clark takes on the responsibility of protecting an overweight, emotionally disturbed friend.

☐ *Across Five Aprils*
by Irene Hunt
1965 Newbery Honor Book

Jethro, who is nine years old during the first April, grows from boy to man when he must run the farm almost alone during the Civil War, when dangers on the home front prove as exciting as those in battle.

☐ *Chive*
by Shelley A. Barre

Eleven-year-old Chive, homeless because his parents have lost their farm, strikes up an unusual friendship with 11-year-old Terry.

The Reality of War
King Matt the First

☐ *George Washington's Socks*
by Elvira Woodruff

In the midst of a backyard campout, five children find themselves transported back into the time of George Washington, where they begin to learn the sober realities of war.

☐ *My Brother Sam Is Dead*
by Christopher and James Lincoln Collier

Recounts the tragedy that strikes the Meeker family during the Revolution, when one son joins the rebel forces while the rest of the family tries to stay neutral in a Tory town.

☐ *AK*
by Peter Dickinson

When a military coup occurs in the war-torn African country of Nagala, teenage Paul is forced to flee into the countryside to avoid enemy soldiers who seek his life.

☐ *The Shining Company*
by Rosemary Sutcliff

In A.D. 600 in northern Britain, Prosper becomes a shield-bearer with the Companions, an army made up of 300 younger sons of minor kings and trained to act as one fighting brotherhood against the invading Saxons.

☐ *April Morning*
by Howard Fast

Fifteen-year-old Adam Cooper relates the events he witnessed in Lexington and Concord on April 19, 1775, after he signs up on the muster roll of the militia and then lives through the first day of conflict with the British.

Good Intentions Go Awry
King Matt the First

☐ *Maniac Magee*
by Jerry Spinelli
1991 Newbery Medal

After his parents die, Jeffrey Lionel Magee's life becomes legendary, as he accomplishes athletic and other feats that awe his contemporaries.

☐ *Shiloh*
by Phyllis Reynolds Naylor
1992 Newbery Medal

When he finds a lost beagle in the hills behind his West Virginia home, Marty tries to hide it from his family and the dog's real owner, a mean-spirited man known to shoot deer out of season and to mistreat his dogs.

☐ *Ben and Annie*
by Joan Tate

Ben has a special friendship with his crippled neighbor, Annie, which is spoiled by misunderstanding.

☐ *The Neverending Story*
by Michael Ende

The magical tale of Bastian, a lonely, solitary boy who steps through the pages of a book into a special kingdom where he learns the true measure of his courage and creates a new world with his wishes.

☐ *Finding Buck McHenry*
by Alfred Slote

Eleven-year-old Jason, believing the school custodian, Mack Henry, to be Buck McHenry, a famous pitcher from the old Negro League, tries to enlist him as a coach for his Little League team by revealing his identity to the world.

Scheming Enemies
King Matt the First

☐ *Lost Magic*
by Berthe Amoss

In the Middle Ages, orphaned Ceridwen learns the art of herbal healing and gains the protection of the local lord until she is accused of witchcraft.

☐ *Quest for a Maid*
by Frances Mary Hendry

Meg realizes she must protect the young Norwegian princess who has been chosen as rightful heir to the Scottish throne from those, including Meg's sorceress sister, who plot the princess's death.

☐ *Black Hearts in Battersea*
by Joan Aiken

An orphan arrives in London and becomes embroiled in a plot against the king.
Part of the Wolves of Willoughby Chase series

☐ *The Wolves of Willoughby Chase*
by Joan Aiken

Surrounded by villains of the first order, brave Bonnie and gentle cousin Sylvia conquer all obstacles in this Victorian melodrama.
Book 1 of the Wolves of Willoughby Chase series

☐ *Tunes for Bears to Dance To*
by Robert Cormier

When 11-year-old Henry is manipulated into betraying his friend, he comes to know true evil.

☐ *Escape to Witch Mountain*
by Alexander Key

When a mysterious man claims to be the uncle of Tia and Tony and acquires court custody, the children run away to prevent him from exploiting their unusual powers.

☐ *Treasure Island*
by Robert Louis Stevenson

The mistress of the inn and her son find a treasure map that leads them to a pirate's fortune.

When Kids Are in Charge
King Matt the First

☐ *Lord of the Flies*
by William Golding

Stranded on an island while an atomic war destroys the rest of the world, a group of young boys reverts to savagery as they struggle to survive.

☐ *The Chocolate War*
by Robert Cormier
PG language

A high school freshman discovers the devastating consequences of refusing to join the school's annual fundraising drive and arousing the wrath of the school bullies.

Sequel: *Beyond the Chocolate War*

☐ *The Outsiders*
by S. E. Hinton

The struggle of three brothers to stay together after their parents' deaths and their quest for identity among the conflicting values of their adolescent society.

☐ *Bel-Air Bambi and the Mall Rats*
by Richard Peck

Bambi, Buffie, and Brick, three totally cool siblings from Los Angeles, move with their parents to Hickory Fork, a small town terrorized by a high school gang.

☐ *No Kidding*
by Bruce Brooks

In his 21st-century society, 14-year-old Sam is allowed to decide the fate of his family after his mother is released from an alcohol rehabilitation center.

Unforeseen Consequences
King Matt the First

☐ *Nothing but the Truth*
by Avi
1992 Newbery Honor Book

A ninth-grader's suspension for singing "The Star Spangled Banner" during homeroom becomes a national news story.

☐ *On My Honor*
by Marian Dane Bauer
1987 Newbery Honor Book

When his best friend drowns while they are both swimming in a treacherous river that they had promised never to go near, Joel is devastated and terrified at having to tell both sets of parents the terrible consequences of their disobedience.

☐ *T-Backs, T-Shirts, COAT, and Suit*
by E. L. Konigsburg

Spending the summer in Florida with her stepfather's sister, who operates a "meals-on-wheels" van, 12-year-old Chloe and her aunt become involved in a controversy surrounding the wearing of T-back bathing suits.

☐ *Brady*
by Jean Fritz

A young Pennsylvania boy takes part in the pre-Civil War antislavery activities.

☐ *The Shadow Club*
by Neal Shusterman

A high school boy and his friends decide to form a club of second-bests and play anonymous tricks on each other's archrivals, but when the harmless pranks become life-threatening, no one in the club will admit responsibility.

Kings
King Matt the First

☐ *The King's Falcon*
by Paula Fox

With the help of a falcon, an ineffectual medieval king trades the troubled, boring life of royalty for the freedom of a falconer.

☐ *The Emperor's Winding Sheet*
by Jill Paton Walsh

An English boy, shipwrecked, hungry, and lost, finds his way into the court of Constantine, where he is interpreted as a symbol of good luck and, as such, ordered to always be kept near the king.

Real-Life Education
King Matt the First

☐ *Ender's Game*
by Orson Scott Card

Ender may be the military genius Earth needs in its war against an alien enemy.

☐ *Hazel Rye*
by Vera and Bill Cleaver

An 11-year-old girl with no appreciation for land and growing things finds her values beginning to change when she agrees to let an impoverished family live in a small house she owns, in exchange for working in the surrounding orange grove.

☐ *The Magic Grandfather*
by Jay Williams

An 11-year-old discovers that not only is his seemingly ne'er-do-well grandfather a bona fide sorcerer, but he himself may have an untapped talent for magic.

Rights
King Matt the First

☐ *North to Freedom*
by Anne Holm

Having escaped from an Eastern European concentration camp where he has spent his life, a 12-year-old boy struggles to cope with an entirely strange world as he flees northward to freedom in Denmark.

☐ *The Pushcart War*
by Jean Merrill

The outbreak of a war between truck drivers and pushcart peddlers brings the mounting problems of traffic to the attention of both the city of New York and the world.

☐ *Words by Heart*
by Ouida Sebestyen

In 1910, a young black girl struggles to fulfill her papa's dream of a better future for their family in the southwestern town where they are the only blacks.

☐ *The Child Buyer*
by John Hersey

A novel in the form of hearings before the Standing Committee on Education, Welfare & Public Morality of a certain State Senate, investigating the conspiracy of Mr. Wissey Jones, with others, to purchase a male child.

Little Women

Louisa May Alcott

Sisters
Ask Me Something Easy
Maybe Yes, Maybe No, Maybe Maybe
Wall of Words
Jacob Have I Loved
Family of Strangers
Beezus and Ramona

Girls Growing Up
Belle Pruitt
Cassie Binegar
The Facts and Fictions of Minna Pratt
Unclaimed Treasures
A Tree Grows in Brooklyn
Summer of the Falcon
Loving Ben

Close-Knit Families
The Railway Children
Nekomah Creek
Cheaper by the Dozen
All About Sam
Anastasia Krupnik
Little House on the Prairie

**Adult Books
for Children**
How Green Was My Valley
The Yearling
Lies My Father Told Me
Captains Courageous
To Kill a Mockingbird

Little Women

Louisa May Alcott

**Independent
Girls**
The Good Master
The Illyrian Adventure
Dust of the Earth
Matilda
True Grit
Dealing with Dragons

**Families in the 19th
Century**
The Golden Age
A Gathering of Days
Oh, Those Harper Girls
Missouri Homestead
Grace
Caddie Woodlawn

**Other Books by
Louisa May Alcott**
Little Men
Jo's Boys
Eight Cousins
Rose in Bloom
Under the Lilacs
Jack and Jill
An Old Fashioned Girl

**Old-Fashioned Classics
About Girls**
A Little Princess
The Secret Garden
Anne of Green Gables
Anne of Avonlea
Pollyanna
Daddy Long-Legs

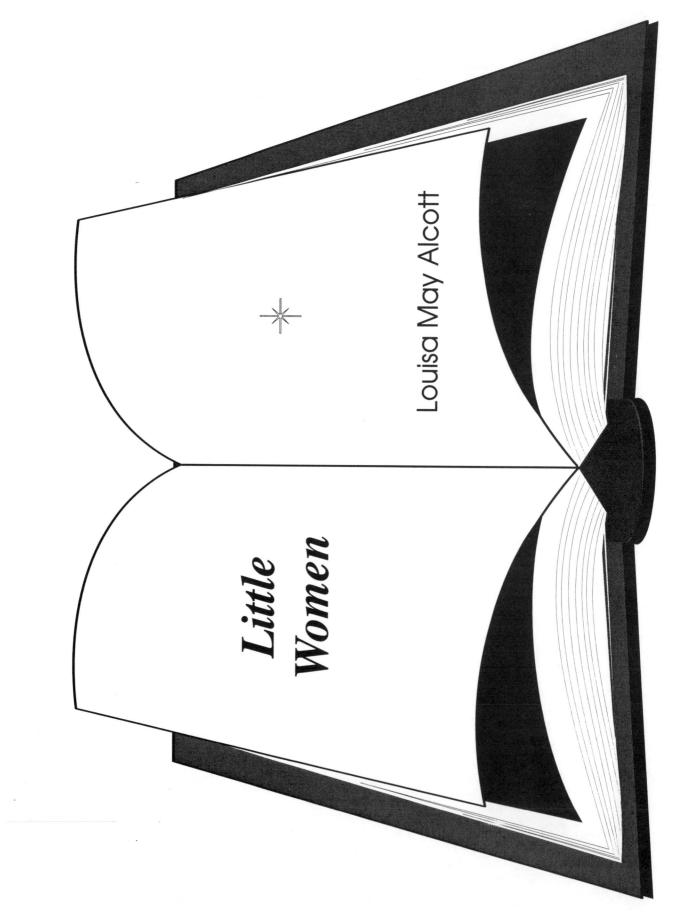

Louisa May Alcott

Little Women

Sisters

Ask Me Something Easy

*Maybe Yes, Maybe No,
Maybe Maybe*

Wall of Words

Jacob Have I Loved

Family of Strangers

Beezus and Ramona

Close-Knit Families

The Railway Children

Nekomah Creek

Cheaper by the Dozen

All About Sam

Anastasia Krupnik

*Little House
on the Prairie*

Old-Fashioned Classics About Girls

A Little Princess

The Secret Garden

Anne of Green Gables

Anne of Avonlea

Pollyanna

Daddy Long-Legs

Girls Growing Up

Belle Pruitt

Cassie Binegar

*The Facts and Fictions
of Minna Pratt*

Unclaimed Treasures

A Tree Grows in Brooklyn

Summer of the Falcon

Loving Ben

Families in the 19th Century

The Golden Age

A Gathering of Days

Oh, Those Harper Girls

Missouri Homestead

Grace

Caddie Woodlawn

Adult Books for Children

*How Green Was My
Valley*

The Yearling

Lies My Father Told Me

Captains Courageous

To Kill a Mockingbird

Independent Girls

The Good Master

The Illyrian Adventure

Dust of the Earth

Matilda

True Grit

Dealing with Dragons

Other Books by Louisa May Alcott

Little Men

Jo's Boys

Eight Cousins

Rose in Bloom

Under the Lilacs

Jack and Jill

An Old Fashioned Girl

Sisters
Little Women

☐ *Ask Me Something Easy*
by Natalie Honeycutt

After her father leaves the family, Addie must cope with her increasingly hostile mother, perfect older sister, and sensitive younger twin sisters.

☐ *Maybe Yes, Maybe No, Maybe Maybe*
by Susan Patron

When her hardworking mother decides to move, eight-year-old PK uses her imagination and storytelling to help her older and younger sisters adjust.

☐ *Wall of Words*
by Tim Kennemore

Kate waits for her father, who has left home to write a novel, to return, while her sister suffers from a phobia about school.

☐ *Jacob Have I Loved*
by Katherine Paterson

1981 Newbery Medal
PG language

Feeling deprived all her life of schooling, friends, mother, and even her name by her twin sister, Louise finally begins to find her identity.

☐ *Family of Strangers*
by Susan Beth Pfeffer

Emotionally disturbed 16-year-old Abby chronicles her growing desperation in a family consisting of unloving parents, one self-destructive older sister, and another older sister who has always seemed perfect.

☐ *Beezus and Ramona*
by Beverly Cleary

Four-year-old Ramona has an imagination that makes her a menace to everyone, particularly her older sister Beezus.

Many sequels

Close-Knit Families
Little Women

☐ *The Railway Children*
by E. Nesbit

When their father is taken away, three children move to the country, where they stay busy saving the train, befriending a nice Old Gentleman, and trying not to quarrel.

☐ *Nekomah Creek*
by Linda Crew

Nine-year-old Robby loves his unconventional family, but attention from a counselor and a bully at school makes him self-conscious about just how unconventional his family might look to outsiders.

☐ *Cheaper by the Dozen*
by Frank B. Gilbreth Jr. and Ernestine Gilbreth Carey

Depicts the lives and adventures of the Gilbreths and their 12 children.
Sequel: *Belles on Their Toes*

☐ *All About Sam*
by Lois Lowry

The adventures of Sam, Anastasia Krupnik's younger brother, from his first day as a newborn through his mischievous times as a toddler.

☐ *Anastasia Krupnik*
by Lois Lowry

Anastasia's 10th year has good things, like falling in love and getting to know her grandmother, and bad things, like finding out about an impending baby brother.

☐ *Little House on the Prairie*
by Laura Ingalls Wilder

A family travels from Wisconsin to a new home on the prairie, where they build a home, meet neighboring Indians, build a well, and fight a prairie fire.
Many sequels

Old-Fashioned Classics About Girls
Little Women

☐☐ *A Little Princess*
by Frances Hodgson Burnett

Sara Crewe, a pupil at Miss Minchin's London school, is left in poverty when her father dies, but is later rescued by a mysterious benefactor.

☐☐ *The Secret Garden*
by Frances Hodgson Burnett

A boy who has lived as a spoiled invalid regains his health when he and his orphaned cousin restore a once lovely garden.

☐☐ *Anne of Green Gables*
by L. M. Montgomery

Anne, an 11-year-old orphan, is sent by mistake to live with a lonely, middle-aged brother and sister on a Prince Edward Island farm and proceeds to make an indelible impression on everyone around her.

☐☐ *Anne of Avonlea*
by L. M. Montgomery

Sixteen-year-old Anne, mischievous and spirited as ever, returns to Avonlea to teach in the village school where she herself was taught.

☐ *Pollyanna*
by Eleanor H. Porter

When a 12-year-old orphan comes to live with her austere and wealthy aunt Polly, her philosophy of gladness brings happiness to the aunt and unloved members of the community.

☐☐ *Daddy Long-Legs*
by Jean Webster

A 17-year-old orphan is sent to a northeastern college for women by an anonymous benefactor.

Girls Growing Up
Little Women

☐ *Belle Pruitt*
by Vera Cleaver

When her baby brother suddenly dies, 11-year-old Belle is left to cope with the devastating effects on her family.

☐ *Cassie Binegar*
by Patricia MacLachlan

During her family's first summer in an old house by the sea, Cassie learns to accept change and to find her own space.

☐ *The Facts and Fictions of Minna Pratt*
by Patricia MacLachlan

An 11-year-old cellist learns about life from her eccentric family, her first boyfriend, and Mozart.

☐ *Unclaimed Treasures*
by Patricia MacLachlan

Willa thinks that she's in love with the father of the boy next door, until she realizes that her true love is the boy himself.

☐ *A Tree Grows in Brooklyn*
by Betty Smith

Young Francie Nolan experiences the problems of growing up in a Brooklyn slum.

☐ *Summer of the Falcon*
by Jean Craighead George

As June Pritchard trains her sparrowhawk, she chafes at her mother's insistence that she assume the responsibilities of her increasing age.

☐ *Loving Ben*
by Elizabeth Laird

Anna's teen years bring maturity and fulfillment as she experiences the birth and death of a loving hydrocephalic brother and works with a child with Down's syndrome.

Families in the 19th Century
Little Women

☐ *The Golden Age*
by Kenneth Grahame

The adventures of five siblings growing up in rural England in the late 19th century.

Sequel: *Dream Days*

☐☐ *A Gathering of Days*
by Joan W. Blos

1980 Newbery Medal

The journal of a 14-year-old girl, kept the last year she lived on the family farm, records daily events in her small New Hampshire town.

☐☐ *Oh, Those Harper Girls*
by Kathleen Karr

In west Texas in 1869, Lily and her five older sisters participate in a series of misguided schemes to save their father's ranch.

☐☐ *Missouri Homestead*
by T. L. Tedrow

In 1884, when Laura, Manly, and their daughter Rose come from South Dakota to Mansfield, Missouri, Laura's outspoken articles against a local timberman cause some problems.

Book 1 of The Days of Laura Ingalls Wilder series

☐☐ *Grace*
by Jill Paton Walsh

After helping her father rescue the survivors of a shipwreck on the coast of England in 1838, Grace Darling finds her quiet life crumbling as she is unwillingly fashioned into a national hero.

☐☐ *Caddie Woodlawn*
by Carol Ryrie Brink

1936 Newbery Medal

The adventures of an 11-year-old tomboy growing up on the Wisconsin frontier.

Adult Books for Children
Little Women

☐ *How Green Was My Valley*
by Richard Llewellyn

A boy faces adversity with courage in a Welsh mining town.

☐☐ *The Yearling*
by Marjorie Kinnan Rawlings

A young boy living in the Florida backwoods is forced to decide the fate of a fawn he has lovingly raised as a pet.

☐☐ *Lies My Father Told Me*
by Norman Allan

A boy grows up in the Jewish ghetto in Canada around the turn of the century.

☐☐ *Captains Courageous*
by Rudyard Kipling

Harvey Cheyne, the spoiled son of an American millionaire, is saved from drowning by a New England fishing schooner and must share the hard life and labor of the crew to prove his worth to the captain and crew.

☐☐ *To Kill a Mockingbird*
by Harper Lee

Eight-year-old Scout Finch tells of life in a small Alabama town where her father is a lawyer, and where she and her brother are thrust into an adult world of racial bigotry and hatred when their father chooses to defend a black man charged with raping a white girl.

Independent Girls
Little Women

☐ *The Good Master*
by Kate Seredy

1936 Newbery Honor Book

Kate, a headstrong tomboy from Budapest, learns gentle ways when she goes to live with an understanding uncle in the country.

☐☐ *The Illyrian Adventure*
by Lloyd Alexander

On a visit to a European kingdom in 1872, a fearless 16-year-old orphan and her guardian research an ancient legend and become enmeshed in a dangerous rebellion.

☐☐ *Dust of the Earth*
by Vera and Bill Cleaver

Fourteen-year-old Fern and her family face challenges and hardships when they move to a farm.

☐☐ *Matilda*
by Roald Dahl

Matilda applies her mental powers to rid the school of the evil, child-hating headmistress, Miss Trunchbull, and restore her nice teacher, Miss Honey, to financial security.

☐☐ *True Grit*
by Charles Portis

Fourteen-year-old Mattie Ross convinces one-eyed Marshall Rooster Cogburn to help her capture the gang of outlaws who murdered her father.

☐☐ *Dealing with Dragons*
by Patricia C. Wrede

Bored with traditional palace life, a princess goes off to live with a group of dragons and soon becomes involved in fighting against some wizards who want to steal the dragon's kingdom.

Other Books by Louisa May Alcott
Little Women

☐ *Little Men*

Adventures in Jo March and her husband Professor Bhaer's school for boys, a place of light, warmth, comfort, and delights where self-knowledge and self-control are acquired along with book learning.

Sequel to *Little Women*

☐☐ *Jo's Boys*

Recounts the further adventures, successes, and failures of the numerous young men of Plumfield school.

Sequel to *Little Men*

☐☐ *Eight Cousins*

Tells of 13-year-old Rose Campbell, an orphan who lived with her Uncle Alec, and the seven lively boy cousins who were her playmates.

☐☐ *Rose in Bloom*

Rose and her seven cousins grow up amidst few disappointments and many pleasures.

Sequel to *Eight Cousins*

☐☐ *Under the Lilacs*

Two runaways from a circus, Ben and his performing dog Sancho, find a home and friends in a country village.

☐☐ *Jack and Jill*

When Jack and Jill tumble off their sled while attempting to slide down a dangerous slope, there is a long, painful convalescence for both of them, made easier by the help of their loyal friends.

☐☐ *An Old Fashioned Girl*

Polly Milton's cheerful temperament and courage enable her to make friends quickly during her first stay in the city.

Maniac Magee

Jerry Spinelli

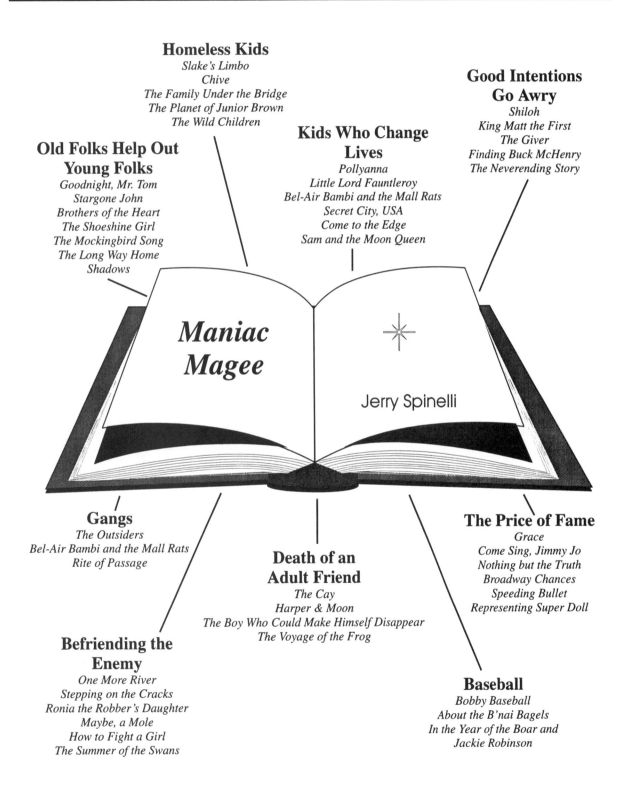

Homeless Kids
Slake's Limbo
Chive
The Family Under the Bridge
The Planet of Junior Brown
The Wild Children

**Old Folks Help Out
Young Folks**
Goodnight, Mr. Tom
Stargone John
Brothers of the Heart
The Shoeshine Girl
The Mockingbird Song
The Long Way Home
Shadows

**Kids Who Change
Lives**
Pollyanna
Little Lord Fauntleroy
Bel-Air Bambi and the Mall Rats
Secret City, USA
Come to the Edge
Sam and the Moon Queen

**Good Intentions
Go Awry**
Shiloh
King Matt the First
The Giver
Finding Buck McHenry
The Neverending Story

*Maniac
Magee*

Jerry Spinelli

Gangs
The Outsiders
Bel-Air Bambi and the Mall Rats
Rite of Passage

**Death of an
Adult Friend**
The Cay
Harper & Moon
The Boy Who Could Make Himself Disappear
The Voyage of the Frog

The Price of Fame
Grace
Come Sing, Jimmy Jo
Nothing but the Truth
Broadway Chances
Speeding Bullet
Representing Super Doll

**Befriending the
Enemy**
One More River
Stepping on the Cracks
Ronia the Robber's Daughter
Maybe, a Mole
How to Fight a Girl
The Summer of the Swans

Baseball
Bobby Baseball
About the B'nai Bagels
*In the Year of the Boar and
Jackie Robinson*

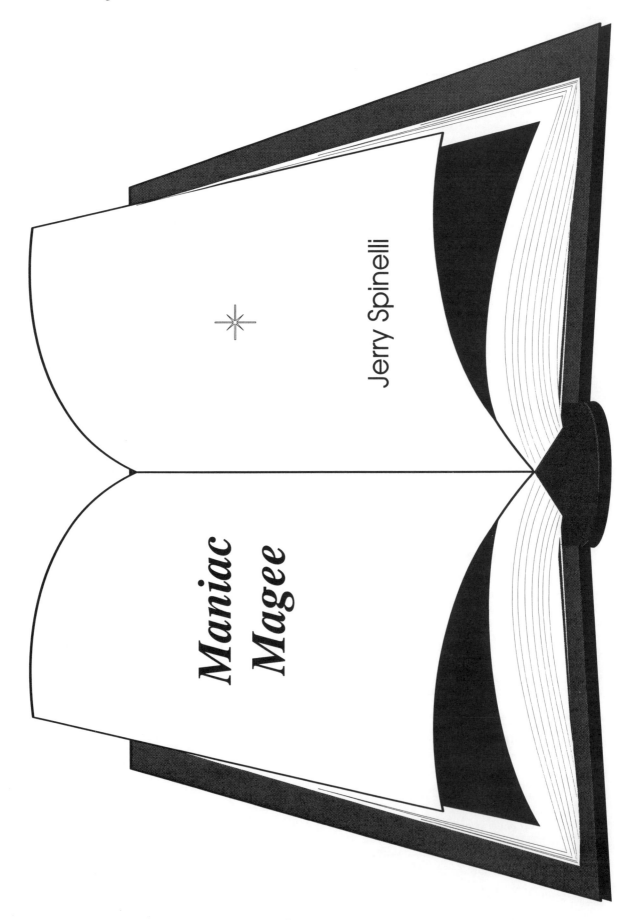

Maniac Magee

Jerry Spinelli

Death of
an Adult Friend

The Cay

Harper & Moon

*The Boy Who Could Make
Himself Disappear*

The Voyage of the Frog

Good Intentions
Go Awry

Shiloh

King Matt the First

The Giver

Finding Buck McHenry

The Neverending Story

Gangs

The Outsiders

*Bel-Air Bambi and the
Mall Rats*

Rite of Passage

Baseball

Bobby Baseball

About the B'nai Bagels

*In the Year of the Boar
and Jackie Robinson*

Old Folks Help
Out Young Folks

Goodnight, Mr. Tom

Stargone John

Brothers of the Heart

The Shoeshine Girl

The Mockingbird Song

The Long Way Home

Shadows

Befriending
the Enemy

One More River

Stepping on the Cracks

*Ronia the Robber's
Daughter*

Maybe, a Mole

How to Fight a Girl

The Summer of the Swans

Kids
Who Change Lives

Pollyanna

Little Lord Fauntleroy

*Bel-Air Bambi and the
Mall Rats*

Secret City, USA

Come to the Edge

Sam and the Moon Queen

The Price of Fame

Grace

Come Sing, Jimmy Jo

Nothing but the Truth

Broadway Chances

Speeding Bullet

Representing Super Doll

Homeless Kids

Slake's Limbo

Chive

*The Family Under
the Bridge*

*The Planet of Junior
Brown*

The Wild Children

Baseball
Maniac Magee

☐ *Bobby Baseball*
by Robert Kimmel Smith

Ten-year-old Bobby is passionate about baseball and convinced that he is a great player. The only problem is to get a chance to prove his skill, especially to his father.

☐ *About the B'nai Bagels*
by E. L. Konigsburg

Mark Setzer tells about his troubles in general and in particular his misfortunes on the Little League team managed by his mother and coached by his brother.

☐ *In the Year of the Boar and Jackie Robinson*
by Betty Bao Lord

In 1947, a Chinese child comes to Brooklyn where she becomes Americanized at school, in her apartment building, and by her love for baseball.

Gangs
Maniac Magee

☐ *The Outsiders*
by S. E. Hinton

The struggle of three brothers to stay together after their parents' deaths and their quest for identity among the conflicting values of their adolescent society.

☐ *Bel-Air Bambi and the Mall Rats*
by Richard Peck

Bambi, Buffie, and Brick, three totally cool siblings from Los Angeles, move with their parents to a small town terrorized by a high school gang.

☐ *Rite of Passage*
by Richard Wright
PG language

When 15-year-old Johnny Gibbs runs off into the streets of Harlem, he meets up with a gang that wants him to participate in a mugging.

Good Intentions Go Awry
Maniac Magee

☐ *Shiloh*
by Phyllis Reynolds Naylor
1992 Newbery Medal

When he finds a lost beagle in the hills behind his West Virginia home, Marty tries to hide it from his family and the dog's real owner, a mean-spirited man known to shoot deer out of season and to mistreat his dogs.

Prequel/sequel: *Timothy of the Cay*

☐ *King Matt the First*
by Janusz Korczak

A child king introduces reforms to give children the same rights as adults.

☐ *The Giver*
by Lois Lowry
1994 Newbery Medal

Given his lifetime assignment at the Ceremony of Twelve, Jonas becomes the receiver of memories shared by only one other in his community and discovers the terrible truth about the society in which he lives.

☐ *Finding Buck McHenry*
by Alfred Slote

Eleven-year-old Jason, believing the school custodian Mack Henry to be Buck McHenry, a famous pitcher from the old Negro League, tries to enlist him as a coach for his Little League team by revealing his identity to the world.

☐ *The Neverending Story*
by Michael Ende

The magical tale of Bastian, a lonely, solitary boy who steps through the pages of a book into a special kingdom where he learns the true measure of his courage and creates a new world with his wishes.

Death of an Adult Friend
Maniac Magee

☐ *The Cay*
by Theodore Taylor

When the freighter on which they are traveling is torpedoed by a German submarine during World War II, an adolescent white boy, blinded by a blow on the head, and an old black man are stranded on a tiny Caribbean island where the boy acquires a new kind of vision, courage, and love from his old companion.

☐ *Harper & Moon*
by Ramon Royal Ross

Although 12-year-old Harper has always liked Moon, an abused, orphaned, older boy, their friendship is tested by a discovery Harper makes when Moon joins the army in 1943.

☐ *The Boy Who Could Make Himself Disappear*
by Kin Platt

A 12-year-old boy with a speech defect gradually withdraws into schizophrenia after moving to live with his mother following the divorce of his harsh and detached parents.

☐ *The Voyage of the Frog*
by Gary Paulsen

When David goes out on his sailboat to scatter his recently deceased uncle's ashes to the wind, he is caught in a fierce storm and must survive many days on his own as he works out his feelings about life and his uncle.

The Price of Fame
Maniac Magee

☐ *Grace*
by Jill Paton Walsh

After helping her father rescue the survivors of a shipwreck, Grace Darling is unwillingly fashioned into a national hero.

☐ *Come Sing, Jimmy Jo*
by Katherine Paterson

When his family becomes a successful country music group and makes him a featured singer, 11-year-old James has to deal with big changes in all aspects of his life, even his name.

☐ *Nothing but the Truth*
by Avi

1992 Newbery Honor Book

A ninth-grader's suspension for singing "The Star Spangled Banner" during homeroom becomes a national news story.

☐ *Broadway Chances*
by Elizabeth Starr Hill

Twelve-year-old Fitzi, finally settled into a normal life after years of street performances with her parents, gets a chance to star in a Broadway musical.

Sequel to *Street Dancer*

☐ *Speeding Bullet*
by Neal Shusterman

After becoming famous and getting the attention of the daughter of a wealthy New York City developer following his rescue of a little girl from a speeding subway train, Nick looks for other people to rescue.

☐ *Representing Super Doll*
by Richard Peck

After being involved in the brittle, superficial world of a beauty contest, a country girl appreciates even more the solid values of her Indiana farm life.

Kids Who Change Lives
Maniac Magee

☐ *Pollyanna*
by Eleanor H. Porter

When a 12-year-old orphan comes to live with her austere and wealthy aunt Polly, her philosophy of gladness bring happiness to the aunt and unloved members of the community.

☐ *Little Lord Fauntleroy*
by Frances Hodgson Burnett

A Brooklyn boy discovers that he is the heir to an earldom and a fortune, and goes to live with his bad-tempered, selfish, and cantankerous grandfather.

☐ *Bel-Air Bambi and the Mall Rats*
by Richard Peck

Bambi, Buffie, and Brick, three totally cool siblings from Los Angeles, move with their parents to Hickory Fork, a small town terrorized by a high school gang.

☐ *Secret City, USA*
by Felice Holman

Against all odds, Benno and his friends in the ghetto turn an abandoned house into a shelter for the homeless.

☐ *Come to the Edge*
by Julia Cunningham

After he is befriended by a sign painter, a confused runaway finds trust and a purpose for living.

☐ *Sam and the Moon Queen*
by Alison Cragin Herzig and Jane Lawrence Mali

Sympathetic to a homeless girl's plight, Sam tries to help her find food for herself and medical aid for her dog.

Befriending the Enemy
Maniac Magee

☐ *One More River*
by Lynne Reid Banks

Fourteen-year-old Lesley is upset when her parents abandon their comfortable life in Canada for a kibbutz in Israel prior to the 1967 war.

☐ *Stepping on the Cracks*
by Mary Downing Hahn

In 1944, while her brother is overseas fighting in World War II, 11-year-old Margaret gets a new view of the school bully Gordy when she finds him hiding his own brother, an army deserter, and decides to help him.

☐ *Ronia the Robber's Daughter*
by Astrid Lindgren

Ronia, who lives with her father and his band of robbers in a castle in the woods, causes trouble when she befriends the son of a rival robber chieftain.

☐ *Maybe, a Mole*
by Julia Cunningham

Vignettes about Maybe, a mole who can see, his friend the fox, and their adventures.

☐ *How to Fight a Girl*
by Thomas Rockwell

Joe and Alan's plan to get revenge on Billy backfires when their secret weapon, the prettiest girl in their fifth-grade class, becomes Billy's friend instead.

Sequel to *How to Eat Fried Worms*

☐ *The Summer of the Swans*
by Betsy Byars

1971 Newbery Medal

A teenage girl gains new insight into herself and her family when her mentally retarded brother gets lost.

Old Folks Help Out Young Folks
Maniac Magee

☐ *Goodnight, Mr. Tom*
by Michelle Magorian

A battered child learns to embrace life when he is adopted by an old man.

☐ *Stargone John*
by Ellen Kindt McKenzie

Six-year-old John experiences ridicule and punishment at his one-room schoolhouse, until an old retired teacher reaches out from her blindness.

☐ *Brothers of the Heart*
by Joan W. Blos

Fourteen-year-old Shem spends six months in the wilderness alone with a dying Indian woman, who helps him survive and mature to the point where he can return to the difficulties of life as a cripple on the frontier.

☐ *The Shoeshine Girl*
by Clyde Robert Bulla

Determined to earn some money, 10-year-old Sarah Ida gets a job at a shoeshine stand.

☐ *The Mockingbird Song*
by Berthe Amoss

Unable to get along with her new stepmother, 11-year-old Lindy goes to live with the elderly lady next door.

☐ *The Long Way Home*
by Barbara Cohen

Sally's relationship with an elderly bus driver helps her to cope with the problems of her mother's cancer.

☐ *Shadows*
by Dennis Haseley

Jamie's lonely life with his aunt and uncle changes when Grandpa comes to visit and teaches him to make shadow pictures.

Homeless Kids
Maniac Magee

☐ *Slake's Limbo*
by Felice Holman

Thirteen-year-old Aremis Slake, hounded by his fears and misfortunes, flees into New York City's subway tunnels, never again, he believes, to emerge.

☐ *Chive*
by Shelley A. Barre

Eleven-year-old Chive, homeless because his parents have lost their farm and are looking for work in the city, strikes up an unusual friendship with 11-year-old Terry and competes with him in a skateboard competition.

☐ *The Family Under the Bridge*
by Natalie Savage Carlson

An old tramp, adopted by three fatherless children when their mother hides them under a bridge on the Seine, finds a home for mother and children and a job for himself.

☐ *The Planet of Junior Brown*
by Virginia Hamilton
1972 Newbery Honor Book

Already a leader in New York's underground world of homeless children, eighth-grader Buddy Clark takes on the responsibility of protecting the overweight, emotionally disturbed friend with whom he has been playing hooky all semester.

☐ *The Wild Children*
by Felice Holman

Left behind when his family is arrested during the Bolshevik Revolution, Alex falls in with a gang of other desperate homeless children.

Morning Girl

Michael Dorris

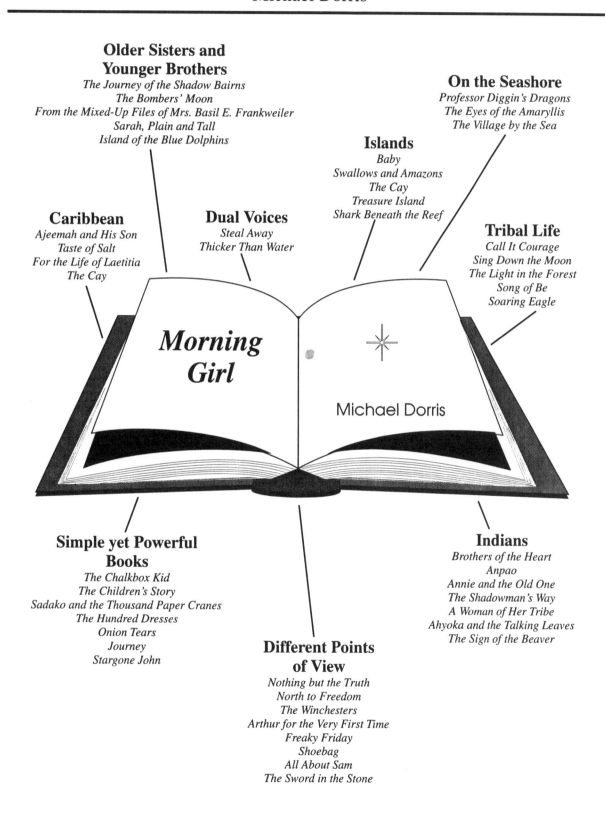

Older Sisters and Younger Brothers
The Journey of the Shadow Bairns
The Bombers' Moon
From the Mixed-Up Files of Mrs. Basil E. Frankweiler
Sarah, Plain and Tall
Island of the Blue Dolphins

On the Seashore
Professor Diggin's Dragons
The Eyes of the Amaryllis
The Village by the Sea

Islands
Baby
Swallows and Amazons
The Cay
Treasure Island
Shark Beneath the Reef

Caribbean
Ajeemah and His Son
Taste of Salt
For the Life of Laetitia
The Cay

Dual Voices
Steal Away
Thicker Than Water

Tribal Life
Call It Courage
Sing Down the Moon
The Light in the Forest
Song of Be
Soaring Eagle

Simple yet Powerful Books
The Chalkbox Kid
The Children's Story
Sadako and the Thousand Paper Cranes
The Hundred Dresses
Onion Tears
Journey
Stargone John

Different Points of View
Nothing but the Truth
North to Freedom
The Winchesters
Arthur for the Very First Time
Freaky Friday
Shoebag
All About Sam
The Sword in the Stone

Indians
Brothers of the Heart
Anpao
Annie and the Old One
The Shadowman's Way
A Woman of Her Tribe
Ahyoka and the Talking Leaves
The Sign of the Beaver

Morning Girl

Michael Dorris

On the Seashore

Professor Diggin's Dragons

The Eyes of the Amaryllis

The Village by the Sea

Dual Voices

Steal Away

Thicker Than Water

Tribal Life

Call It Courage

Sing Down the Moon

The Light in the Forest

Song of Be

Soaring Eagle

Indians

Brothers of the Heart

Anpao

Annie and the Old One

The Shadowman's Way

A Woman of Her Tribe

Ahyoka and the Talking Leaves

The Sign of the Beaver

Older Sisters and Younger Brothers

The Journey of the Shadow Bairns

The Bombers' Moon

From the Mixed-Up Files of Mrs. Basil E. Frankweiler

Sarah, Plain and Tall

Island of the Blue Dolphins

Caribbean

Ajeemah and His Son

Taste of Salt

For the Life of Laetitia

The Cay

Islands

Baby

Swallows and Amazons

The Cay

Treasure Island

Shark Beneath the Reef

Different Points of View

Nothing but the Truth

North to Freedom

The Winchesters

Arthur for the Very First Time

Freaky Friday

Shoebag

All About Sam

The Sword in the Stone

Simple yet Powerful Books

The Chalkbox Kid

The Children's Story

Sadako and the Thousand Paper Cranes

The Hundred Dresses

Onion Tears

Journey

Stargone John

On the Seashore
Morning Girl

☐ *Professor Diggin's Dragons*
by Felice Holman

An eccentric professor turns a trip to the seashore into a most unusual adventure for a group of children.

☐ *The Eyes of the Amaryllis*
by Natalie Babbitt

When 11-year-old Jenny goes to stay with her widowed grandmother, who lives by the seaside waiting for a sign from her drowned husband, she learns a great deal about the nature of love and the ways of the sea.

☐ *The Village by the Sea*
by Paula Fox

When her father enters the hospital to have open-heart surgery, 10-year-old Emma is sent to Peconic Bay to live with her tormented aunt, and finds the experience painful until she meets a friend who suggests making a miniature village in the sand.

Dual Voices
Morning Girl

☐ *Steal Away*
by Jennifer Armstrong

In 1855 two 13-year-old girls, one white and one black, run away from a southern farm and make the difficult journey north to freedom, living to recount their story 41 years later to two similar young girls.

☐ *Thicker Than Water*
by Penelope Farmer

Both Will and his cousin Becky have some some adjusting to do when he comes to live with her family after his mother's death, especially when the ghost of a child coal miner begins his insistent haunting of Will.

Tribal Life
Morning Girl

☐ *Call It Courage*
by Armstrong Sperry
1941 Newbery Medal

Based on a Polynesian legend, this is the story of a youth, the son of a Polynesian chief whose people worship courage. Though he is afraid of the sea, he sets out alone in his canoe to conquer his fear and prove his courage to himself and his tribe.

☐ *Sing Down the Moon*
by Scott O'Dell
1971 Newbery Honor Book

A young Navajo girl recounts the events of 1864, when her tribe was forced to march to Fort Sumner, New Mexico, as prisoners of the white soldiers.

☐ *The Light in the Forest*
by Conrad Richter

After being raised as an Indian for 11 years following his capture at the age of four, John Butler is forcibly returned to his white parents but continues to long for the freedom of Indian life.

☐ *Song of Be*
by Lesley Beake

Be, a young Bushman woman searching in the desert for the peace she remembers from her childhood, realizes that she and her people must reconcile new personal and political realities with ancient traditions.

☐ *Soaring Eagle*
by Mary Peace Finley

Julio, a 13-year-old boy in 1845, finds friendship and a clue to his identity while living with the Cheyenne tribe that rescued him on the Santa Fe Trail.

Indians
Morning Girl

☐ *Brothers of the Heart*
by Joan W. Blos

Fourteen-year-old Shem spends six months in the wilderness alone with a dying Indian woman, who helps him survive and mature.

☐ *Anpao*
by Jamake Highwater
1978 Newbery Honor Book

Traditional tales from North American tribes woven into one story that relates the adventures of one boy as he grows to manhood.

☐ *Annie and the Old One*
by Miska Miles
1972 Newbery Honor Book

A Navajo girl unravels a day's weaving on a rug whose completion will mean the death of her grandmother.

☐ *The Shadowman's Way*
by Paul Pitts

Nelson Sam always managed to stay out of trouble on the reservation—until now.

☐ *A Woman of Her Tribe*
by Margaret A. Robinson

Fifteen-year-old Annette, whose dead father was a Nootka Indian, seeks to find her own way in deciding which cultural heritage she should pursue.

☐ *Ahyoka and the Talking Leaves*
by Peter and Connie Roop

Ahyoka helps her father Sequoyah in his quest to create a system of writing for his people.

☐ *The Sign of the Beaver*
by Elizabeth George Speare
1984 Newbery Honor Book

Left alone to guard the family's wilderness home, a boy is hard-pressed to survive until local Indians teach him their skills.

Older Sisters and Younger Brothers

Morning Girl

☐ *The Journey of the Shadow Bairns*
by Margaret J. Anderson

When her parents die suddenly, leaving only a one-way passage to Canada, a young Scottish girl decides she and her four-year-old brother will pursue family plans to relocate.

☐ *The Bombers' Moon*
by Betty Vander Els

In the summer of 1942, an American missionary family living in China is separated when the two children are evacuated to India with their school class to escape the Japanese invasion.

☐ *From the Mixed-Up Files of Mrs. Basil E. Frankweiler*
by E. L. Konigsburg
1968 Newbery Medal

Two suburban children run away from home and go to the Metropolitan Museum of Art, where their ingenuity enables them to live in luxury.

☐ *Sarah, Plain and Tall*
by Patricia MacLachlan
1986 Newbery Medal

When their father invites a mail-order bride to come live with them in their prairie home, Caleb and Anna are captivated by their new mother and hope that she will stay.

☐ *Island of the Blue Dolphins*
by Scott O'Dell
1961 Newbery Medal

Records the courage and self-reliance of an Indian girl who lived alone for 18 years on an isolated island off the California coast when her tribe emigrated and she was left behind.

Caribbean

Morning Girl

☐ *Ajeemah and His Son*
by James Berry

A father and his 18-year-old son are each affected differently by their experiences as slaves in Jamaica in the early 19th century.

☐ *Taste of Salt*
by Francis Temple

In the hospital after being beaten by Macoutes, 17-year-old Djo tells the story of his impoverished life to a young woman who, like him, has been working with the social reformer Father Aristide to fight the repression in Haiti.

☐ *For the Life of Laetitia*
by Merle Hodge

As the first in her family to go to secondary school, 12-year-old Lacey struggles with a variety of problems, including a cruel teacher and a difficult home life with her father and stepmother.

☐ *The Cay*
by Theodore Taylor

When the freighter on which they are traveling is torpedoed by a German submarine during World War II, an adolescent white boy, blinded by a blow on the head, and an old black man are stranded on a tiny Caribbean island, where the boy acquires a new kind of vision, courage, and love from his old companion.

Prequel/sequel: *Timothy of the Cay*

Islands

Morning Girl

☐ *Baby*
by Patricia MacLachlan

Taking care of a baby left with them at the end of the tourist season helps a family come to terms with the death of their own infant son.

☐ *Swallows and Amazons*
by Arthur Ransome

Introduces the lovable Walker family, the camp on Wild Cat Island, the able Catboat Swallow, and the two intrepid amazons, Nancy and Peggy Blackett.

☐ *The Cay*
by Theodore Taylor

When the freighter on which they are traveling is torpedoed by a German submarine during World War II, an adolescent white boy, blinded by a blow on the head, and an old black man are stranded on a tiny Caribbean island where the boy acquires a new kind of vision, courage, and love from his old companion.

Prequel/sequel: *Timothy of the Cay*

☐ *Treasure Island*
by Robert Louis Stevenson

While going through the possessions of a deceased guest who owed them money, the mistress of the inn and her son find a treasure map that leads them to a pirate's fortune.

☐ *Shark Beneath the Reef*
by Jean Craighead George

On the island of Coronado, a young Mexican fisherman comes of age as he becomes aware of the politics, corruption, and changes around him.

Different Points of View

Morning Girl

☐ *Nothing but the Truth*
by Avi
1992 Newbery Honor Book

A ninth-grader's suspension for singing "The Star Spangled Banner" becomes a national news story.

☐ *North to Freedom*
by Anne Holm

Having escaped from a concentration camp where he has spent his life, a 12-year-old boy struggles to cope with an entirely strange world.

☐ *The Winchesters*
by James Lincoln Collier

Fourteen-year-old Chris, a poor relation of the wealthy Winchesters, must choose sides when his classmates' parents go on strike at the Winchester mill.

☐ *Arthur for the Very First Time*
by Patricia MacLachlan

Arthur spends a summer with his unconventional aunt and uncle.

☐ *Freaky Friday*
by Mary Rodgers

A 13-year-old girl gains understanding of her mother when she has to spend a day in her mother's body.

☐ *Shoebag*
by Mary James

A cockroach finds himself changed into a little boy.

☐ *All About Sam*
by Lois Lowry

The adventures of Sam starting with his first day as a newborn.

☐ *The Sword in the Stone*
by T. H. White

Arthur becomes a wiser person as a result of Merlin's lessons.

Simple yet Powerful Books

Morning Girl

☐ *The Chalkbox Kid*
by Clyde Robert Bulla
Nine-year-old Gregory creates a surprising and very different garden.

☐ *The Children's Story*
by James Clavell
A new teacher uses charm and fallacious logic to brainwash a class of second-graders after the U.S. has been conquered.

☐ *Sadako and the Thousand Paper Cranes*
by Eleanor Coerr
Hospitalized with the dreaded atom bomb disease, a child in Hiroshima races to fold 1,000 paper cranes, believing that by doing so she will become healthy.

☐ *The Hundred Dresses*
by Eleanor Estes
1945 Newbery Honor Book
In winning a medal she is no longer there to receive, a little Polish girl teaches her classmates a lesson.

☐ *Onion Tears*
by Diana Kidd
A Vietnamese girl tries to come to terms with her grief over the loss of her family and her new life with an Australian family.

☐ *Journey*
by Patricia MacLachlan
Two children are abandoned by their mother at their grandparents' house.

☐ *Stargone John*
by Ellen Kindt McKenzie
Six-year-old John experiences ridicule and punishment at his one-room schoolhouse, until an old retired teacher reaches out from her blindness to share with him the world of reading and writing.

The Moves Make the Man

Bruce Brooks

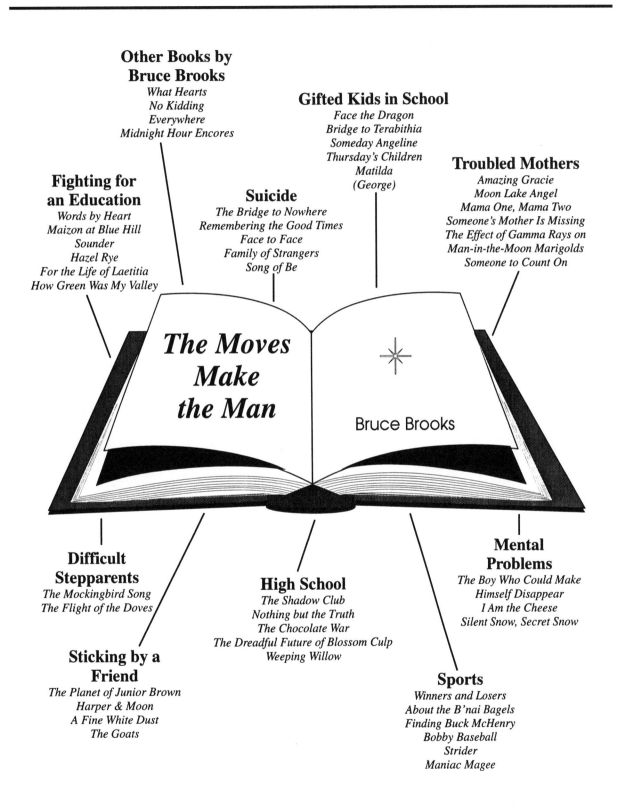

Other Books by
Bruce Brooks
What Hearts
No Kidding
Everywhere
Midnight Hour Encores

Gifted Kids in School
Face the Dragon
Bridge to Terabithia
Someday Angeline
Thursday's Children
Matilda
(George)

Troubled Mothers
Amazing Gracie
Moon Lake Angel
Mama One, Mama Two
Someone's Mother Is Missing
The Effect of Gamma Rays on
Man-in-the-Moon Marigolds
Someone to Count On

Fighting for
an Education
Words by Heart
Maizon at Blue Hill
Sounder
Hazel Rye
For the Life of Laetitia
How Green Was My Valley

Suicide
The Bridge to Nowhere
Remembering the Good Times
Face to Face
Family of Strangers
Song of Be

The Moves
Make
the Man

Bruce Brooks

Difficult
Stepparents
The Mockingbird Song
The Flight of the Doves

High School
The Shadow Club
Nothing but the Truth
The Chocolate War
The Dreadful Future of Blossom Culp
Weeping Willow

Mental
Problems
The Boy Who Could Make
Himself Disappear
I Am the Cheese
Silent Snow, Secret Snow

Sticking by a
Friend
The Planet of Junior Brown
Harper & Moon
A Fine White Dust
The Goats

Sports
Winners and Losers
About the B'nai Bagels
Finding Buck McHenry
Bobby Baseball
Strider
Maniac Magee

109

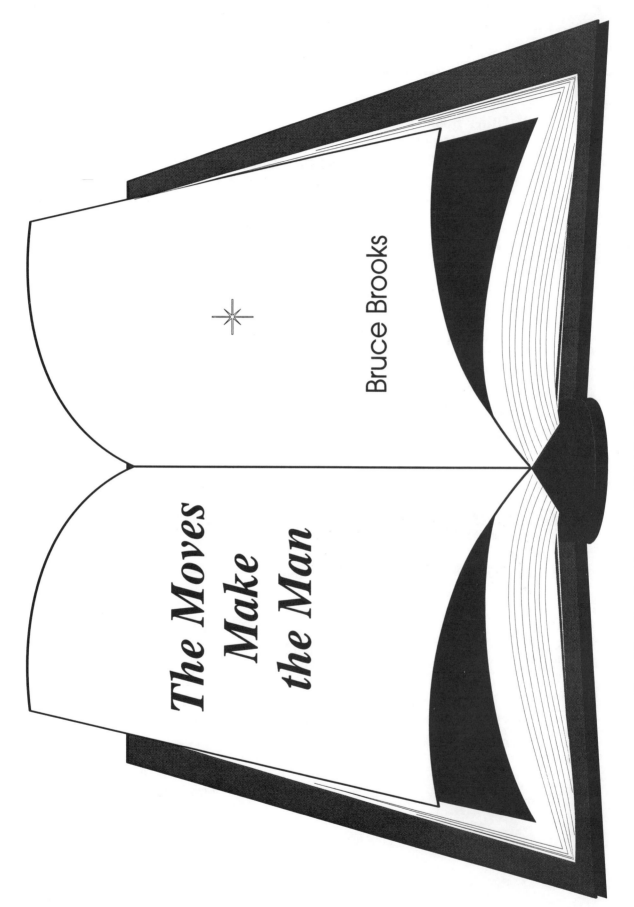

Bruce Brooks

*The Moves
Make
the Man*

Sports

Winners and Losers

About the B'nai Bagels

Finding Buck McHenry

Bobby Baseball

Strider

Maniac Magee

Suicide

The Bridge to Nowhere

Remembering the Good Times

Face to Face

Family of Strangers

Song of Be

High School

The Shadow Club

Nothing but the Truth

The Chocolate War

The Dreadful Future of Blossom Culp

Weeping Willow

Fighting for an Education

Words by Heart

Maizon at Blue Hill

Sounder

Hazel Rye

For the Life of Laetitia

How Green Was My Valley

Troubled Mothers

Amazing Gracie

Moon Lake Angel

Mama One, Mama Two

Someone's Mother Is Missing

The Effect of Gamma Rays on Man-in-the-Moon Marigolds

Someone to Count On

Mental Problems

The Boy Who Could Make Himself Disappear

I Am the Cheese

Silent Snow, Secret Snow

Other Books by Bruce Brooks

What Hearts

No Kidding

Everywhere

Midnight Hour Encores

Difficult Stepparents

The Mockingbird Song

The Flight of the Doves

Sticking by a Friend

The Planet of Junior Brown

Harper & Moon

A Fine White Dust

The Goats

Gifted Kids
in School

Face the Dragon

Bridge to Terabithia

Someday Angeline

Thursday's Children

Matilda

(George)

Fighting for an Education
The Moves Make the Man

☐ *Words by Heart*
by Ouida Sebestyen

In 1910, a young black girl struggles to fulfill her papa's dream of a better future for their family in a town where they are the only blacks.

☐ *Maizon at Blue Hill*
by Jacqueline Woodson

After winning a scholarship to an academically challenging boarding school, Maizon finds herself one of only five blacks there.

Sequel to *Last Summer with Maizon*

☐ *Sounder*
by William H. Armstrong

1970 Newbery Medal

When his sharecropper father is jailed for stealing food for his family, a young black boy grows in courage and understanding with the help of the dog Sounder and learns to read and write.

Sequel: *Sourland*

☐ *Hazel Rye*
by Vera and Bill Cleaver

An 11-year-old girl with no appreciation for land and growing things finds her values beginning to change when she agrees to let an impoverished family live in a small house she owns.

☐ *For the Life of Laetitia*
by Merle Hodge

As the first in her family to go to secondary school, 12-year-old Lacey struggles with a variety of problems, including a cruel teacher and a difficult home life with her father and stepmother.

☐ *How Green Was My Valley*
by Richard Llewellyn

A boy faces hardship growing up in a Welsh coal mining town.

High School
The Moves Make the Man

☐ *The Shadow Club*
by Neal Shusterman

A high school boy and his friends decide to form a club of second-bests and play anonymous tricks on each other's archrivals, but when the harmless pranks become life-threatening, no one in the club will admit responsibility.

☐ *Nothing but the Truth*
by Avi

1992 Newbery Honor Book

A ninth-grader's suspension for singing "The Star Spangled Banner" during homeroom becomes a national news story.

☐ *The Chocolate War*
by Robert Cormier

PG language

A freshman discovers the devastating consequences of refusing to join the school's annual fund-raising drive and arousing the wrath of the school bullies.

Sequel: *Beyond the Chocolate War*

☐ *The Dreadful Future of Blossom Culp*
by Richard Peck

Blossom, not the most popular member of her freshman class in 1914, travels ahead 70 years and returns in time to make Halloween a memorable night for her classmates and teachers.

☐ *Weeping Willow*
by Ruth White

PG sex

Despite all the problems she faces at home, Tiny Lambert's experiences at Black Gap High School help her begin to feel good about herself—until the day that she is raped by her stepfather.

Suicide
The Moves Make the Man

☐ *The Bridge to Nowhere*
by Megan McDonald

Seventh-grader Hallie is adjusting to friendship with an exciting older boy when her father, temporarily out of work, becomes an angry stranger in his own home.

☐ *Remembering the Good Times*
by Richard Peck

Trav, Kate, and Buck's special friendship may not be enough to save Trav as he pressures himself relentlessly to succeed, in his own eyes as well as in the eyes of his parents.

☐ *Face to Face*
by Marion Dane Bauer

Picked on at school by bullies, 13-year-old Michael confronts his fears during a trip to Colorado to see his father, who works as a whitewater rafting guide and who Michael has not seen in eight years.

☐ *Family of Strangers*
by Susan Beth Pfeffer

PG language

Through letters and essays, emotionally disturbed 16-year-old Abby chronicles her growing desperation in a family consisting of parents who seem devoid of love, one older sister bent on self-destruction, and another older sister who has always seemed perfect.

☐ *Song of Be*
by Lesley Beake

Be, a young Bushman woman searching in the desert for the peace she remembers from her childhood, realizes that she and her people must reconcile new personal and political realities with ancient traditions.

Sports
The Moves Make the Man

☐ *Winners and Losers*
by Stephen Hoffius

When a heart condition curtails his friend Daryl's track career, Curt takes Daryl's place as lead contender for the championship and as the new obsession of Daryl's father.

☐ *About the B'nai Bagels*
by E. L. Konigsburg

Mark tells about his troubles on the Little League team managed by his mother and coached by his brother.

☐ *Finding Buck McHenry*
by Alfred Slote

Eleven-year-old Jason, believing the school custodian to be a famous pitcher from the old Negro League, tries to enlist him as a coach for his Little League team by revealing his identity to the world.

☐ *Bobby Baseball*
by Robert Kimmel Smith

Ten-year-old Bobby is passionate about baseball and convinced that he is a great player. The only problem is to get a chance to prove his skill to his father.

☐ *Strider*
by Beverly Cleary

Leigh tells how he comes to terms with his parents' divorce, acquires joint custody of an abandoned dog, and joins the track team at school.

Sequel to *Dear Mr. Henshaw*

☐ *Maniac Magee*
by Jerry Spinelli

1991 Newbery Medal

After his parents die, Jeffrey Lionel Magee's life becomes legendary, as he accomplishes athletic and other feats that awe his contemporaries.

Troubled Mothers
The Moves Make the Man

☐ *Amazing Gracie*
by A. E. Cannon
A high school girl has a lot to deal with when her mother, who suffers from depression, remarries; a new brother is acquired; and the family moves to Salt Lake City.

☐ *Moon Lake Angel*
by Vera and Bill Cleaver
Kitty, whose mother does not want a child, stays with her aunt and learns to accept her mother's weaknesses.

☐ *Mama One, Mama Two*
by Patricia MacLachlan
A child lives with a foster family until her own mother can care for her.

☐ *Someone's Mother Is Missing*
by Harry Mazer
When her emotionally disturbed mother disappears from their home, Lisa searches for her.

☐ *The Effect of Gamma Rays on Man-in-the-Moon Marigolds*
by Paul Zindel
A two-act play depicting an embittered mother who vents her frustrations upon her two daughters.

☐ *Someone to Count On*
by Patricia Hermes
When 11-year-old Sam visits her grandfather's ranch, she finds life very different from the one she has known with her vagabond mother and discovers what really matters to her.

Mental Problems
The Moves Make the Man

☐ *The Boy Who Could Make Himself Disappear*
by Kin Platt
A 12-year-old boy with a speech defect gradually withdraws into schizophrenia after moving to live with his mother following the divorce of his harsh and detached parents.

☐ *I Am the Cheese*
by Robert Cormier
A young boy desperately tries to unlock his hidden past.

☐ *Silent Snow, Secret Snow*
by Conrad Aiken
As Paul gradually withdraws from reality, he sees his world engulfed by a deep snow that exists only in his mind.

Other Books by Bruce Brooks
The Moves Make the Man

☐ *What Hearts*
1993 Newbery Honor Book
After his mother divorces his father and remarries, Asa's sharp intellect helps him deal with his new world.

☐ *No Kidding*
In the 21st century, 14-year-old Sam must decide the fate of his family after his mother is released from an alcohol rehabilitation center.

☐ *Everywhere*
Afraid that his grandfather will die after a heart attack, a nine-year-old boy agrees to perform a ritual called soul switching.

☐ *Midnight Hour Encores*
A 16-year-old cellist and musical prodigy travels cross-country with her father to meet her mother, who abandoned her as a baby.

Difficult Stepparents
The Moves Make the Man

☐ *The Mockingbird Song*
by Berthe Amoss
Unable to get along with her new stepmother, 11-year-old Lindy goes to live with the elderly lady next door.

☐ *The Flight of the Doves*
by Walter Macken
An English boy and his younger sister run away from their abusive stepfather and set out to reach their grandmother in western Ireland.

Gifted Kids in School
The Moves Make the Man

Face the Dragon
by Joyce Sweeney

After skipping the ninth grade and entering high school in a program for gifted students, 14-year-old Eric and his best friend Paul undergo a dynamic change in their relationship.

Bridge to Terabithia
by Katherine Paterson
1978 Newbery Medal

The life of a 10-year-old boy in rural Virginia expands when he becomes friends with a newcomer who subsequently meets an untimely death trying to reach their hideaway, Terabithia, during a storm.

Someday Angeline
by Louis Sachar

As an eight-year-old genius in the sixth grade, Angeline is not too popular, but she tries to adjust to being different.

Thursday's Children
by Rumer Godden

As he tags along to his spoiled sister's ballet classes, Doone discovers and develops his own rare and special talents.

Matilda
by Roald Dahl

Matilda applies her untapped mental powers to rid the school of the evil, child-hating headmistress, Miss Trunchbull.

(George)
by E. L. Konigsburg

When 12-year-old Benjamin refuses to see what is going on in his chemistry lab, the little man who lives inside of him must finally speak out in public.

Sticking by a Friend
The Moves Make the Man

The Planet of Junior Brown
by Virginia Hamilton
1972 Newbery Honor Book

Already a leader in New York's underground world of homeless children, Buddy takes on the responsibility of protecting an overweight, emotionally disturbed friend.

Harper & Moon
by Ramon Royal Ross

Twelve-year-old Harper's friendship with Moon, an abused, orphaned, older boy, is tested by a discovery Harper makes.

A Fine White Dust
by Cynthia Rylant
1987 Newbery Honor Book

The visit of the traveling Preacher Man to a small town gives new impetus to 13-year-old Peter's struggle to reconcile his own deeply felt religious belief with the beliefs and nonbeliefs of his family and friends.

The Goats
by Brock Cole

Stripped and marooned on a small island by their fellow campers, a boy and a girl form an uneasy bond that grows into a deep friendship when they decide to run away.

North to Freedom

Anne Holm

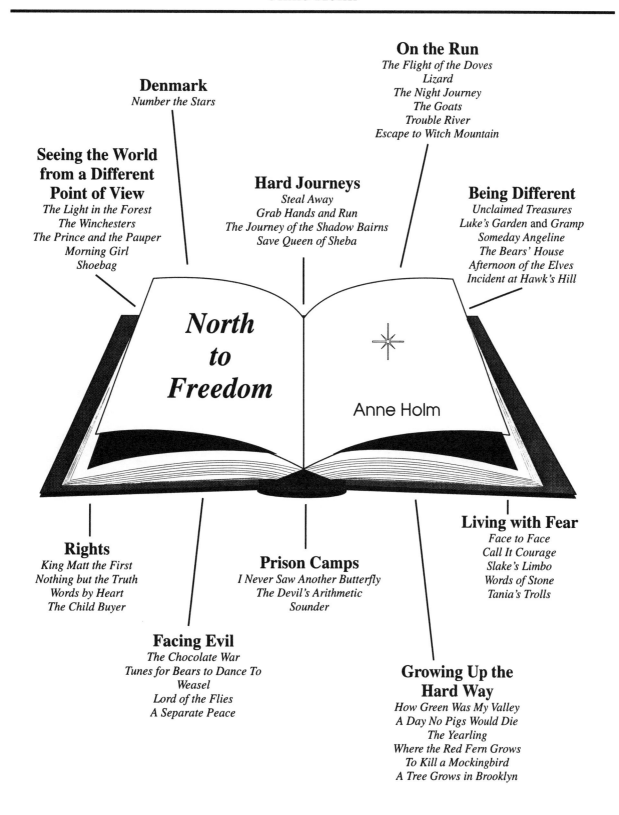

On the Run
The Flight of the Doves
Lizard
The Night Journey
The Goats
Trouble River
Escape to Witch Mountain

Denmark
Number the Stars

**Seeing the World
from a Different
Point of View**
The Light in the Forest
The Winchesters
The Prince and the Pauper
Morning Girl
Shoebag

Hard Journeys
Steal Away
Grab Hands and Run
The Journey of the Shadow Bairns
Save Queen of Sheba

Being Different
Unclaimed Treasures
Luke's Garden and *Gramp*
Someday Angeline
The Bears' House
Afternoon of the Elves
Incident at Hawk's Hill

*North
to
Freedom*

Anne Holm

Living with Fear
Face to Face
Call It Courage
Slake's Limbo
Words of Stone
Tania's Trolls

Rights
King Matt the First
Nothing but the Truth
Words by Heart
The Child Buyer

Prison Camps
I Never Saw Another Butterfly
The Devil's Arithmetic
Sounder

Facing Evil
The Chocolate War
Tunes for Bears to Dance To
Weasel
Lord of the Flies
A Separate Peace

**Growing Up the
Hard Way**
How Green Was My Valley
A Day No Pigs Would Die
The Yearling
Where the Red Fern Grows
To Kill a Mockingbird
A Tree Grows in Brooklyn

North
to
Freedom

Anne Holm

Prison Camps

I Never Saw Another Butterfly

The Devil's Arithmetic

Sounder

Hard Journeys

Steal Away

Grab Hands and Run

The Journey of the Shadow Bairns

Save Queen of Sheba

On the Run

The Flight of the Doves

Lizard

The Night Journey

The Goats

Trouble River

Escape to Witch Mountain

Rights

King Matt the First

Nothing but the Truth

Words by Heart

The Child Buyer

Denmark

Number the Stars

Living with Fear

Face to Face

Call It Courage

Slake's Limbo

Words of Stone

Tania's Trolls

Facing Evil

The Chocolate War

Tunes for Bears to Dance To

Weasel

Lord of the Flies

A Separate Peace

Seeing the World from a Different Point of View

The Light in the Forest

The Winchesters

The Prince and the Pauper

Morning Girl

Shoebag

Being Different

Unclaimed Treasures

Luke's Garden and *Gramp*

Someday Angeline

The Bears' House

Afternoon of the Elves

Incident at Hawk's Hill

Growing Up the Hard Way

How Green Was My Valley

A Day No Pigs Would Die

The Yearling

Where the Red Fern Grows

To Kill a Mockingbird

A Tree Grows in Brooklyn

Prison Camps
North to Freedom

❏ *I Never Saw Another Butterfly*
Hana Volavkovak, ed.

A selection of children's poems and drawings from the Terezin concentration camp.

❏ *The Devil's Arithmetic*
by Jane Yolen

Time travel places Hanna in a small Jewish village in Nazi-occupied Poland.

❏ *Sounder*
by William H. Armstrong
1970 Newbery Medal

When his sharecropper father is jailed for stealing food for his family, a young black boy grows in courage and understanding with the help of the dog Sounder and learns to read and write.

Sequel: *Sourland*

Hard Journeys
North to Freedom

❏ *Steal Away*
by Jennifer Armstrong

In 1855 two 13-year-old girls, one white and one black, run away from a southern farm and make the difficult journey north.

❏ *Grab Hands and Run*
by Frances Temple

After his father disappears, 12-year-old Felipe, his mother, and his sister make their way from their home in El Salvador to Canada.

❏ *The Journey of the Shadow Bairns*
by Margaret J. Anderson

When her parents die, leaving only a one-way passage to Canada, a Scottish girl decides she and her four-year-old brother will pursue family plans to relocate.

❏ *Save Queen of Sheba*
by Louise Moeri

After miraculously surviving a Sioux Indian raid, a brother and sister set out to find the rest of the settlers.

On the Run
North to Freedom

❏ *The Flight of the Doves*
by Walter Macken

A 12-year-old English boy and his seven-year-old sister run away from their abusive stepfather and set out to reach their grandmother in western Ireland.

❏ *Lizard*
by Dennis Covington

Sent to live at a school for retarded boys, Lizard, a bright, deformed youngster, escapes with the help of a visiting actor.

❏ *The Night Journey*
by Kathryn Lasky

Rache ignores her parents' wishes and persuades her great-grandmother to relate the story of her escape from czarist Russia.

❏ *The Goats*
by Brock Cole

Stripped and marooned on a small island by their fellow campers, a boy and a girl form an uneasy bond that grows into a deep friendship when they decide to run away and disappear without a trace.

❏ *Trouble River*
by Betsy Byars

In order to escape the Indians, young Dewey negotiates the rapids of Trouble River with his grandmother on a homemade raft.

❏ *Escape to Witch Mountain*
by Alexander Key

When a mysterious man claims to be Tia and Tony's uncle and acquires court custody, the children, aware of his evil intent, run away to prevent him from exploiting their unusual powers.

Rights
North to Freedom

❏ *King Matt the First*
by Janusz Korczak

A child king introduces reforms to give children the same rights as adults.

❏ *Nothing but the Truth*
by Avi
1992 Newbery Honor Book

A ninth-grader's suspension for singing "The Star Spangled Banner" during homeroom becomes a national news story.

❏ *Words by Heart*
by Ouida Sebestyen

In 1910, a young black girl struggles to fulfill her papa's dream of a better future for their family in the southwestern town where they are the only blacks.

❏ *The Child Buyer*
by John Hersey

A novel in the form of hearings before the Standing Committee on Education, Welfare & Public Morality of a certain State Senate, investigating the conspiracy of Mr. Wissey Jones, with others, to purchase a male child.

Denmark
North to Freedom

☐ *Number the Stars*
by Lois Lowry
1990 Newbery Medal

In 1943, during the German occupation of Denmark, 10-year-old Annemarie learns how to be brave and courageous when she helps shelter her Jewish friend from the Nazis.

Living with Fear
North to Freedom

☐ *Face to Face*
by Marion Dane Bauer

Picked on at school by bullies, 13-year-old Michael confronts his fears during a trip to Colorado to see his father, who works as a whitewater rafting guide and who Michael has not seen in eight years.

☐ *Call It Courage*
by Armstrong Sperry
1941 Newbery Medal

Based on a Polynesian legend, this is the story of a youth, the son of a Polynesian chief whose people worship courage. Though he is afraid of the sea, he sets out alone in his canoe to conquer his fear and prove his courage to himself and his tribe.

☐ *Slake's Limbo*
by Felice Holman

Thirteen-year-old Aremis Slake, hounded by his fears and misfortunes, flees into New York City's subway tunnels, never again, he believes, to emerge.

☐ *Words of Stone*
by Kevin Henkes

Busy trying to deal with his many fears and his troubled feelings for his dead mother, 10-year-old Blaze has his life changed when he meets the boisterous and irresistible Joselle.

☐ *Tania's Trolls*
by Lisa Westberg Peters

A formidable grandmother helps young Tania overcome her stage fright.

Facing Evil
North to Freedom

☐ *The Chocolate War*
by Robert Cormier

A high school freshman discovers the devastating consequences of refusing to join the school's annual fund-raising drive and arousing the wrath of the school bullies.

Sequel: *Beyond the Chocolate War*

☐ *Tunes for Bears to Dance To*
by Robert Cormier

Eleven-year-old Henry escapes his family's problems by watching the woodcarving of Mr. Levine, an elderly Holocaust survivor, but when Henry is manipulated into betraying his friend, he comes to know true evil.

☐ *Weasel*
by Cynthia DeFelice

Alone in the frontier wilderness in the winter of 1839 while his father is recovering from an injury, 11-year-old Nathan runs afoul of the renegade killer known as Weasel and makes a surprising discovery about the concept of revenge.

☐ *Lord of the Flies*
by William Golding

Stranded on an island while an atomic war destroys the rest of the world, a group of young boys reverts to savagery as they struggle to survive.

☐ *A Separate Peace*
by John Knowles

Gene Forrester looks back 15 years to a World War II year in which he and his best friend Phineas were roommates in a New Hampshire boarding school. Their friendship is marred by Finny's crippling fall, an event for which Gene is responsible.

Seeing the World from a Different Point of View
North to Freedom

☐ *The Light in the Forest*
by Conrad Richter

After being raised as an Indian for 11 years following his capture at the age of four, John Butler is forcibly returned to his white parents but continues to long for the freedom of Indian life.

☐ *The Winchesters*
by James Lincoln Collier

Fourteen-year-old Chris, a poor relation of the wealthy Winchesters, must choose whether to be on the side of management or labor when his classmates' parents go on strike at the Winchester mill in response to a wage cut.

☐ *The Prince and the Pauper*
by Mark Twain

When young Edward VI of England and a poor boy who resembles him exchange places, each learns something about the other's very different station in life.

☐ *Morning Girl*
by Michael Dorris

Morning Girl, who loves the day, and her younger brother Star Boy, who loves the night, take turns describing their life on an island in pre-Colombian America; in Morning Girl's last narrative, she witnesses the arrival of the first Europeans in her world.

☐ *Shoebag*
by Mary James

Shoebag, a happy cockroach who finds himself suddenly changed into a little boy, changes the lives of those around him before returning to his former life as an insect.

Growing Up the Hard Way
North to Freedom

📖 *How Green Was My Valley*
by Richard Llewellyn

A boy grows up in a Welsh mining town.

📖 *A Day No Pigs Would Die*
by Robert Newton Peck

A 13-year-old farm boy whose father slaughters pigs for a living learns to do what's got to be done, especially regarding his pet pig, who cannot produce a litter.

📖 *The Yearling*
by Marjorie Kinnan Rawlings

A young boy living in the Florida backwoods is forced to decide the fate of a fawn he has raised as a pet.

📖 *Where the Red Fern Grows*
by Wilson Rawls

The adventures of a 10-year-old boy and the two dogs he bought with money he had earned.

📖 *To Kill a Mockingbird*
by Harper Lee

Eight-year-old Scout Finch and her brother are thrust into an adult world of racial bigotry and hatred when their father chooses to defend a black man charged with raping a white girl.

📖 *A Tree Grows in Brooklyn*
by Betty Smith

Francie Nolan experiences the problems of growing up in a Brooklyn slum.

Being Different
North to Freedom

📖 *Unclaimed Treasures*
by Patricia MacLachlan

Willa, who wants to feel extraordinary, thinks that she's in love with the father of the boy next door until she realizes that her true love is the boy himself.

📖 *Luke's Garden and Gramp*
by Joan Tate

In one short novel, a boy is destroyed because he is different; in the other, a boy finds a way to make his grandfather feel useful again.

📖 *Someday Angeline*
by Louis Sachar

As an eight-year-old genius in the sixth grade, Angeline is not too popular, but she tries to adjust to being different.

📖 *The Bears' House*
by Marilyn Sachs

Fran Ellen is ostracized by her class because she sucks her thumb and smells bad, but her dreadful home life is a secret she tries to keep from them all.

📖 *Afternoon of the Elves*
by Janet Taylor Lisle

1990 Newbery Honor Book

As Hillary works in the miniature village, allegedly built by elves, in Sara-Kate's backyard, she becomes more and more curious about Sara-Kate's real life inside her big, gloomy house with her mysterious, silent mother.

📖 *Incident at Hawk's Hill*
by Allan W. Eckert

1972 Newbery Honor Book

A shy, lonely six-year-old wanders into the Canadian prairie and spends a summer under the protection of a badger.

On My Honor

Marian Dane Bauer

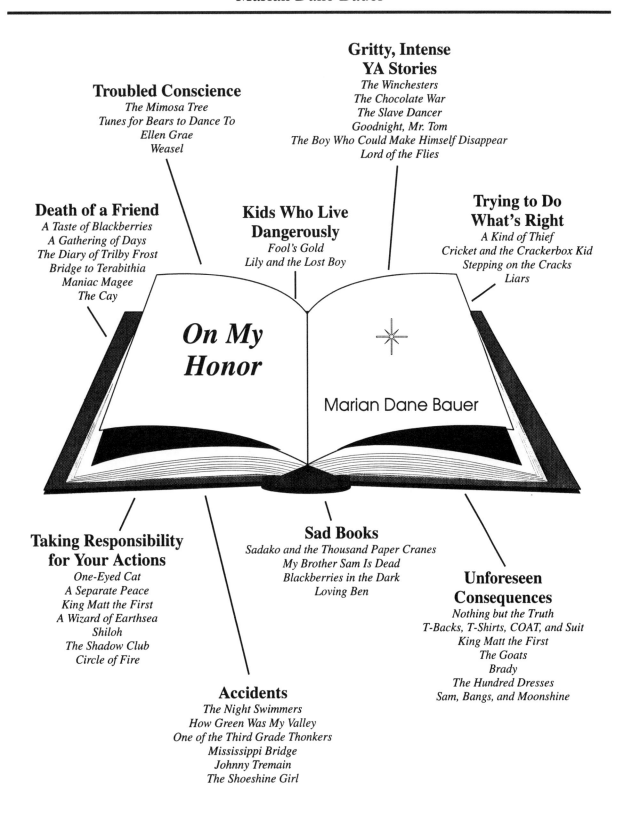

Troubled Conscience
The Mimosa Tree
Tunes for Bears to Dance To
Ellen Grae
Weasel

**Gritty, Intense
YA Stories**
The Winchesters
The Chocolate War
The Slave Dancer
Goodnight, Mr. Tom
The Boy Who Could Make Himself Disappear
Lord of the Flies

Death of a Friend
A Taste of Blackberries
A Gathering of Days
The Diary of Trilby Frost
Bridge to Terabithia
Maniac Magee
The Cay

**Kids Who Live
Dangerously**
Fool's Gold
Lily and the Lost Boy

**Trying to Do
What's Right**
A Kind of Thief
Cricket and the Crackerbox Kid
Stepping on the Cracks
Liars

*On My
Honor*

Marian Dane Bauer

**Taking Responsibility
for Your Actions**
One-Eyed Cat
A Separate Peace
King Matt the First
A Wizard of Earthsea
Shiloh
The Shadow Club
Circle of Fire

Sad Books
Sadako and the Thousand Paper Cranes
My Brother Sam Is Dead
Blackberries in the Dark
Loving Ben

**Unforeseen
Consequences**
Nothing but the Truth
T-Backs, T-Shirts, COAT, and Suit
King Matt the First
The Goats
Brady
The Hundred Dresses
Sam, Bangs, and Moonshine

Accidents
The Night Swimmers
How Green Was My Valley
One of the Third Grade Thonkers
Mississippi Bridge
Johnny Tremain
The Shoeshine Girl

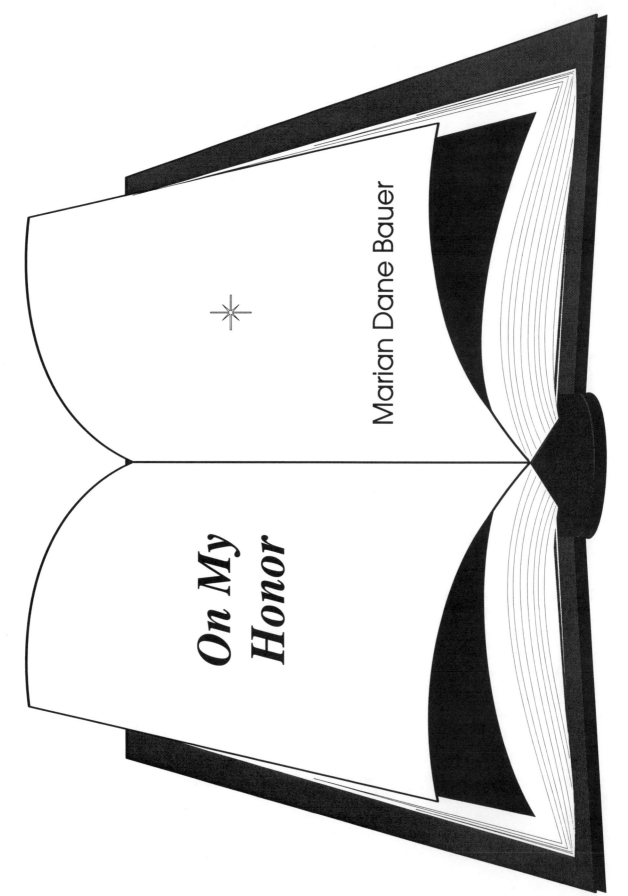

On My Honor

Marian Dane Bauer

Taking Responsibility for Your Actions

One-Eyed Cat

A Separate Peace

King Matt the First

A Wizard of Earthsea

Shiloh

The Shadow Club

Circle of Fire

Unforeseen Consequences

Nothing but the Truth

T-Backs, T-Shirts, COAT, and Suit

King Matt the First

The Goats

Brady

The Hundred Dresses

Sam, Bangs, and Moonshine

Accidents

The Night Swimmers

How Green Was My Valley

One of the Third Grade Thonkers

Mississippi Bridge

Johnny Tremain

The Shoeshine Girl

Trying to Do What's Right

A Kind of Thief

Cricket and the Crackerbox Kid

Stepping on the Cracks

Liars

Troubled Conscience

The Mimosa Tree

Tunes for Bears to Dance To

Ellen Grae

Weasel

Gritty, Intense YA Stories

The Winchesters

The Chocolate War

The Slave Dancer

Goodnight, Mr. Tom

The Boy Who Could Make Himself Disappear

Lord of the Flies

Kids Who Live Dangerously

Fool's Gold

Lily and the Lost Boy

Sad Books

Sadako and the Thousand Paper Cranes

My Brother Sam Is Dead

Blackberries in the Dark

Loving Ben

Death of a Friend

A Taste of Blackberries

A Gathering of Days

The Diary of Trilby Frost

Bridge to Terabithia

Maniac Magee

The Cay

Taking Responsibility for Your Actions
On My Honor

☐ *One-Eyed Cat*
by Paula Fox

1985 Newbery Honor Book

An 11-year-old shoots a stray cat with his new air rifle.

☐ *A Separate Peace*
by John Knowles

Gene's friendship with Phineas is marred by Finny's crippling fall, an event for which Gene is responsible.

☐ *King Matt the First*
by Janusz Korczak

A child king introduces reforms to give children the same rights as adults.

☐ *A Wizard of Earthsea*
by Ursula Le Guin

A boy attempts to subdue the evil he unleashed on the world as an apprentice to the Master Wizard.

Book 1 of the Earthsea series

☐ *Shiloh*
by Phyllis Reynolds Naylor

1992 Newbery Medal

When he finds a lost beagle, Marty tries to hide it from his family and the dog's real owner, a mean-spirited man known to shoot deer out of season and to mistreat his dogs.

☐ *The Shadow Club*
by Neal Shusterman

A high school boy and his friends decide to form a club and play anonymous tricks on each other's rivals, but when the harmless pranks become life-threatening, no one in the club will admit responsibility.

☐ *Circle of Fire*
by William Hooks

Eleven-year-old Harrison overhears a local bigot planning a Ku Klux Klan raid on a band of Irish tinkers.

Unforeseen Consequences
On My Honor

☐ *Nothing but the Truth*
by Avi

1992 Newbery Honor Book

A ninth-grader's suspension for singing "The Star Spangled Banner" during homeroom becomes a national news story.

☐ *T-Backs, T-Shirts, COAT, and Suit*
by E. L. Konigsburg

Twelve-year-old Chloe and her aunt become involved in a controversy surrounding the wearing of T-back bathing suits.

☐ *King Matt the First*
by Janusz Korczak

A child king introduces reforms to give children the same rights as adults.

☐ *The Goats*
by Brock Cole

Stripped and marooned on an island by their fellow campers, a boy and a girl decide to run away and disappear without a trace.

☐ *Brady*
by Jean Fritz

A young Pennsylvania boy takes part in the pre-Civil War antislavery activities.

☐ *The Hundred Dresses*
by Eleanor Estes

1945 Newbery Honor Book

In winning a medal she is no longer there to receive, a tight-lipped little Polish girl teaches her classmates a lesson.

☐ *Sam, Bangs, and Moonshine*
by Evaline Ness

1967 Caldecott Medal

Relates the experiences of a little girl as she learns to tell the difference between make-believe and real life.

Accidents
On My Honor

☐ *The Night Swimmers*
by Betsy Byars

With their mother dead and their father working nights, Retta tries to be mother to her two younger brothers.

☐ *How Green Was My Valley*
by Richard Llewellyn

A boy faces adversity with courage in a Welsh mining town.

☐ *One of the Third Grade Thonkers*
by Phyllis Reynolds Naylor

Ashamed of his wimpy younger cousin, eight-year-old Jimmy is determined to keep him out of his special club for rough, tough, and terrible boys, until an accident involving Jimmy's father demonstrates for him the true meaning of courage.

☐ *Mississippi Bridge*
by Mildred Taylor

During a heavy rainstorm in 1930s rural Mississippi, a 10-year-old white boy sees a bus driver order all the black passengers off a crowded bus to make room for late-arriving white passengers and then sees the bus set off across a bridge over the raging Rosa Lee Creek.

☐ *Johnny Tremain*
by Esther Forbes

A teenager in colonial Boston becomes deeply involved in the Revolutionary cause.

☐ *The Shoeshine Girl*
by Clyde Robert Bulla

Determined to earn some money, 10-year-old Sarah Ida gets a job at a shoeshine stand.

Trying to Do What's Right
On My Honor

☐ *A Kind of Thief*
by Vivien Alcock

When her father is suddenly arrested and put into prison, 13-year-old Elinor finds that she has to face many unpleasant truths about him and their way of life.

☐ *Cricket and the Crackerbox Kid*
by Alane Ferguson

Pampered, 11-year-old rich kid Cricket thinks she has finally found a friend in Dominic, who lives in the low-income houses called crackerboxes, until they quarrel over ownership of a dog, and their classroom becomes a courtroom to decide who is right.

☐ *Stepping on the Cracks*
by Mary Downing Hahn

In 1944, while her brother is overseas fighting in World War II, 11-year-old Margaret gets a new view of the school bully Gordy when she finds him hiding his own brother, an army deserter, and decides to help him.

☐ *Liars*
by P. J. Petersen

Life in the remote town of Alder Creek, California, is boring for eighth-grader Sam and his friends, until his newly awakened ability to tell when a person is lying involves him in a series of mysterious events.

Troubled Conscience
On My Honor

☐ *The Mimosa Tree*
by Vera and Bill Cleaver

Shortly after the Proffitts arrive in the Chicago slums from North Carolina, their stepmother leaves the family, and 14-year-old Marvella becomes the sole support for her blind father and the four younger children.

☐ *Tunes for Bears to Dance To*
by Robert Cormier

Eleven-year-old Henry escapes his family's problems by watching the woodcarving of Mr. Levine, an elderly Holocaust survivor, but when Henry is manipulated into betraying his friend, he comes to know true evil.

☐ *Ellen Grae*
by Vera and Bill Cleaver

Ellen Grae is an imaginative girl in whom simple-minded Ira confides. Ellen finds herself greatly confused between her affection for Ira and her sense of what is right.

☐ *Weasel*
by Cynthia DeFelice

Alone in the frontier wilderness in the winter of 1839 while his father is recovering from an injury, 11-year-old Nathan runs afoul of the renegade killer known as Weasel and makes a surprising discovery about the concept of revenge.

Gritty, Intense YA Stories
On My Honor

☐ *The Winchesters*
by James Lincoln Collier

Fourteen-year-old Chris, a poor relation of the wealthy Winchesters, must choose whether to be on the side of management or labor when his classmates' parents go on strike at the Winchester mill.

☐ *The Chocolate War*
by Robert Cormier

A high school freshman discovers the devastating consequences of refusing to join the school's annual fund-raising drive and arousing the wrath of the school bullies.

Sequel: *Beyond the Chocolate War*

☐ *The Slave Dancer*
by Paula Fox

1974 Newbery Medal

Kidnapped by the crew of an Africa-bound ship, a 13-year-old boy discovers to his horror that he is on a slaver and his job is to play music for the exercise periods of the human cargo.

☐ *Goodnight, Mr. Tom*
by Michelle Magorian

A battered child learns to embrace life when he is adopted by an old man in the English countryside during World War II.

☐ *The Boy Who Could Make Himself Disappear*
by Kin Platt

A 12-year-old boy with a speech defect gradually withdraws into schizophrenia after moving to live with his mother following the divorce of his harsh and detached parents.

☐ *Lord of the Flies*
by William Golding

Stranded on an island, a group of young boys reverts to savagery as they struggle to survive.

Kids
Who Live Dangerously
On My Honor

☐ *Fool's Gold*
by Zilpha Keatley Snyder

Secretly claustrophobic, Rudy tries to find a way to distract his friends from pursuing their plan of exploring an abandoned gold mine.

☐ *Lily and the Lost Boy*
by Paula Fox

Eleven-year-old Lily has grown close to her 13-year-old brother Paul on the Greek island Thasos, until the unpredictable behavior of another American boy disrupts their lives.

Sad Books
On My Honor

☐ *Sadako and the Thousand Paper Cranes*
by Eleanor Coerr

Hospitalized with leukemia, a child in Hiroshima races to fold 1,000 paper cranes to verify the legend that by doing so she will become healthy.

☐ *My Brother Sam Is Dead*
by Christopher and James Lincoln Collier

During the Revolution, one son joins the rebel forces while the rest of the family tries to stay neutral in a Tory town.

☐ *Blackberries in the Dark*
by Mavis Jukes

Nine-year-old Austin visits his grandmother after his grandfather dies, and together they try to come to terms with their loss.

☐ *Loving Ben*
by Elizabeth Laird

Anna experiences the birth and death of a loved and loving hydrocephalic brother and works with a child with Down's syndrome.

Death of a Friend
On My Honor

☐☐*A Taste of Blackberries*
by Doris B. Smith

A young boy tries to adjust to the accidental death of his best friend.

☐☐*A Gathering of Days*
by Joan W. Blos

1980 Newbery Medal

The journal of a 14-year-old girl records daily events in her small town, her father's remarriage, and the death of her best friend.

☐☐*The Diary of Trilby Frost*
by Dianne Glaser

At the turn of the century, teenager Trilby Frost records in her diary her growing realization that life continues even though her father, younger brother, and closest friend die.

☐☐*Bridge to Terabithia*
by Katherine Paterson

1978 Newbery Medal

The life of a 10-year-old boy expands when he becomes friends with a newcomer who subsequently dies trying to reach their hideaway, Terabithia, during a storm.

☐☐*Maniac Magee*
by Jerry Spinelli

1991 Newbery Medal

Jeffrey Lionel Magee's life becomes legendary, as he accomplishes athletic and other feats that awe his contemporaries.

☐☐*The Cay*
by Theodore Taylor

When their ship is torpedoed by a German submarine, a white boy, blinded by a blow on the head, and an old black man are stranded on a tiny island, where the boy acquires a new kind of vision, courage, and love from his old companion.

Prequel/sequel: *Timothy of the Cay*

The Phantom Tollbooth

Norton Juster

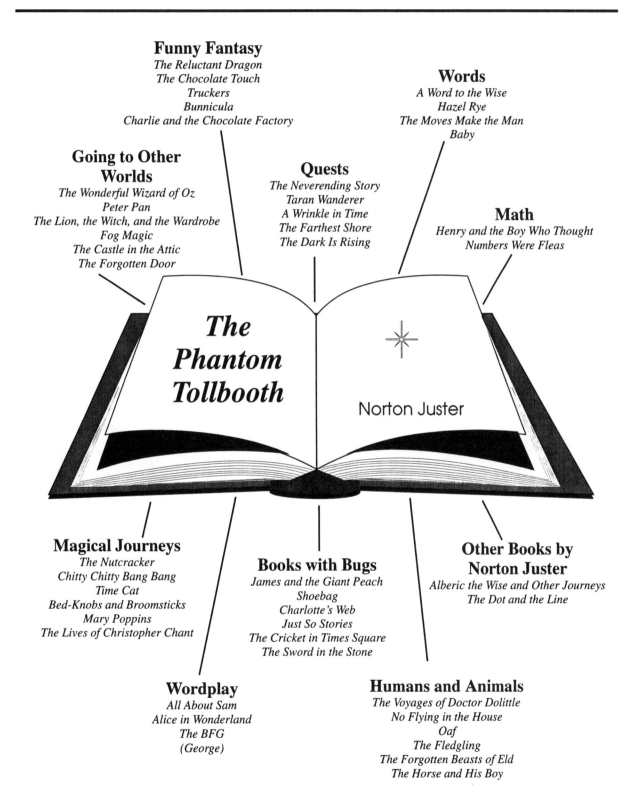

Funny Fantasy
The Reluctant Dragon
The Chocolate Touch
Truckers
Bunnicula
Charlie and the Chocolate Factory

Words
A Word to the Wise
Hazel Rye
The Moves Make the Man
Baby

Going to Other Worlds
The Wonderful Wizard of Oz
Peter Pan
The Lion, the Witch, and the Wardrobe
Fog Magic
The Castle in the Attic
The Forgotten Door

Quests
The Neverending Story
Taran Wanderer
A Wrinkle in Time
The Farthest Shore
The Dark Is Rising

Math
Henry and the Boy Who Thought Numbers Were Fleas

The Phantom Tollbooth

Norton Juster

Magical Journeys
The Nutcracker
Chitty Chitty Bang Bang
Time Cat
Bed-Knobs and Broomsticks
Mary Poppins
The Lives of Christopher Chant

Books with Bugs
James and the Giant Peach
Shoebag
Charlotte's Web
Just So Stories
The Cricket in Times Square
The Sword in the Stone

Other Books by Norton Juster
Alberic the Wise and Other Journeys
The Dot and the Line

Wordplay
All About Sam
Alice in Wonderland
The BFG
(George)

Humans and Animals
The Voyages of Doctor Dolittle
No Flying in the House
Oaf
The Fledgling
The Forgotten Beasts of Eld
The Horse and His Boy

The Phantom Tollbooth

Norton Juster

Other Books by Norton Juster

Alberic the Wise and Other Journeys

The Dot and the Line

Wordplay

All About Sam

Alice in Wonderland

The BFG

(George)

Words

A Word to the Wise

Hazel Rye

The Moves Make the Man

Baby

Math

Henry and the Boy Who Thought Numbers Were Fleas

Quests

The Neverending Story

Taran Wanderer

A Wrinkle in Time

The Farthest Shore

The Dark Is Rising

Going to Other Worlds

The Wonderful Wizard of Oz

Peter Pan

The Lion, the Witch, and the Wardrobe

Fog Magic

The Castle in the Attic

The Forgotten Door

Books with Bugs

James and the Giant Peach

Shoebag

Charlotte's Web

Just So Stories

The Cricket in Times Square

The Sword in the Stone

Magical Journeys

The Nutcracker

Chitty Chitty Bang Bang

Time Cat

Bed-Knobs and Broomsticks

Mary Poppins

The Lives of Christopher Chant

Funny Fantasy

The Reluctant Dragon

The Chocolate Touch

Truckers

Bunnicula

Charlie and the Chocolate Factory

Humans
and Animals

The Voyages of Doctor Dolittle

No Flying in the House

Oaf

The Fledgling

The Forgotten Beasts of Eld

The Horse and His Boy

Math
The Phantom Tollbooth

📖 *Henry and the Boy Who Thought Numbers Were Fleas*
by Marjorie Kaplan

Henry the dog helps his owner's little brother, Sam, learn the multiplication tables.

Words
The Phantom Tollbooth

📖 *A Word to the Wise*
by Alison Cragin Herzig and Jane Lawrence Mali

The thesaurus stolen from their teacher alters the lives of eight fifth-graders in a special reading group.

📖 *Hazel Rye*
by Vera and Bill Cleaver

An 11-year-old girl with no appreciation for land and growing things finds her values beginning to change when she agrees to let an impoverished family live in a small house she owns, in exchange for working in the surrounding orange grove.

📖 *The Moves Make the Man*
by Bruce Brooks

1985 Newbery Honor Book

A black boy and an emotionally troubled white boy in North Carolina form a precarious friendship.

📖 *Baby*
by Patricia MacLachlan

Taking care of a baby left with them at the end of the tourist season helps a family come to terms with the death of their own infant son.

Wordplay
The Phantom Tollbooth

📖 *All About Sam*
by Lois Lowry

The adventures of Sam, Anastasia Krupnik's younger brother, from his first day as a newborn through his mischievous times as a toddler.

📖 *Alice in Wonderland*
by Lewis Carroll

A little girl falls down a rabbit hole and discovers a world of nonsensical and amusing characters.

📖 *The BFG*
by Roald Dahl

Kidsnatched from her orphanage by a BFG (Big Friendly Giant) who spends his life blowing happy dreams to children, Sophie concocts with him a plan to save the world from nine other man-gobbling cannybul giants.

📖 *(George)*
by E. L. Konigsburg

When 12-year-old Benjamin refuses to see what is going on in his chemistry lab, the little man who lives inside of him must finally speak out in public for the safety of all concerned.

Other Books by Norton Juster
The Phantom Tollbooth

📖 *Alberic the Wise and Other Journeys*

In the days of the Renaissance, Alberic leads the reader among the folds of a rich tapestry in his search for wisdom.

📖 *The Dot and the Line*

A romance in higher mathematics, wherein a line falls in love with a vain dot.

Magical Journeys
The Phantom Tollbooth

☐ *The Nutcracker*
by E. T. A. Hoffman

After hearing how her toy nutcracker got his ugly face, a little girl helps break the spell and changes him into a handsome prince.

☐ *Chitty Chitty Bang Bang*
by Ian Fleming

Two children persuade their inventor father to purchase and restore an old car, which turns out to have magical powers.

☐ *Time Cat*
by Lloyd Alexander

Gareth, a cat with miraculous powers, takes his human friend Jason with him when he travels through time to visit countries all over the world during different periods of history.

☐ *Bed-Knobs and Broomsticks*
by Mary Norton

With the powers they acquire from a spinster who is studying to be a witch, three children go on a number of exciting and gruesome trips.

☐ *Mary Poppins*
by P. L. Travers

The Banks children's new nanny arrives on the east wind and introduces Jane and Michael to some delightful people and experiences.

☐ *The Lives of Christopher Chant*
by Diana Wynne Jones

Young Christopher Chant, in training to become the next head controller of magic in the world, becomes a key figure in a battle with renegade sorcerers because he has nine lives.

Books with Bugs
The Phantom Tollbooth

☐ *James and the Giant Peach*
by Roald Dahl

Wonderful adventures abound after James escapes from his fearful aunts by rolling away inside a giant peach.

☐ *Shoebag*
by Mary James

Shoebag, a happy cockroach who finds himself suddenly changed into a little boy, changes the lives of those around him before returning to his former life as an insect.

☐ *Charlotte's Web*
by E. B. White

1953 Newbery Honor Book

Wilbur the pig is desolate when he discovers that he is destined to be the farmer's Christmas dinner, until his spider friend Charlotte decides to help him.

☐ *Just So Stories*
by Rudyard Kipling

A collection of 12 humorous tales about animals and insects that tell how certain things came to be.

☐ *The Cricket in Times Square*
by George Selden

1961 Newbery Honor Book

With the help of a mouse and a cat, a musical cricket improves business at the newsstand run by Mario and his family.

☐ *The Sword in the Stone*
by T. H. White

Wart, as Arthur is called, becomes a wiser, more thoughtful person and a worthy king as a result of Merlin's lessons.

Going to Other Worlds
The Phantom Tollbooth

☐ *The Wonderful Wizard of Oz*
by L. Frank Baum

After a cyclone transports her to the land of Oz, Dorothy must seek out the great wizard in order to return to Kansas.

Many sequels

☐ *Peter Pan*
by J. M. Barrie

Peter Pan teaches Wendy and her brothers to fly to Neverland, where they share some exciting adventures with Indians and pirates.

☐ *The Lion, the Witch, and the Wardrobe*
by C. S. Lewis

Four English schoolchildren find their way into a magical land where they help Aslan free Narnia from the spell of the White Witch.

Book 1 of the Chronicles of Narnia

☐ *Fog Magic*
by Julia L. Sauer

1944 Newbery Honor Book

Greta loved and understood the fog, and it was in the fog that Greta was transported to a secret world of her own.

☐ *The Castle in the Attic*
by Elizabeth Winthrop

A gift of a toy castle, complete with a silver knight, introduces William to an adventure involving magic and a personal quest.

Sequel: *The Battle for the Castle*

☐ *The Forgotten Door*
by Alexander Key

John has fallen through a forgotten door to the strange planet Earth and is in great danger. Soon the family who befriends him is in great danger too. Time is running out. He must find the secret passage quickly or he may never get home.

Quests
The Phantom Tollbooth

☐ *The Neverending Story*
by Michael Ende

The magical tale of Bastian, a lonely, solitary boy who steps through the pages of a book into a special kingdom where he learns the true measure of his courage and creates a new world with his wishes.

☐ *Taran Wanderer*
by Lloyd Alexander

Accompanied by his faithful friend Gurgi, Taran Wanderer goes questing for his parentage, hoping it will prove noble for the sake of a beautiful princess.

Book 4 of the Chronicles of Prydain

☐ *A Wrinkle in Time*
by Madeleine L'Engle

1963 Newbery Medal

Three extraterrestrial beings take Meg and her friends to another world, where they become involved with unearthly strangers and a search for Meg's father, who has disappeared while engaged in secret work for the government.

Book 1 of the Chronos Quartet

☐ *The Farthest Shore*
by Ursula Le Guin

A young prince joins forces with a master wizard on a journey to discover a cause and remedy for the loss of magic in Earthsea.

Book 3 of the Earthsea series

☐ *The Dark Is Rising*
by Susan Cooper

1974 Newbery Honor Book

On his 11th birthday Will Stanton discovers that he is the last of the Old Ones, destined to seek the six magical Signs that will enable the Old Ones to triumph over the evil forces of the Dark.

Book 2 of The Dark Is Rising series

Funny Fantasy
The Phantom Tollbooth

The Reluctant Dragon
by Kenneth Grahame

The boy who finds the dragon in the cave knows it is a kindly, harmless one, but how can he convince the frightened villagers, and especially St. George the dragonkiller, that there is no call for concern?

The Chocolate Touch
by Patrick Skene Catling

A boy acquires a magical gift that turns everything his lips touch into chocolate.

Truckers
by Terry Pratchett

Reluctant to believe that there's a world outside the department store where they live, Torrit, Dorcas, and the other nomes look to Masklin, a newly arrived "outsider," to lead them to a safe haven when the store goes out of business.
Book 1 of the Bromeliad

Bunnicula
by Deborah and James Howe

Though scoffed at by Harold the dog, Chester the cat tries to warn his human family that their foundling baby bunny must be a vampire.
First of a series

Charlie and the Chocolate Factory
by Roald Dahl

Each of five children lucky enough to discover an entry ticket into Mr. Willy Wonka's mysterious chocolate factory takes advantage of the situation in his or her own way.
Sequel: *Charlie and the Great Glass Elevator*

Humans and Animals
The Phantom Tollbooth

The Voyages of Doctor Dolittle
by Hugh Lofting
1923 Newbery Medal

The adventures of a kind-hearted doctor, who is fond of animals and understands their language, as he travels to Africa with some of his favorite pets to cure the monkeys of a terrible sickness.

No Flying in the House
by Betty Brock

A mysterious girl and her miniature talking dog come to live with a childless old lady.

Oaf
by Julia Cunningham

Eight-year-old Oaf, seeking his fortune with a band of talking animals, seeks to rescue five dwarfs and a dancing fox from their cruel master.

The Fledgling
by Jane Langton

Georgie's fondest hope, to be able to fly, is fleetingly fulfilled when she is befriended by a Canada goose.

The Forgotten Beasts of Eld
by Patricia McKillip

A wizard, accustomed only to the company of great legendary beasts, is introduced to the human world, with all its sorrows and delights, when a baby comes into her care.

The Horse and His Boy
by C. S. Lewis

Bree, a talking horse, and Shasta, a young boy, are joined by a princess and her talking horse to help save Narnia from invasion.
Book 4 of the Chronicles of Narnia

The Planet of Junior Brown

Virginia Hamilton

Emotional Problems
The Boy Who Could Make Himself Disappear
Stargone John
Family of Strangers
Incident at Hawk's Hill
The Catcher in the Rye
Bless the Beasts and Children
There's a Boy in the Girls' Bathroom
I Am the Cheese

**Friends Who Stick by You
in Tough Times**
The Moves Make the Man
The Goats
Number the Stars
A Fine White Dust
The Neverending Story
Afternoon of the Elves

Homeless Kids
Slake's Limbo
Sam and the Moon Queen
Secret City, USA
The Wild Children
Maniac Magee
Chive
The Family Under the Bridge

Black Children in the City
Rite of Passage
The Me Nobody Knows
The Jazz Man
The Shimmershine Queens
Circle of Gold

Secret Places
J. T.
The Velvet Room
The Secret Garden
My Side of the Mountain
Through the Hidden Door
The Chalkbox Kid
Up from Jericho Tel

*The Planet
of
Junior Brown*

Virginia Hamilton

Troubled Young Artists
Goodnight, Mr. Tom
Bridge to Terabithia
The Cartoonist
The Monument
My Name Is Sus5an Smith. The 5 Is Silent
The Broken Bridge
Words of Stone

Great YA Novels
Nothing but the Truth
The Chocolate War
Lord of the Flies
The Outsiders
A Separate Peace
Don't Look and It Won't Hurt
The Pigman

**Taking Responsibility
for Others**
The Indian in the Cupboard
The Shoeshine Girl
The Summer of the Swans
King Matt the First
Shiloh
Stepping on the Cracks
Quest for a Maid

139

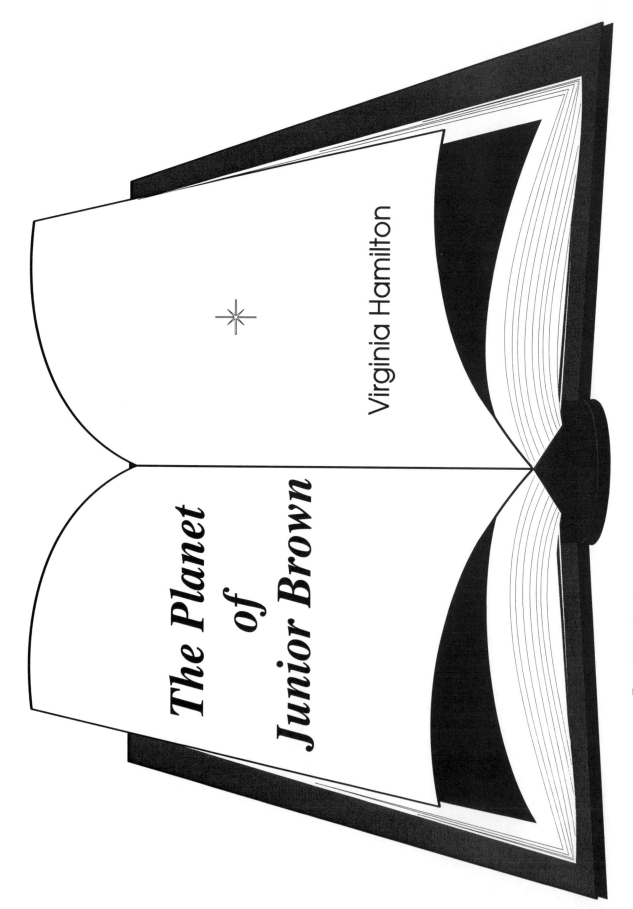

The Planet
of
Junior Brown

Virginia Hamilton

Homeless Kids

Slake's Limbo

Sam and the Moon Queen

Secret City, USA

The Wild Children

Maniac Magee

Chive

The Family Under the Bridge

Emotional Problems

The Boy Who Could Make Himself Disappear

Stargone John

Family of Strangers

Incident at Hawk's Hill

The Catcher in the Rye

Bless the Beasts and Children

There's a Boy in the Girls' Bathroom

I Am the Cheese

Troubled Young Artists

Goodnight, Mr. Tom

Bridge to Terabithia

The Cartoonist

The Monument

My Name Is Sus5an Smith. The 5 Is Silent

The Broken Bridge

Words of Stone

Secret Places

J. T.

The Velvet Room

The Secret Garden

My Side of the Mountain

Through the Hidden Door

The Chalkbox Kid

Up from Jericho Tel

Taking Responsibility for Others

The Indian in the Cupboard

The Shoeshine Girl

The Summer of the Swans

King Matt the First

Shiloh

Stepping on the Cracks

Quest for a Maid

Friends Who Stick by You in Tough Times

The Moves Make the Man

The Goats

Number the Stars

A Fine White Dust

The Neverending Story

Afternoon of the Elves

Great YA Novels

Nothing but the Truth

The Chocolate War

Lord of the Flies

The Outsiders

A Separate Peace

Don't Look and It Won't Hurt

The Pigman

Black Children in the City

Rite of Passage

The Me Nobody Knows

The Jazz Man

The Shimmershine Queens

Circle of Gold

Homeless Kids
The Planet of Junior Brown

☐ *Slake's Limbo*
by Felice Holman

Thirteen-year-old Aremis Slake, hounded by his fears and misfortunes, flees into New York City's subway tunnels.

☐ *Sam and the Moon Queen*
by Alison Cragin Herzig and Jane Lawrence Mali

Sympathetic to a homeless girl's plight, Sam tries to help her find food for herself and medical aid for her dog.

☐ *Secret City, USA*
by Felice Holman

Against all odds, Benno and his friends in the ghetto turn an abandoned house into a shelter for the homeless.

☐ *The Wild Children*
by Felice Holman

Left behind when his family is arrested during the Bolshevik Revolution, Alex falls in with a gang of other desperate homeless children.

☐ *Maniac Magee*
by Jerry Spinelli

1991 Newbery Medal

After his parents die, Jeffrey Lionel Magee's life becomes legendary, as he accomplishes athletic and other feats.

☐ *Chive*
by Shelley A. Barre

Eleven-year-old Chive, homeless because his parents have lost their farm, strikes up an unusual friendship with 11-year-old Terry.

☐ *The Family Under the Bridge*
by Natalie Savage Carlson

1959 Newbery Honor Book

An old tramp is adopted by three fatherless children when their mother hides them under a bridge.

Emotional Problems
The Planet of Junior Brown

☐ *The Boy Who Could Make Himself Disappear*
by Kin Platt

A 12-year-old boy with a speech defect gradually withdraws into schizophrenia after moving to live with his mother following the divorce of his harsh and detached parents.

☐ *Stargone John*
by Ellen Kindt McKenzie

Six-year-old John is emotionally withdrawn until an old retired teacher reaches out from her blindness.

☐ *Family of Strangers*
by Susan Beth Pfeffer

PG language

Sixteen-year-old Abby is growing desperate in a family consisting of parents who seem devoid of love, and a self-destructive sister.

☐ *Incident at Hawk's Hill*
by Allan W. Eckert

1972 Newbery Honor Book

A shy, lonely six-year-old spends a summer under the protection of a badger.

☐ *The Catcher in the Rye*
by J. D. Salinger

About to be kicked out of school, Holden Caulfield embarks on a journey of self-discovery.

☐ *Bless the Beasts and Children*
by Glendon Swarthout

A group of disturbed boys searches for a way to improve their lives.

☐ *There's a Boy in the Girls' Bathroom*
by Louis Sachar

An unmanageable 11-year-old misfit gets to know the new school counselor, who is a sort of misfit too.

☐ *I Am the Cheese*
by Robert Cormier

A boy tries to unlock his past, yet knows he must hide those memories if he is to remain alive.

Troubled Young Artists
The Planet of Junior Brown

☐ *Goodnight, Mr. Tom*
by Michelle Magorian

A battered child learns to embrace life when he is adopted by an old man in the English countryside.

☐ *Bridge to Terabithia*
by Katherine Paterson

1978 Newbery Medal

The life of a 10-year-old boy expands when he becomes friends with a newcomer.

☐ *The Cartoonist*
by Betsy Byars

Threatened with the loss of his private place in the attic, a young boy determines to keep it at all costs.

☐ *The Monument*
by Gary Paulsen

Thirteen-year-old Rocky has her life changed by the remarkable artist who comes to her small town to design a war memorial.

☐ *My Name Is Sus5an Smith. The 5 Is Silent*
by Louise Plummer

After years spent idolizing and championing her long-absent and much-reviled uncle Willy, 17-year-old Susan meets him by chance in Boston.

☐ *The Broken Bridge*
by Philip Pullman

Sixteen-year-old Ginny, the artist daughter of an English father and a Haitian mother, learns that her mother may still be alive.

☐ *Words of Stone*
by Kevin Henkes

Busy trying to deal with his troubled feelings for his dead mother, 10-year-old Blaze has his life changed when he meets the boisterous and irresistible Joselle.

Secret Places
The Planet of Junior Brown

☐ *J. T.*
by Jane Wagner

J. T. begins to change when he discovers there is more satisfaction in caring for an injured cat than in listening to a stolen transistor radio.

☐ *The Velvet Room*
by Zilpha Keatley Snyder

Robin finds a haven from the world and the confusion she feels in the velvet room of the deserted McGurdy mansion.

☐ *The Secret Garden*
by Frances Hodgson Burnett

A boy who has lived as a spoiled invalid regains his health when he and his orphaned cousin restore a once lovely garden.

☐ *My Side of the Mountain*
by Jean Craighead George

1960 Newbery Honor Book

Young Sam Gribley leaves New York City and spends a year living by himself in a remote area of the Catskill Mountains.

Sequel: *On the Far Side of the Mountain*

☐ *Through the Hidden Door*
by Rosemary Wells

Two young boys stumble upon the remains of an ancient underground mystery civilization.

☐ *The Chalkbox Kid*
by Clyde Robert Bulla

Nine-year-old Gregory's house does not have room for a garden, but he creates a surprising and very different garden in an unusual place.

☐ *Up from Jericho Tel*
by E. L. Konigsburg

The spirit of a dead actress turns two children invisible and sends them out among a group of street performers to search for a missing necklace.

Black Children in the City
The Planet of Junior Brown

❑ *Rite of Passage*
by Richard Wright
PG language

When 15-year-old Johnny Gibbs is told that he is really a foster child, he runs off into the streets of Harlem and meets up with a gang that wants him to participate in a mugging.

❑ *The Me Nobody Knows*
Stephen M. Joseph, ed.
Poems by children of the ghetto.

❑ *The Jazz Man*
by Mary Hays Weik
1967 Newbery Honor Book

Zeke spends a lot of time watching his neighbor, a jazz pianist, through the window, until he is abandoned by his parents.

❑ *The Shimmershine Queens*
by Camille Yarbrough

Two fifth-graders try to lift themselves and their classmates out of a less-than-beautiful urban present by encouraging dreams and the desire to achieve them.

❑ *Circle of Gold*
by Candy Dawson Boyd

Mattie is determined to get her mother a beautiful gold pin for Mother's Day, even though she has not saved enough money and has just lost her job.

Great YA Novels
The Planet of Junior Brown

❑ *Nothing but the Truth*
by Avi
1992 Newbery Honor Book

A ninth-grader's suspension for singing "The Star Spangled Banner" during homeroom becomes a national news story.

❑ *The Chocolate War*
by Robert Cormier

A high school freshman discovers the devastating consequences of arousing the wrath of the school bullies.
Sequel: *Beyond the Chocolate War*

❑ *Lord of the Flies*
by William Golding

Stranded on an island, a group of young boys reverts to savagery as they struggle to survive.

❑ *The Outsiders*
by S. E. Hinton

The struggle of three brothers to stay together after their parents' deaths.

❑ *A Separate Peace*
by John Knowles

Gene and Phineas's friendship is marred by Finny's crippling fall, an event for which Gene is responsible and one that eventually leads to tragedy.

❑ *Don't Look and It Won't Hurt*
by Richard Peck

A teenage girl struggles to understand her place within her family and the world.

❑ *The Pigman*
by Paul Zindel

Two high school sophomores from unhappy homes form a close friendship with a lonely old man with a terrible secret.

Friends Who Stick by You in Tough Times
The Planet of Junior Brown

❑ *The Moves Make the Man*
by Bruce Brooks
1985 Newbery Honor Book

A black boy and an emotionally troubled white boy form a precarious friendship.

❑ *The Goats*
by Brock Cole

A boy and a girl form an uneasy bond that grows into a deep friendship when they decide to run away.

❑ *Number the Stars*
by Lois Lowry
1990 Newbery Medal

In 1943, during the German occupation of Denmark, 10-year-old Annemarie learns how to be brave and courageous when she helps shelter her Jewish friend from the Nazis.

❑ *A Fine White Dust*
by Cynthia Rylant
1987 Newbery Honor Book

The visit of the traveling Preacher Man gives new impetus to 13-year-old Peter's struggle to reconcile his own deeply felt religious belief with the beliefs and nonbeliefs of his family and friends.

❑ *The Neverending Story*
by Michael Ende

Bastian, a lonely, solitary boy, steps through the pages of a book into a special kingdom where he learns the true measure of his courage and creates a new world with his wishes.

❑ *Afternoon of the Elves*
by Janet Taylor Lisle
1990 Newbery Honor Book

As Hillary works in the miniature village in Sara-Kate's backyard, she becomes curious about Sara-Kate's real life inside her big, gloomy house with her mysterious, silent mother.

Taking Responsibility for Others
The Planet of Junior Brown

❑ *The Indian in the Cupboard*
by Lynne Reid Banks

A nine-year-old boy finds himself involved in adventure when a plastic Indian comes to life.
Book 1 of the Indian in the Cupboard series

❑ *The Shoeshine Girl*
by Clyde Robert Bulla

Ten-year-old Sarah Ida gets a job at a shoeshine stand and learns a great many things besides shining shoes.

❑ *The Summer of the Swans*
by Betsy Byars
1971 Newbery Medal

A teenage girl gains new insight into herself and her family when her mentally retarded brother gets lost.

❑ *King Matt the First*
by Janusz Korczak

A child king introduces reforms to give children the same rights as adults.

❑ *Shiloh*
by Phyllis Reynolds Naylor
1992 Newbery Medal

When he finds a lost beagle, Marty tries to hide it from the dog's real owner, a mean-spirited man known to mistreat his dogs.

❑ *Stepping on the Cracks*
by Mary Downing Hahn

Eleven-year-old Margaret gets a new view of the school bully when she finds him hiding his brother, an army deserter.

❑ *Quest for a Maid*
by Frances Mary Hendry

Meg realizes she must protect the young Norwegian princess who has been chosen as rightful heir to the Scottish throne from those, including Meg's sorceress sister, who plot the princess's death.

The Secret Garden

Frances Hodgson Burnett

Other Books by Frances Hodgson Burnett
Little Lord Fauntleroy
A Little Princess
The Lost Prince

Orphans Who Change Other People's Lives
Pollyanna
Anne of Green Gables
Trial Valley
Come to the Edge
Lost Magic
Sir Gibbie
Maniac Magee

19th-Century England
Black Beauty
The December Rose
The Case of the Baker Street Irregular
Black Hearts in Battersea

The Power of Gardens and Working Outdoors
Miracles on Maple Hill
The Chalkbox Kid
J. T.
Afternoon of the Elves
Lost Magic

Spoiled Kids
Captains Courageous
Macaroon
The Whipping Boy
The Voyage of the Dawn Treader
Shoebag

The Secret Garden

Frances Hodgson Burnett

Rural England
The Railway Children
The Children of Green Knowe
Swallows and Amazons
Goodnight, Mr. Tom
The Hollow Land
The Stone Book Quartet
Badger on the Barge

Boy-Girl Friendship
Bridge to Terabithia
The Goats
Cricket and the Crackerbox Kid
The Broccoli Tapes
Words of Stone

Kids Who Change Lives
Hazel Rye
Sam and the Moon Queen
Secret City, USA
Bel-Air Bambi and the Mall Rats
The Thanksgiving Treasure
Luke's Garden and *Gramp*

Secret Places
The Moves Make the Man
My Side of the Mountain
The Planet of Junior Brown
From the Mixed-Up Files of Mrs. Basil E. Frankweiler
Up from Jericho Tel
Through the Hidden Door

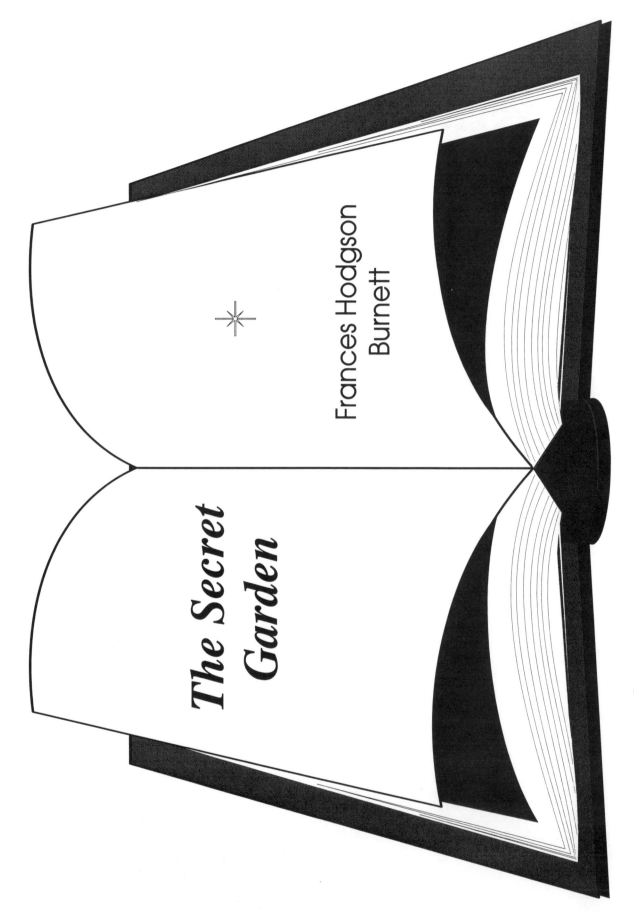

The Secret Garden

Frances Hodgson Burnett

Orphans Who Change Other People's Lives

Pollyanna

Anne of Green Gables

Trial Valley

Come to the Edge

Lost Magic

Sir Gibbie

Maniac Magee

Kids Who Change Lives

Hazel Rye

Sam and the Moon Queen

Secret City, USA

Bel-Air Bambi and the Mall Rats

The Thanksgiving Treasure

Luke's Garden and *Gramp*

The Power of Gardens and Working Outdoors

Miracles on Maple Hill

The Chalkbox Kid

J. T.

Afternoon of the Elves

Lost Magic

Rural England

The Railway Children

The Children of Green Knowe

Swallows and Amazons

Goodnight, Mr. Tom

The Hollow Land

The Stone Book Quartet

Badger on the Barge

Boy-Girl Friendship

Bridge to Terabithia

The Goats

Cricket and the Crackerbox Kid

The Broccoli Tapes

Words of Stone

Secret Places

The Moves Make the Man

My Side of the Mountain

The Planet of Junior Brown

From the Mixed-Up Files of Mrs. Basil E. Frankweiler

Up from Jericho Tel

Through the Hidden Door

Spoiled Kids

Captains Courageous

Macaroon

The Whipping Boy

The Voyage of the Dawn Treader

Shoebag

19th-Century England

Black Beauty

The December Rose

The Case of the Baker Street Irregular

Black Hearts in Battersea

Other Books by Frances Hodgson Burnett

Little Lord Fauntleroy

A Little Princess

The Lost Prince

Rural England
The Secret Garden

☐ *The Railway Children*
by E. Nesbit

When their father is taken away, three children move to the country, where they stay busy saving the train from accidents.

☐ *The Children of Green Knowe*
by L. M. Boston

Tolly becomes friends with three children who lived in the 17th century.

☐ *Swallows and Amazons*
by Arthur Ransome

Introduces the Walker family, the camp on Wild Cat Island, the able Catboat Swallow, and the two intrepid amazons, Nancy and Peggy.

☐ *Goodnight, Mr. Tom*
by Michelle Magorian

A battered child learns to embrace life when he is adopted by an old man.

☐ *The Hollow Land*
by Jane Gardam

Short stories about young Harry, who comes from London year after year to spend the summer at Light Trees Farm.

☐ *The Stone Book Quartet*
by Alan Garner

Four short stories about four generations of an English rural family of stonecutters and smiths.

☐ *Badger on the Barge*
by Janni Howker

A collection of five short stories set in the small towns of northern England.

The Power of Gardens and Working Outdoors
The Secret Garden

☐ *Miracles on Maple Hill*
by Virginia Sorensen
1957 Newbery Medal

Ten-year-old Marly and her family move from the city to grandmother's old Pennsylvania farmhouse, hoping that the outdoor life will restore Father's health.

☐ *The Chalkbox Kid*
by Clyde Robert Bulla

Nine-year-old Gregory's house does not have room for a garden, but he creates a surprising and very different garden in an unusual place.

☐ *J. T.*
by Jane Wagner

J. T. begins to change when he discovers there is more satisfaction in caring for an injured cat than in listening to a stolen transistor radio.

☐ *Afternoon of the Elves*
by Janet Taylor Lisle
1990 Newbery Honor Book

As Hillary works in the miniature village, allegedly built by elves, in Sara-Kate's backyard, she becomes more and more curious about Sara-Kate's real life inside her big, gloomy house with her mysterious, silent mother.

☐ *Lost Magic*
by Berthe Amoss

In the Middle Ages, orphaned Ceridwen learns the art of herbal healing and gains the protection of the local lord until she is accused of witchcraft.

Kids Who Change Lives
The Secret Garden

☐ *Hazel Rye*
by Vera and Bill Cleaver

An 11-year-old girl with no appreciation for land and growing things finds her values beginning to change when she agrees to let an impoverished family live in a small house she owns, in exchange for working in her orange grove.

☐ *Sam and the Moon Queen*
by Alison Cragin Herzig and Jane Lawrence Mali

Sympathetic to a homeless girl's plight, Sam tries to help her find food for herself and medical aid for her dog.

☐ *Secret City, USA*
by Felice Holman

Against all odds, Benno and his friends in the ghetto turn an abandoned house into a shelter for the homeless.

☐ *Bel-Air Bambi and the Mall Rats*
by Richard Peck

Bambi, Buffie, and Brick, three totally cool siblings from Los Angeles, move with their parents to Hickory Fork, a small town terrorized by a high school gang.

☐ *The Thanksgiving Treasure*
by Gail Rock

Addie's Thanksgiving gesture toward a crotchety old man enriches both their lives.
Sequel to *The House Without a Christmas Tree*

☐ *Luke's Garden and Gramp*
by Joan Tate

In one short novel, a boy is destroyed because he is different; in the other, a boy finds a way to make his grandfather feel useful again.

Orphans Who Change Other People's Lives
The Secret Garden

☐ *Pollyanna*
by Eleanor H. Porter

When a 12-year-old orphan comes to live with her austere and wealthy aunt, she brings happiness to the aunt and unloved members of the community.

☐ *Anne of Green Gables*
by L. M. Montgomery

Anne, an 11-year-old orphan, is sent by mistake to live with a lonely, middle-aged brother and sister on a farm.

☐ *Trial Valley*
by Vera and Bill Cleaver

The Luther children, who have raised themselves since their father's death, find an abandoned boy.
Sequel to *Where the Lilies Bloom*

☐ *Come to the Edge*
by Julia Cunningham

A confused runaway is befriended by a sign painter.

☐ *Lost Magic*
by Berthe Amoss

In the Middle Ages, orphaned Ceridwen learns the art of healing until she is accused of witchcraft.

☐ *Sir Gibbie*
by George MacDonald

After his father's tragic death and after witnessing a violent murder, Gibbie finds his life changed.
Also called *The Baronet's Song*

☐ *Maniac Magee*
by Jerry Spinelli
1991 Newbery Medal

After his parents die, Jeffrey Lionel Magee's life becomes legendary, as he accomplishes athletic and other feats that awe his contemporaries.

Boy-Girl Friendship
The Secret Garden

Bridge to Terabithia
by Katherine Paterson

1978 Newbery Medal

The life of a 10-year-old boy expands when he becomes friends with a newcomer, and together they create a secret hideaway, Terabithia.

The Goats
by Brock Cole

Stripped and marooned on a small island by their fellow campers, a boy and a girl form an uneasy bond that grows into a deep friendship when they decide to run away and disappear without a trace.

Cricket and the Crackerbox Kid
by Alane Ferguson

Pampered, 11-year-old rich kid Cricket thinks she has finally found a friend in Dominic, who lives in the low-income houses called crackerboxes, until they quarrel over ownership of a dog, and their classroom becomes a courtroom to decide who is right.

The Broccoli Tapes
by Jan Slepian

During a stay of several months in Hawaii with her family, Sara reports her experiences by tape back to her sixth-grade class in Boston, detailing her adoption of a wild cat, a friendship with a troubled Hawaiian boy, and the death of a beloved grandmother.

Words of Stone
by Kevin Henkes

Busy trying to deal with his many fears and his troubled feelings for his dead mother, 10-year-old Blaze has his life changed when he meets the boisterous and irresistible Joselle.

Secret Places
The Secret Garden

The Moves Make the Man
by Bruce Brooks

1985 Newbery Honor Book

A black boy and an emotionally troubled white boy in North Carolina form a precarious friendship.

My Side of the Mountain
by Jean Craighead George

1960 Newbery Honor Book

Young Sam Gribley leaves New York City and spends a year living by himself in a remote area of the Catskill Mountains.

Sequel: *On the Far Side of the Mountain*

The Planet of Junior Brown
by Virginia Hamilton

1972 Newbery Honor Book

Already a leader in New York's underground world of homeless children, Buddy Clark takes on the responsibility of protecting an overweight, emotionally disturbed friend.

From the Mixed-Up Files of Mrs. Basil E. Frankweiler
by E. L. Konigsburg

1968 Newbery Medal

Two suburban children run away from their Connecticut home and go to New York's Metropolitan Museum of Art, where their ingenuity enables them to live in luxury.

Up from Jericho Tel
by E. L. Konigsburg

The spirit of a dead actress turns two children invisible and sends them out among a group of colorful street performers to search for a missing necklace.

Through the Hidden Door
by Rosemary Wells

Two young boys stumble upon the remains of an ancient underground mystery civilization.

Spoiled Kids
The Secret Garden

Captains Courageous
by Rudyard Kipling

Harvey Cheyne, the spoiled son of an American millionaire, is saved from drowning by a New England fishing schooner and must share the hard life and labor of the crew to prove his worth to the captain and crew.

Macaroon
by Julia Cunningham

A raccoon decides to spend the winter in a child's warm home—a disagreeable child, so that his departure in the spring will not be regretted—but he selects such a nasty, spoiled little girl that he can't help trying to reform her.

The Whipping Boy
by Sid Fleischman

1987 Newbery Medal

A bratty prince and his whipping boy have many adventures when they inadvertently trade places after becoming involved with dangerous outlaws.

The Voyage of the Dawn Treader
by C. S. Lewis

Lucy and Edmund, accompanied by their peevish cousin Eustace, sail to the magic land of Narnia, where Eustace is temporarily transformed into a green dragon because of his selfish behavior and skepticism.

Book 3 of the Chronicles of Narnia

Shoebag
by Mary James

Shoebag, a happy cockroach who finds himself suddenly changed into a little boy, changes the lives of those around him before returning to his former life as an insect.

19th-Century England
The Secret Garden

Black Beauty
by Anna Sewell

A horse in 19th-century England recounts his experiences with both good and bad masters.

The December Rose
by Leon Garfield

A young sweep's fall down the wrong chimney lands him in the center of espionage, treachery, and murder.

The Case of the Baker Street Irregular
by Robert Newman

A young boy seeks the help of Sherlock Holmes when his tutor is kidnapped and he himself is threatened with the same fate.

Black Hearts in Battersea
by Joan Aiken

An orphan arrives in London and becomes embroiled in a plot against the king.

Part of the Wolves of Willoughby Chase series

Other Books by
Frances Hodgson Burnett
The Secret Garden

📖*Little Lord Fauntleroy*
A Brooklyn boy discovers that he is the heir to an earldom and a fortune and goes to live with his bad-tempered, selfish, and cantankerous grandfather.

📖📖*A Little Princess*
Sara Crewe is left in poverty when her father dies, but is later rescued by a mysterious benefactor.

A shorter version is called *Sarah Crewe.*

📖*The Lost Prince*
The lost prince is coming home to rule his people. Now Marco is to cross Europe with his friend The Rat, disguised as beggar boys, to bear the great message.

Shiloh

Phyllis Reynolds Naylor

Taking Responsibility for Another Living Being
The Indian in the Cupboard
One-Eyed Cat
Stepping on the Cracks
The Planet of Junior Brown
Quest for a Maid

Boys and Their Dogs
Strider
Sounder
Stone Fox
Old Yeller
Where the Red Fern Grows
The Dog Who Wouldn't Be
Aldo Peanut Butter

Virginia and West Virginia
Bridge to Terabithia
Park's Quest
A Blue-Eyed Daisy
Missing May
Our Mountain
Shadows
Misty of Chincoteague

Good Intentions Go Awry
Finding Buck McHenry
Maniac Magee
King Matt the First
The Neverending Story
Give Us a Great Big Smile, Rosy Cole
The Giver

Arguments over Ownership
Cricket and the Crackerbox Kid
Henry Huggins
Toad Food and Measle Soup

Shiloh

Phyllis Reynolds Naylor

Deciding What's Right
Weasel
Stepping on the Cracks
A Kind of Thief
Nothing but the Truth
On My Honor

Honesty
The Hundred Dresses
The Bandit of Mok Hill
Sam, Bangs, and Moonshine
Liars
Circle of Gold
Jennifer, Hecate, Macbeth, William McKinley, and Me, Elizabeth

Mistreated Animals
Poor Badger
Black Beauty
The Call of the Wild
Oaf

Kids Fighting Mean Adults
The Light in the Forest
On the Far Side of the Mountain
Sport
Circle of Fire
Emil and the Detectives
The Flight of the Doves
Matilda

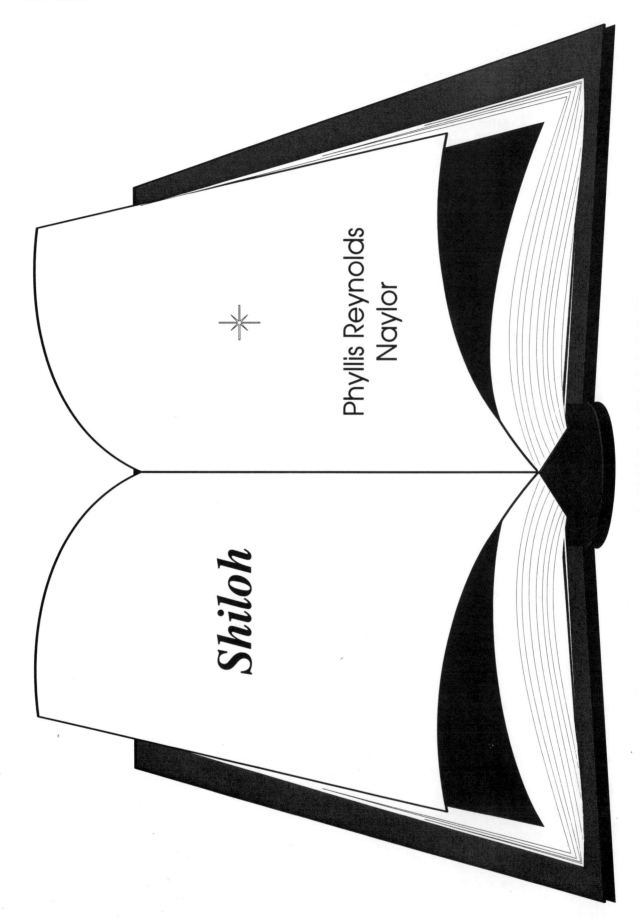

Shiloh

Phyllis Reynolds Naylor

Good Intentions Go Awry

Finding Buck McHenry

Maniac Magee

King Matt the First

The Neverending Story

*Give Us a Great Big
Smile, Rosy Cole*

The Giver

Virginia and West Virginia

Bridge to Terabithia

Park's Quest

A Blue-Eyed Daisy

Missing May

*Our Mountain
Shadows*

Misty of Chincoteague

Mistreated Animals

Poor Badger

Black Beauty

The Call of the Wild

Oaf

Arguments over Ownership

*Cricket and
the Crackerbox Kid*

Henry Huggins

*Toad Food
and Measle Soup*

Boys and Their Dogs

Strider

Sounder

Stone Fox

Old Yeller

*Where the Red
Fern Grows*

The Dog Who Wouldn't Be

Aldo Peanut Butter

Honesty

The Hundred Dresses

The Bandit of Mok Hill

*Sam, Bangs, and
Moonshine*

Liars

Circle of Gold

*Jennifer, Hecate, Mac-
beth, William McKinley,
and Me, Elizabeth*

Deciding What's Right

Weasel

Stepping on the Cracks

A Kind of Thief

Nothing but the Truth

On My Honor

Kids Fighting Mean Adults

The Light in the Forest

*On the Far Side of
the Mountain*

Sport

Circle of Fire

Emil and the Detectives

The Flight of the Doves

Matilda

Taking Responsibility for Another Living Being

*The Indian in the
Cupboard*

One-Eyed Cat

Stepping on the Cracks

*The Planet of Junior
Brown*

Quest for a Maid

Good Intentions Go Awry
Shiloh

Finding Buck McHenry
by Alfred Slote

Eleven-year-old Jason, believing the school custodian, Mack Henry, to be Buck McHenry, a famous pitcher from the old Negro League, tries to enlist him as a coach for his Little League team by revealing his identity to the world.

Maniac Magee
by Jerry Spinelli

1991 Newbery Medal

After his parents die, Jeffrey Lionel Magee's life becomes legendary, as he accomplishes athletic and other feats that awe his contemporaries.

King Matt the First
by Janusz Korczak

A child king introduces reforms to give children the same rights as adults.

The Neverending Story
by Michael Ende

The magical tale of Bastian, a lonely, solitary boy who steps through the pages of a book into a special kingdom where he learns the true measure of his courage and creates a new world with his wishes.

Give Us a Great Big Smile, Rosy Cole
by Sheila Greenwald

When Uncle Ralph gets out his camera, determined to make Rosy and her violin his next book, Rosy's troubles begin.

The Giver
by Lois Lowry

1994 Newbery Medal

Jonas becomes the receiver of memories shared by only one other and discovers the terrible truth about the society in which he lives.

Virginia and West Virginia
Shiloh

Bridge to Terabithia
by Katherine Paterson

1978 Newbery Medal

The life of a 10-year-old boy in rural Virginia expands when he becomes friends with a newcomer.

Park's Quest
by Katherine Paterson

Eleven-year-old Park makes some startling discoveries when he travels to his grandfather's farm to learn about his father, who died in the Vietnam War.

A Blue-Eyed Daisy
by Cynthia Rylant

Relates episodes in the life of 11-year-old Ellie and her family, who live in a coal mining town in West Virginia.

Missing May
by Cynthia Rylant

After the death of the beloved aunt who has raised her, 12-year-old Summer and her uncle Ob leave their West Virginia trailer in search of the strength to go on living.

Our Mountain
by Ellen Harvey Showell

Two brothers living in the mountains describe their family, home, and favorite pastimes.

Shadows
by Dennis Haseley

Jamie's lonely life with his aunt and uncle in rural West Virginia changes when Grandpa comes to visit.

Misty of Chincoteague
by Marguerite Henry

1948 Newbery Honor Book

Two children's determination to own a Chincoteague pony is greatly increased when the Phantom and her colt are among those rounded up for the yearly auction.

Many sequels

Mistreated Animals
Shiloh

Poor Badger
by K. M. Peyton

Having become passionately devoted to a pony who is being mistreated by his owner, nine-year-old Ros decides to steal him in the night.

Black Beauty
by Anna Sewell

A horse in 19th-century England recounts his experiences with both good and bad masters.

The Call of the Wild
by Jack London

Buck is stolen from his home and pressed into service as a sled dog, and he becomes the leader of a wolf pack.

Oaf
by Julia Cunningham

Eight-year-old Oaf seeks to rescue five dwarfs and a dancing fox from their cruel master.

Arguments over Ownership
Shiloh

Cricket and the Crackerbox Kid
by Alane Ferguson

Cricket thinks she has finally found a friend in Dominic, until they quarrel over ownership of a dog, and their classroom becomes a courtroom to decide who is right.

Henry Huggins
by Beverly Cleary

Henry finds a stray dog, but it is a battle to get it home and keep it.

Toad Food and Measle Soup
by Christine McDonnell

Leo finds a lost dog, surprises the class on book report day, and survives his mother's experiments with vegetarian cooking.

Boys and Their Dogs
Shiloh

☐ *Strider*
by Beverly Cleary

In a series of diary entries, Leigh tells how he comes to terms with his parents' divorce, acquires joint custody of an abandoned dog, and joins the track team.
Sequel to *Dear Mr. Henshaw*

☐ *Sounder*
by William H. Armstrong
1970 Newbery Medal

When his sharecropper father is jailed for stealing food for his family, a young black boy grows in courage and understanding with the help of the dog Sounder and learns to read and write.
Sequel: *Sourland*

☐ *Stone Fox*
by John R. Gardiner

Little Willie hopes to pay the back taxes on his grandfather's farm with the purse from a dogsled race he enters.

☐ *Old Yeller*
by Fred Gipson
1957 Newbery Honor Book

In the late 1860s, a big yellow dog and a 14-year-old boy form a close, loving relationship.

☐ *Where the Red Fern Grows*
by Wilson Rawls

The adventures of a 10-year-old boy and the two dogs he bought with money he had earned.

☐ *The Dog Who Wouldn't Be*
by Farley Mowat

The author's boyhood experiences with his dog Mutt and two pet owls.

☐ *Aldo Peanut Butter*
by Johanna Hurwitz

Peanut and Butter, two dogs Aldo gets for his 11th birthday, create chaos inside the house while his parents are out of town.

Honesty
Shiloh

☐ *The Hundred Dresses*
by Eleanor Estes
1945 Newbery Honor Book

In winning a medal she is no longer there to receive, a tight-lipped girl teaches her classmates a lesson.

☐ *The Bandit of Mok Hill*
by Evelyn Sibley Lampman

Twelve-year-old Angel Palma leaves his life among the street orphans of early San Francisco to travel to the gold fields, and looks for an old friend who has become a renowned bandit.

☐ *Sam, Bangs, and Moonshine*
by Evaline Ness
1967 Caldecott Medal

Relates the experiences of a little girl as she learns to tell the difference between make-believe and real life.

☐ *Liars*
by P. J. Petersen

Life in a remote town is boring for eighth-grader Sam until his newly awakened ability to tell when a person is lying involves him in a series of mysterious events.

☐ *Circle of Gold*
by Candy Dawson Boyd

Mattie is determined to get her mother a beautiful gold pin for Mother's Day, even though she has not saved enough money and has just lost her job.

☐ *Jennifer, Hecate, Macbeth, William McKinley, and Me, Elizabeth*
by E. L. Konigsburg

Elizabeth is very lonely until she meets Jennifer, who claims to be a witch and who teaches Elizabeth to become a witch herself.

Deciding What's Right
Shiloh

☐ *Weasel*
by Cynthia DeFelice

Alone in the frontier wilderness in the winter of 1839 while his father is recovering from an injury, 11-year-old Nathan runs afoul of the renegade killer known as Weasel and makes a surprising discovery about the concept of revenge.

☐ *Stepping on the Cracks*
by Mary Downing Hahn

Eleven-year-old Margaret gets a new view of the school bully Gordy when she finds him hiding his brother, an army deserter.

☐ *A Kind of Thief*
by Vivien Alcock

When her father is arrested and put into prison, 13-year-old Elinor finds that she has to face many unpleasant truths about him.

☐ *Nothing but the Truth*
by Avi
1992 Newbery Honor Book

A ninth-grader's suspension for singing "The Star Spangled Banner" during homeroom becomes a national news story.

☐ *On My Honor*
by Marian Dane Bauer
1987 Newbery Honor Book

When his best friend drowns while they are both swimming in a treacherous river that they had promised never to go near, Joel is devastated and terrified at having to tell both sets of parents.

Kids Fighting Mean Adults
Shiloh

☐ *The Light in the Forest*
by Conrad Richter

After being raised as an Indian, John Butler is forcibly returned to his white parents.

☐ *On the Far Side of the Mountain*
by Jean Craighead George

Sam's peaceful existence in his wilderness home is disrupted when his pet falcon is confiscated by a conservation officer.
Sequel to *My Side of the Mountain*

☐ *Sport*
by Louise Fitzhugh

Eleven-year-old Sport lives happily with his absentminded father, but his ruthless and wealthy mother suddenly wants custody of him.

☐ *Circle of Fire*
by William Hooks

Eleven-year-old Harrison overhears a notorious local bigot planning a Ku Klux Klan raid on a band of Irish tinkers.

☐ *Emil and the Detectives*
by Erich Kastner

A German boy and his friends use their ingenuity to catch a thief.

☐ *The Flight of the Doves*
by Walter Macken

A 12-year-old English boy and his seven-year-old sister run away from their abusive stepfather and set out to reach their grandmother in western Ireland.

☐ *Matilda*
by Roald Dahl

Matilda applies her untapped mental powers to rid the school of the evil, child-hating headmistress, Miss Trunchbull.

Taking Responsibility for Another Living Being

Shiloh

☐ *The Indian in the Cupboard*
by Lynne Reid Banks

A nine-year-old boy receives a plastic Indian for his birthday and finds himself involved in adventure when the Indian comes to life.

Book 1 of the Indian in the Cupboard series

☐ *One-Eyed Cat*
by Paula Fox

1985 Newbery Honor Book

An 11-year-old shoots a stray cat with his new air rifle, subsequently suffers from guilt, and eventually assumes responsibility for it.

☐ *Stepping on the Cracks*
by Mary Downing Hahn

In 1944, while her brother is overseas fighting in World War II, 11-year-old Margaret gets a new view of the school bully Gordy when she finds him hiding his own brother, an army deserter, and decides to help him.

☐ *The Planet of Junior Brown*
by Virginia Hamilton

1972 Newbery Honor Book

Already a leader in New York's underground world of homeless children, eighth-grader Buddy Clark takes on the responsibility of protecting the overweight, emotionally disturbed friend with whom he has been playing hooky all semester.

☐ *Quest for a Maid*
by Frances Mary Hendry

Meg realizes she must protect the young Norwegian princess who has been chosen as rightful heir to the Scottish throne from those, including Meg's sorceress sister, who plot the princess's death.

Shoebag

Mary James

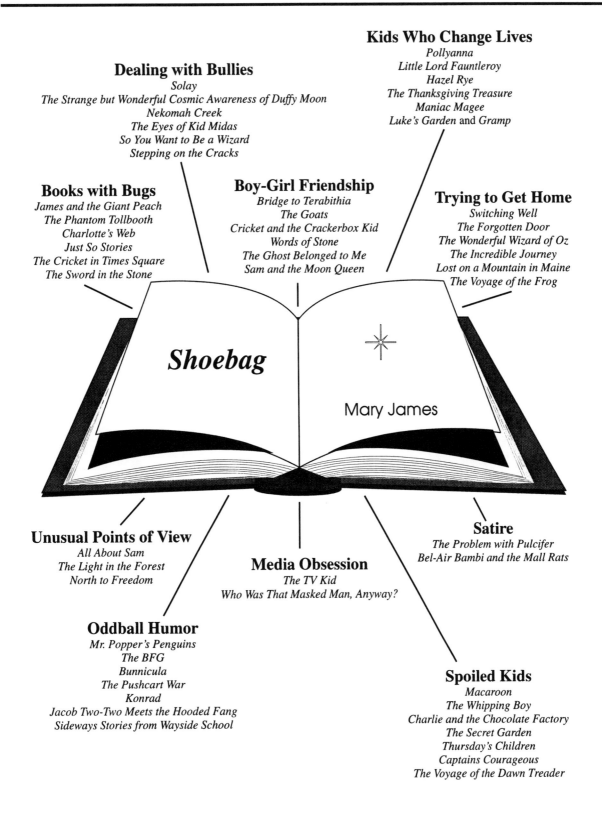

Kids Who Change Lives
Pollyanna
Little Lord Fauntleroy
Hazel Rye
The Thanksgiving Treasure
Maniac Magee
Luke's Garden and *Gramp*

Dealing with Bullies
Solay
The Strange but Wonderful Cosmic Awareness of Duffy Moon
Nekomah Creek
The Eyes of Kid Midas
So You Want to Be a Wizard
Stepping on the Cracks

Books with Bugs
James and the Giant Peach
The Phantom Tollbooth
Charlotte's Web
Just So Stories
The Cricket in Times Square
The Sword in the Stone

Boy-Girl Friendship
Bridge to Terabithia
The Goats
Cricket and the Crackerbox Kid
Words of Stone
The Ghost Belonged to Me
Sam and the Moon Queen

Trying to Get Home
Switching Well
The Forgotten Door
The Wonderful Wizard of Oz
The Incredible Journey
Lost on a Mountain in Maine
The Voyage of the Frog

Shoebag

Mary James

Unusual Points of View
All About Sam
The Light in the Forest
North to Freedom

Media Obsession
The TV Kid
Who Was That Masked Man, Anyway?

Satire
The Problem with Pulcifer
Bel-Air Bambi and the Mall Rats

Oddball Humor
Mr. Popper's Penguins
The BFG
Bunnicula
The Pushcart War
Konrad
Jacob Two-Two Meets the Hooded Fang
Sideways Stories from Wayside School

Spoiled Kids
Macaroon
The Whipping Boy
Charlie and the Chocolate Factory
The Secret Garden
Thursday's Children
Captains Courageous
The Voyage of the Dawn Treader

157

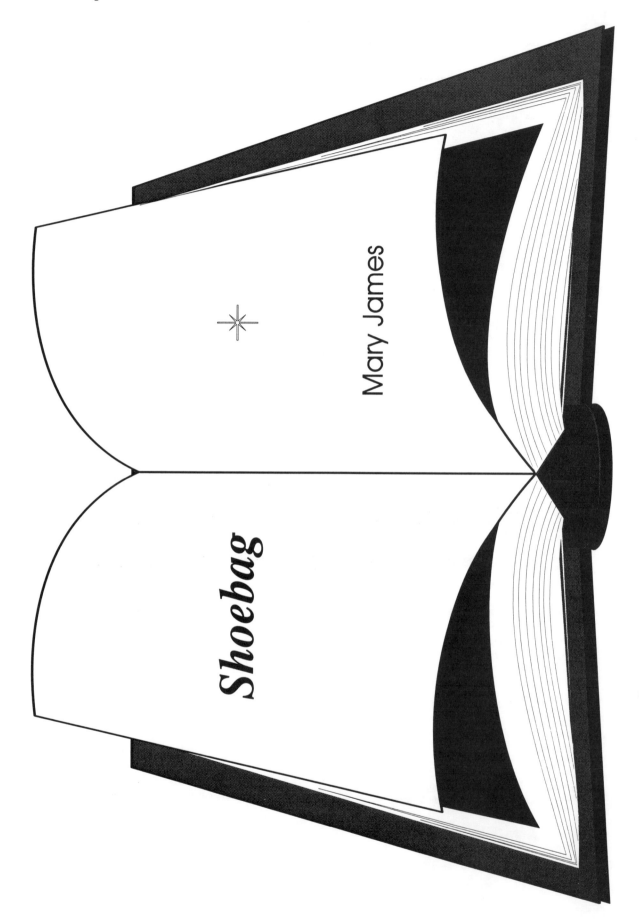

Shoebag

Mary James

Books with Bugs

James and the Giant Peach

The Phantom Tollbooth

Charlotte's Web

Just So Stories

The Cricket in Times Square

The Sword in the Stone

Spoiled Kids

Macaroon

The Whipping Boy

Charlie and the Chocolate Factory

The Secret Garden

Thursday's Children

Captains Courageous

The Voyage of the Dawn Treader

Trying to Get Home

Switching Well

The Forgotten Door

The Wonderful Wizard of Oz

The Incredible Journey

Lost on a Mountain in Maine

The Voyage of the Frog

Media Obsession

The TV Kid

Who Was That Masked Man, Anyway?

Satire

The Problem with Pulcifer

Bel-Air Bambi and the Mall Rats

Unusual Points of View

All About Sam

The Light in the Forest

North to Freedom

Dealing with Bullies

Solay

The Strange but Wonderful Cosmic Awareness of Duffy Moon

Nekomah Creek

The Eyes of Kid Midas

So You Want to Be a Wizard

Stepping on the Cracks

Kids Who Change Lives

Pollyanna

Little Lord Fauntleroy

Hazel Rye

The Thanksgiving Treasure

Maniac Magee

Luke's Garden and *Gramp*

Boy-Girl Friendship

Bridge to Terabithia

The Goats

Cricket and the Crackerbox Kid

Words of Stone

The Ghost Belonged to Me

Sam and the Moon Queen

Oddball Humor

Mr. Popper's Penguins

The BFG

Bunnicula

The Pushcart War

Konrad

*Jacob Two-Two Meets the
Hooded Fang*

*Sideways Stories from
Wayside School*

Media Obsession
Shoebag

☐ *The TV Kid*
by Betsy Byars

To escape failure, boredom, and loneliness, a young boy plunges into the world of television.

☐ *Who Was That Masked Man, Anyway?*
by Avi

Sixth-grader Frankie Wattleson gets in trouble at home and at school because of his preoccupation with his favorite radio programs.

Trying to Get Home
Shoebag

☐ *Switching Well*
by Peni R. Griffin

Two 12-year-old girls—Ada in 1891 and Amber in 1991—switch places and try desperately to return to their own times.

☐ *The Forgotten Door*
by Alexander Key

John has fallen through a forgotten door to the strange planet Earth and is in great danger. Soon the family who befriends him is in great danger too. Time is running out. He must find the secret passage quickly or he may never get home.

☐ *The Wonderful Wizard of Oz*
by L. Frank Baum

After a cyclone transports her to the land of Oz, Dorothy must seek out the great wizard.
Many sequels

☐ *The Incredible Journey*
by Sheila Burnford

A Siamese cat, an old bull terrier, and a young Labrador retriever travel together 250 miles through the wilderness to find their family.

☐ *Lost on a Mountain in Maine*
by Donn Fendler as told to Joseph B. Egan

A 12-year-old describes his nine-day struggle to survive after being separated from his companions in the mountains of Maine in 1939.

☐ *The Voyage of the Frog*
by Gary Paulsen

David is caught in a fierce storm in a sailboat and must survive on his own.

Spoiled Kids
Shoebag

☐ *Macaroon*
by Julia Cunningham

A raccoon decides to spend the winter in a disagreeable child's home, so that his departure in the spring will not be regretted.

☐ *The Whipping Boy*
by Sid Fleischman

1987 Newbery Medal

A bratty prince and his whipping boy have many adventures when they inadvertently trade places.

☐ *Charlie and the Chocolate Factory*
by Roald Dahl

Five children discover an entry ticket into Mr. Willy Wonka's mysterious chocolate factory.
Sequel: *Charlie and the Great Glass Elevator*

☐ *The Secret Garden*
by Frances Hodgson Burnett

A boy who has lived as a spoiled invalid regains his health when he and his orphaned cousin restore a once lovely garden.

☐ *Thursday's Children*
by Rumer Godden

As he tags along to his spoiled sister's ballet classes, Doone discovers his own special talents.

☐ *Captains Courageous*
by Rudyard Kipling

The spoiled son of a millionaire is saved from drowning by a fishing schooner and must share the hard life and labor of the crew.

☐ *The Voyage of the Dawn Treader*
by C. S. Lewis

Lucy and Edmond, accompanied by their peevish cousin Eustace, sail to Narnia, where Eustace is temporarily transformed into a dragon.
Book 3 of the Chronicles of Narnia

Books with Bugs
Shoebag

☐ *James and the Giant Peach*
by Roald Dahl

Wonderful adventures abound after James escapes from his fearful aunts by rolling away inside a giant peach.

☐ *The Phantom Tollbooth*
by Norton Juster

A journey through a land where he learns the importance of words and numbers provides a cure for Milo's boredom.

☐ *Charlotte's Web*
by E. B. White

1953 Newbery Honor Book

Wilbur the pig is desolate when he discovers that he is destined to be the farmer's Christmas dinner, until his spider friend Charlotte decides to help him.

☐ *Just So Stories*
by Rudyard Kipling

A collection of 12 humorous tales about animals and insects that tell how certain things came to be.

☐ *The Cricket in Times Square*
by George Selden

1961 Newbery Honor Book

With the help of a mouse and a cat, a musical cricket improves business at the newsstand run by Mario and his family.

☐ *The Sword in the Stone*
by T. H. White

Wart, as Arthur is called, becomes a wiser, more thoughtful person and a worthy king as a result of Merlin's lessons.

Kids Who Change Lives
Shoebag

☐ *Pollyanna*
by Eleanor H. Porter

When a 12-year-old orphan comes to live with her austere and wealthy aunt Polly, she brings happiness to the aunt and unloved members of the community.

☐ *Little Lord Fauntleroy*
by Frances Hodgson Burnett

A Brooklyn boy discovers that he is the heir to an earldom and goes to live with his bad-tempered and selfish grandfather.

☐ *Hazel Rye*
by Vera and Bill Cleaver

An 11-year-old girl with no appreciation for land and growing things finds her values beginning to change when she agrees to let an impoverished family live in a small house she owns, in exchange for working in her orange grove.

☐ *The Thanksgiving Treasure*
by Gail Rock

Addie's Thanksgiving gesture toward a crotchety old man enriches both their lives.

Sequel to *The House Without a Christmas Tree*

☐ *Maniac Magee*
by Jerry Spinelli

1991 Newbery Medal

After his parents die, Jeffrey Lionel Magee's life becomes legendary, as he accomplishes athletic and other feats that awe his contemporaries.

☐ *Luke's Garden and Gramp*
by Joan Tate

In one short novel, a boy is destroyed because he is different; in the other, a boy finds a way to make his grandfather feel useful again.

Dealing with Bullies
Shoebag

☐ *Solay*
by Mark Jonathan Harris

Ten-year-old Melissa, a favorite target of bullies, gains confidence through her relationship with a visitor from another planet.

☐ *The Strange but Wonderful Cosmic Awareness of Duffy Moon*
by Jean Robinson

Picked on by younger boys, Duffy Moon becomes a student of cosmic awareness and develops talents and powers beyond those he expected.

☐ *Nekomah Creek*
by Linda Crew

Unwanted attention from a counselor and a bully at school makes nine-year-old Robby self-conscious about just how unconventional his family might look to outsiders.

☐ *The Eyes of Kid Midas*
by Neal Shusterman

Kevin is entranced when he finds a pair of sunglasses that turn his desires into reality, but then things start to get out of control.

☐ *So You Want to Be a Wizard*
by Diane Duane

Thirteen-year-old Nita, tormented by a gang of bullies, finds the help she needs in a library book on wizardry.

☐ *Stepping on the Cracks*
by Mary Downing Hahn

In 1944, 11-year-old Margaret gets a new view of the school bully Gordy when she finds him hiding his brother, an army deserter.

Unusual Points of View
Shoebag

☐ *All About Sam*
by Lois Lowry

The adventures of Sam, from his first day as a newborn through his mischievous times as a toddler.

☐ *The Light in the Forest*
by Conrad Richter

After being raised as an Indian for 11 years, John Butler is forcibly returned to his white parents.

☐ *North to Freedom*
by Anne Holm

Having escaped from a concentration camp where he has spent his life, a 12-year-old boy struggles to cope with an entirely strange world.

Satire
Shoebag

☐ *The Problem with Pulcifer*
by Florence Parry Heide

Pulcifer's preference for books is considered a grave problem by the television-addicted world around him.

☐ *Bel-Air Bambi and the Mall Rats*
by Richard Peck

Three totally cool siblings from Los Angeles move with their parents to Hickory Fork, a small town terrorized by a gang.

Oddball Humor
Shoebag

☐ *Mr. Popper's Penguins*
by Richard and Florence Atwater
1939 Newbery Honor Book

The delivery of a crate containing a penguin changes the life and fortunes of Mr. Popper.

☐ *The BFG*
by Roald Dahl

Sophie concocts a plan to save the world from nine man-gobbling cannybul giants.

☐ *Bunnicula*
by Deborah and James Howe

Chester the cat tries to warn his human family that their foundling baby bunny must be a vampire.
First of series

☐ *The Pushcart War*
by Jean Merrill

War breaks out between truck drivers and pushcart peddlers in New York.

☐ *Konrad*
by Christine Nostlinger

By mistake, an unconventional lady receives a perfectly behaved, factory-made child in the mail.

☐ *Jacob Two-Two Meets the Hooded Fang*
by Mordecai Richler

Unjustly imprisoned by the Hooded Fang, Jacob Two-Two awaits the aid of the members of Child Power.

☐ *Sideways Stories from Wayside School*
by Louis Sachar

Humorous episodes from the classroom on the 30th floor of Wayside School.
Sequel: *Wayside School Is Falling Down*

Boy-Girl Friendship
Shoebag

☐ *Bridge to Terabithia*
by Katherine Paterson
1978 Newbery Medal

The life of a 10-year-old boy in rural Virginia expands when he becomes friends with a newcomer.

☐ *The Goats*
by Brock Cole

Stripped and marooned on a small island by their fellow campers, a boy and a girl form an uneasy bond that grows into a deep friendship when they decide to run away and disappear without a trace.

☐ *Cricket and the Crackerbox Kid*
by Alane Ferguson

Pampered, 11-year-old rich kid Cricket thinks she has finally found a friend in Dominic, until they quarrel over ownership of a dog, and their classroom becomes a courtroom to decide who is right.

☐ *Words of Stone*
by Kevin Henkes

Busy trying to deal with his many fears and his troubled feelings for his dead mother, 10-year-old Blaze has his life changed when he meets the boisterous and irresistible Joselle.

☐ *The Ghost Belonged to Me*
by Richard Peck

In 1913 in the Midwest, a quartet of characters share adventures, from exploding steamboats to exorcising a ghost.

☐ *Sam and the Moon Queen*
by Alison Cragin Herzig and Jane Lawrence Mali

Sympathetic to a homeless girl's plight, Sam tries to help her find food for herself and medical aid for her dog.

Slake's Limbo

Felice Holman

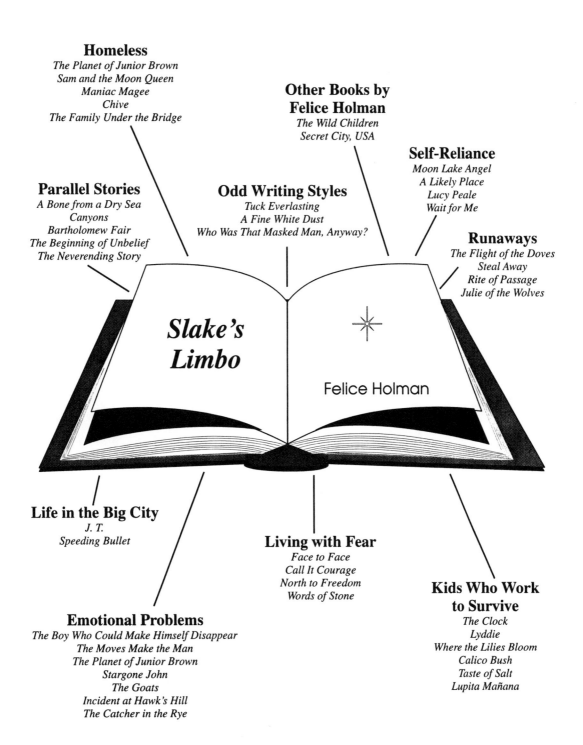

Homeless
The Planet of Junior Brown
Sam and the Moon Queen
Maniac Magee
Chive
The Family Under the Bridge

Other Books by Felice Holman
The Wild Children
Secret City, USA

Self-Reliance
Moon Lake Angel
A Likely Place
Lucy Peale
Wait for Me

Parallel Stories
A Bone from a Dry Sea
Canyons
Bartholomew Fair
The Beginning of Unbelief
The Neverending Story

Odd Writing Styles
Tuck Everlasting
A Fine White Dust
Who Was That Masked Man, Anyway?

Runaways
The Flight of the Doves
Steal Away
Rite of Passage
Julie of the Wolves

Slake's Limbo

Felice Holman

Life in the Big City
J. T.
Speeding Bullet

Living with Fear
Face to Face
Call It Courage
North to Freedom
Words of Stone

Kids Who Work to Survive
The Clock
Lyddie
Where the Lilies Bloom
Calico Bush
Taste of Salt
Lupita Mañana

Emotional Problems
The Boy Who Could Make Himself Disappear
The Moves Make the Man
The Planet of Junior Brown
Stargone John
The Goats
Incident at Hawk's Hill
The Catcher in the Rye

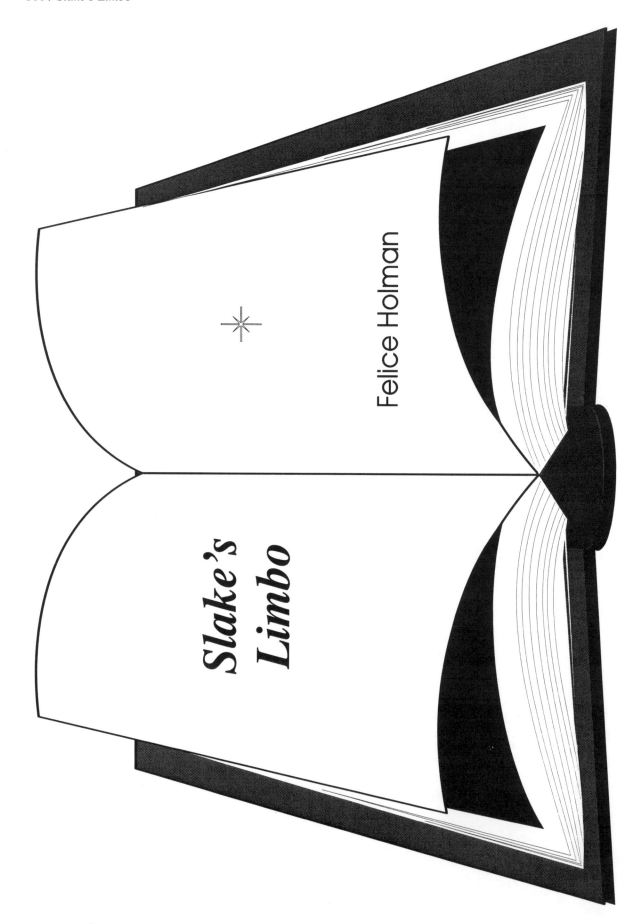

Slake's Limbo

Felice Holman

Other Books by Felice Holman

The Wild Children

Secret City, USA

Odd Writing Styles

Tuck Everlasting

A Fine White Dust

Who Was That Masked Man, Anyway?

Homeless

The Planet of Junior Brown

Sam and the Moon Queen

Maniac Magee

Chive

The Family Under the Bridge

Parallel Stories

A Bone from a Dry Sea

Canyons

Bartholomew Fair

The Beginning of Unbelief

The Neverending Story

Self-Reliance

Moon Lake Angel

A Likely Place

Lucy Peale

Wait for Me

Life in the Big City

J. T.

Speeding Bullet

Kids Who Work to Survive

The Clock

Lyddie

Where the Lilies Bloom

Calico Bush

Taste of Salt

Lupita Mañana

Living with Fear

Face to Face

Call It Courage

North to Freedom

Words of Stone

Emotional Problems

The Boy Who Could Make Himself Disappear

The Moves Make the Man

The Planet of Junior Brown

Stargone John

The Goats

Incident at Hawk's Hill

The Catcher in the Rye

Runaways

The Flight of the Doves

Steal Away

Rite of Passage

Julie of the Wolves

Other Books by Felice Holman
Slake's Limbo

The Wild Children
Left behind when his family is arrested during the Bolshevik Revolution, Alex falls in with a gang of other desperate homeless children.

Secret City, USA
Against all odds, Benno and his friends in the ghetto turn an abandoned house into a shelter for the homeless.

Odd Writing Styles
Slake's Limbo

Tuck Everlasting
by Natalie Babbitt
The Tuck family is confronted with an agonizing situation when they discover that a 10-year-old girl and a malicious stranger now share their secret about a spring whose water prevents one from growing older.

A Fine White Dust
by Cynthia Rylant
1987 Newbery Honor Book
The visit of the traveling Preacher Man to a small North Carolina town gives new impetus to 13-year-old Peter's struggle to reconcile his own deeply felt religious belief with the beliefs and nonbeliefs of his family and friends.

Who Was That Masked Man, Anyway?
by Avi
In the early 1940s, when nearly everyone else is thinking about World War II, sixth-grader Frankie Wattleson gets in trouble at home and at school because of his preoccupation with his favorite radio programs.

Homeless
Slake's Limbo

The Planet of Junior Brown
by Virginia Hamilton
1972 Newbery Honor Book
Already a leader in New York's underground world of homeless children, eighth-grader Buddy Clark takes on the responsibility of protecting the overweight, emotionally disturbed friend with whom he has been playing hooky all semester.

Sam and the Moon Queen
by Alison Cragin Herzig and Jane Lawrence Mali
Sympathetic to a homeless girl's plight, Sam tries to help her find food for herself and medical aid for her dog.

Maniac Magee
by Jerry Spinelli
1991 Newbery Medal
After his parents die, Jeffrey Lionel Magee's life becomes legendary, as he accomplishes athletic and other feats that awe his contemporaries.

Chive
by Shelley A. Barre
Eleven-year-old Chive, homeless because his parents have lost their farm and are looking for work in the city, strikes up an unusual friendship with 11-year-old Terry and competes with him in a skateboard competition.

The Family Under the Bridge
by Natalie Savage Carlson
1959 Newbery Honor Book
An old tramp, adopted by three fatherless children when their mother hides them under a bridge on the Seine, finds a home for mother and children and a job for himself.

Parallel Stories
Slake's Limbo

A Bone from a Dry Sea
by Peter Dickinson
An intelligent female member of a prehistoric tribe advances the lot of her people, and the daughter of a paleontologist is visiting him on a dig in Africa when important fossil remains are discovered.

Canyons
by Gary Paulsen
Finding a skull on a camping trip, Brennan becomes involved with the fate of a young Apache Indian who lived in the late 1890s.

Bartholomew Fair
by Mary Stolz
On an August day in 1597, six people attend London's Bartholomew's Fair and come away with unforgettable experiences.

The Beginning of Unbelief
by Robin Jones
While keeping a journal to record some upheavals in his life, 15-year-old Hal creates within its pages a science fiction story starring his alter ego, Zach.

The Neverending Story
by Michael Ende
The magical tale of Bastian, who steps through the pages of a book into a kingdom where he learns the true measure of his courage.

Self-Reliance
Slake's Limbo

☐ *Moon Lake Angel*
by Vera and Bill Cleaver

Kitty, whose mother does not want to deal with a child, stays with Aunt Petal and eventually learns to accept her mother's weaknesses.

☐ *A Likely Place*
by Paula Fox

A little boy who can't spell or ever seem to please his parents spends a week with a kooky baby-sitter and makes a special friend.

☐ *Lucy Peale*
by Colby Rodowsky
PG sex

Failing to get sympathy from her strict fundamentalist father when a rape leaves her pregnant, Lucy flees her home on Maryland's Eastern Shore and attempts to find self-reliance in nearby Ocean City.

☐ *Wait for Me*
by Susan Shreve

As she begins fifth grade, Molly feels left behind by her older sisters and brother and neglected by her former best friends.

Life in the Big City
Slake's Limbo

☐ *J. T.*
by Jane Wagner

J. T. begins to change when he discovers there is more satisfaction in caring for an injured cat than in listening to a stolen transistor radio.

☐ *Speeding Bullet*
by Neal Shusterman

After becoming famous and getting the attention of the daughter of a wealthy New York City developer following his rescue of a little girl from a speeding subway train, Nick looks for other people to rescue.

Kids Who Work to Survive
Slake's Limbo

☐ *The Clock*
by James Lincoln Collier and Christopher Collier

In 1810, trapped in a grueling job in the local textile mill, 15-year-old Annie becomes the victim of the cruel overseer and plots revenge against him.

☐ *Lyddie*
by Katherine Paterson

Impoverished Vermont farm girl Lyddie Worthen is determined to gain her independence by becoming a factory worker in the 1840s.

☐ *Where the Lilies Bloom*
by Vera and Bill Cleaver

In the Great Smoky Mountains, a 14-year-old girl struggles to keep her family together after their father dies.

☐ *Calico Bush*
by Rachel Field
1932 Newbery Honor Book

Having left France with her grandmother and uncle to seek a home in America, 13-year-old Marguerite is now alone in the world and an indentured servant on her way to Maine.

☐ *Taste of Salt*
by Francis Temple

In the hospital after being beaten by Macoutes, 17-year-old Djo tells the story of his impoverished life to a young woman who, like him, has been working with the social reformer Father Aristide to fight the repression in Haiti.

☐ *Lupita Mañana*
by Patricia Beatty

To help her poverty-stricken family, 13-year-old Lupita enters California as an illegal alien and starts to work while constantly on the watch for "la migra."

Living with Fear
Slake's Limbo

☐ *Face to Face*
by Marion Dane Bauer

Picked on at school by bullies, 13-year-old Michael confronts his fears during a trip to Colorado to see his father, who works as a whitewater rafting guide and who Michael has not seen in eight years.

☐ *Call It Courage*
by Armstrong Sperry
1941 Newbery Medal

Based on a Polynesian legend, this is the story of a youth, the son of a Polynesian chief whose people worship courage. Though he is afraid of the sea, he sets out alone in his canoe to conquer his fear and prove his courage to himself and his tribe.

☐ *North to Freedom*
by Anne Holm

Having escaped from an Eastern European concentration camp where he has spent his life, a 12-year-old boy struggles to cope with an entirely strange world as he flees northward to freedom in Denmark.

☐ *Words of Stone*
by Kevin Henkes

Busy trying to deal with his many fears and his troubled feelings for his dead mother, 10-year-old Blaze has his life changed when he meets the boisterous and irresistible Joselle.

Emotional Problems
Slake's Limbo

☐ *The Boy Who Could Make Himself Disappear*
by Kin Platt

A 12-year-old boy with a speech defect gradually withdraws into schizophrenia after moving to live with his mother following the divorce of his harsh and detached parents.

☐ *The Moves Make the Man*
by Bruce Brooks

1985 Newbery Honor Book

A black boy and an emotionally troubled white boy form a precarious friendship.

☐ *The Planet of Junior Brown*
by Virginia Hamilton

1972 Newbery Honor Book

Buddy takes on the responsibility of protecting an overweight, emotionally disturbed friend.

☐ *Stargone John*
by Ellen Kindt McKenzie

Six-year-old John experiences ridicule and punishment at his one-room schoolhouse, until an old retired teacher reaches out from her blindness.

☐ *The Goats*
by Brock Cole

A boy and a girl form an uneasy bond that grows into a deep friendship when they decide to run away.

☐ *Incident at Hawk's Hill*
by Allan W. Eckert

1972 Newbery Honor Book

A shy, lonely six-year-old wanders into the prairie and spends a summer under the protection of a badger.

☐ *The Catcher in the Rye*
by J. D. Salinger

Unable to conform and knowing he is about to be dropped by his school, Holden Caulfield embarks on a journey of self-discovery.

Runaways
Slake's Limbo

☐ *The Flight of the Doves*
by Walter Macken

A 12-year-old English boy and his seven-year-old sister run away from their abusive stepfather and set out to reach their grandmother in western Ireland, despite the publicity about their flight and a police search for them.

☐ *Steal Away*
by Jennifer Armstrong

In 1855 two 13-year-old girls, one white and one black, run away from a southern farm and make the difficult journey north to freedom, living to recount their story 41 years later to two similar young girls.

☐ *Rite of Passage*
by Richard Wright

PG language

When 15-year-old Johnny Gibbs is told that he is really a foster child, he runs off into the streets of Harlem and meets up with a gang that wants him to participate in a mugging.

☐ *Julie of the Wolves*
by Jean Craighead George

1973 Newbery Medal

While running away from home and an unwanted marriage, a 13-year-old Eskimo girl becomes lost on the North Slope of Alaska and is befriended by a wolf pack.

Sounder

William H. Armstrong

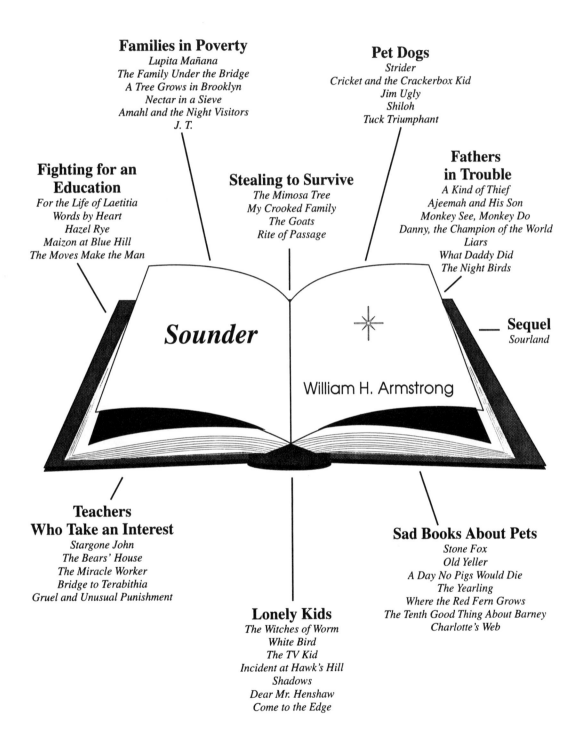

Families in Poverty
Lupita Mañana
The Family Under the Bridge
A Tree Grows in Brooklyn
Nectar in a Sieve
Amahl and the Night Visitors
J. T.

Pet Dogs
Strider
Cricket and the Crackerbox Kid
Jim Ugly
Shiloh
Tuck Triumphant

Fighting for an Education
For the Life of Laetitia
Words by Heart
Hazel Rye
Maizon at Blue Hill
The Moves Make the Man

Stealing to Survive
The Mimosa Tree
My Crooked Family
The Goats
Rite of Passage

Fathers in Trouble
A Kind of Thief
Ajeemah and His Son
Monkey See, Monkey Do
Danny, the Champion of the World
Liars
What Daddy Did
The Night Birds

Sounder

William H. Armstrong

Sequel
Sourland

Teachers Who Take an Interest
Stargone John
The Bears' House
The Miracle Worker
Bridge to Terabithia
Gruel and Unusual Punishment

Lonely Kids
The Witches of Worm
White Bird
The TV Kid
Incident at Hawk's Hill
Shadows
Dear Mr. Henshaw
Come to the Edge

Sad Books About Pets
Stone Fox
Old Yeller
A Day No Pigs Would Die
The Yearling
Where the Red Fern Grows
The Tenth Good Thing About Barney
Charlotte's Web

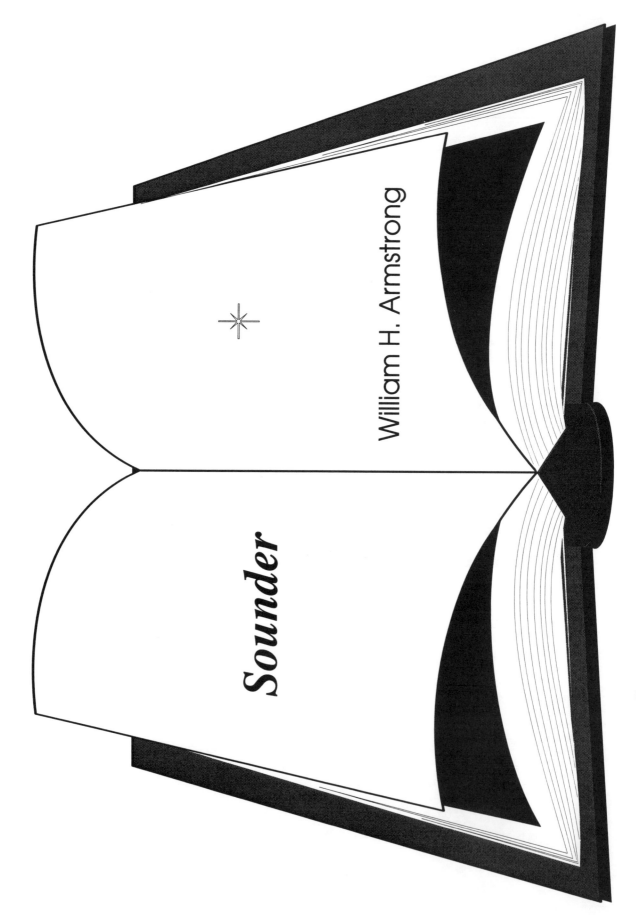

Sounder

William H. Armstrong

Families in Poverty

Lupita Mañana

The Family Under the Bridge

A Tree Grows in Brooklyn

Nectar in a Sieve

Amahl and the Night Visitors

J. T.

Stealing to Survive

The Mimosa Tree

My Crooked Family

The Goats

Rite of Passage

Sequel

Sourland

Sad Books About Pets

Stone Fox

Old Yeller

A Day No Pigs Would Die

The Yearling

Where the Red Fern Grows

The Tenth Good Thing About Barney

Charlotte's Web

Lonely Kids

The Witches of Worm

White Bird

The TV Kid

Incident at Hawk's Hill

Shadows

Dear Mr. Henshaw

Come to the Edge

Fathers in Trouble

A Kind of Thief

Ajeemah and His Son

Monkey See, Monkey Do

Danny, the Champion of the World

Liars

What Daddy Did

The Night Birds

Fighting for an Education

For the Life of Laetitia

Words by Heart

Hazel Rye

Maizon at Blue Hill

The Moves Make the Man

Pet Dogs

Strider

Cricket and the Crackerbox Kid

Jim Ugly

Shiloh

Tuck Triumphant

Teachers Who Take an Interest

Stargone John

The Bears' House

The Miracle Worker

Bridge to Terabithia

Gruel and Unusual Punishment

Families in Poverty
Sounder

☐ *Lupita Mañana*
by Patricia Beatty

To help her poverty-stricken family, 13-year-old Lupita enters California as an illegal alien and starts to work while constantly on the watch for "la migra."

☐ *The Family Under the Bridge*
by Natalie Savage Carlson
1959 Newbery Honor Book

An old tramp, adopted by three fatherless children when their mother hides them under a bridge, finds a home for mother and children and a job for himself.

☐ *A Tree Grows in Brooklyn*
by Betty Smith

Young Francie Nolan experiences the problems of growing up in a Brooklyn slum.

☐ *Nectar in a Sieve*
by Kamala Markandaya

The story of a peasant woman in a primitive village in India whose whole life was a gallant and persistent battle to care for those she loved.

☐ *Amahl and the Night Visitors*
by Giancarlo Menotti

Relates how a crippled young shepherd comes to accompany the three kings on their way to pay homage to the newborn Jesus.

☐ *J. T.*
by Jane Wagner

J. T. begins to change when he discovers there is more satisfaction in caring for an injured cat than in listening to a stolen radio.

Stealing to Survive
Sounder

☐ *The Mimosa Tree*
by Vera and Bill Cleaver

Shortly after the Proffitts arrive in the Chicago slums from North Carolina, their stepmother leaves the family, and 14-year-old Marvella becomes the sole support for her blind father and the four younger children.

☐ *My Crooked Family*
by James Lincoln Collier

Living with irresponsible parents in a seedy part of a big city in 1910, 13-year-old Roger falls in with a gang of murderous burglars and discovers an unpleasant secret about his father.

☐ *The Goats*
by Brock Cole

Stripped and marooned on a small island by their fellow campers, a boy and a girl form an uneasy bond that grows into a deep friendship when they decide to run away and disappear without a trace.

☐ *Rite of Passage*
by Richard Wright
PG language

When 15-year-old Johnny Gibbs is told that he is really a foster child, he runs off into the streets of Harlem and meets up with a gang that wants him to participate in a mugging.

Sequel
Sounder

☐ *Sourland*

For Anson Stone and his three motherless children, the quiet black man who enters their lives as teacher and friend fills a lonely void but also brings home a tragic reality.

Sad Books About Pets
Sounder

☐ *Stone Fox*
by John R. Gardiner

Little Willie hopes to pay the back taxes on his grandfather's farm with the purse from a dogsled race he enters.

☐ *Old Yeller*
by Fred Gipson
1957 Newbery Honor Book

In the late 1860s in Texas, a big yellow dog and a 14-year-old boy form a close, loving relationship.

☐ *A Day No Pigs Would Die*
by Robert Newton Peck

To a 13-year-old Vermont farm boy, maturity comes early as he learns to do what's got to be done, especially regarding his pet pig, who cannot produce a litter.

☐ *The Yearling*
by Marjorie Kinnan Rawlings

A young boy living in the Florida backwoods is forced to decide the fate of a fawn he has lovingly raised as a pet.

☐ *Where the Red Fern Grows*
by Wilson Rawls

The adventures of a 10-year-old boy and the two dogs he bought with money he had earned.

☐ *The Tenth Good Thing About Barney*
by Judith Viorst

In an attempt to overcome his grief, a boy tries to think of the 10 best things about his dead cat.

☐ *Charlotte's Web*
by E. B. White
1953 Newbery Honor Book

Wilbur the pig is desolate when he discovers that he is destined to be the farmer's Christmas dinner, until his friend Charlotte decides to help him.

Lonely Kids
Sounder

☐*The Witches of Worm*
by Zilpha Keatley Snyder
1973 Newbery Honor Book

A lonely 12-year-old is convinced that the cat she finds is possessed by a witch and is responsible for her own strange behavior.

☐*White Bird*
by Clyde Robert Bulla

A lonely boy is found and reared by a hermit in the wilderness in the 1880s.

☐*The TV Kid*
by Betsy Byars

To escape failure, boredom, and loneliness, a young boy plunges with all his imagination into the world of television.

☐*Incident at Hawk's Hill*
by Allan W. Eckert
1972 Newbery Honor Book

A shy, lonely six-year-old wanders into the Canadian prairie and spends a summer under the protection of a badger.

☐*Shadows*
by Dennis Haseley

Jamie's lonely life with his aunt and uncle changes when Grandpa comes to visit and teaches him to make shadow pictures.

☐*Dear Mr. Henshaw*
by Beverly Cleary
1984 Newbery Medal

In his letters to his favorite author, 10-year-old Leigh reveals his problems in coping with his parents' divorce, being the new boy in school, and generally finding his own place in the world.

☐*Come to the Edge*
by Julia Cunningham

After he is befriended by a sign painter, a confused runaway finds trust and a purpose for living.

Fathers in Trouble
Sounder

☐*A Kind of Thief*
by Vivien Alcock

When her father is put into prison, 13-year-old Elinor finds that she has to face many unpleasant truths about him.

☐*Ajeemah and His Son*
by James Berry

A father and his 18-year-old son are each affected differently by their experiences as slaves in Jamaica in the early 19th century.

☐*Monkey See, Monkey Do*
by Barthe DeClements

Jerry's adored father seems unable to stay out of jail, causing the sixth-grader anguish at home and in school.

☐*Danny, the Champion of the World*
by Roald Dahl

Danny describes his relationship with his father, a poacher, and the special adventure they share together.

☐*Liars*
by P. J. Petersen

Life in a remote town is boring for eighth-grader Sam and his friends, until his newly awakened ability to tell when a person is lying involves him in a series of mysterious events.

☐*What Daddy Did*
by Neal Shusterman

A 14-year-old learns that his father is to be released from prison after serving time for killing the boy's mother.

☐*The Night Birds*
by Tormod Haugen

Jake struggles to come to grips with terrors, including his father's bouts of depression and his own nightmares.

Fighting for an Education
Sounder

☐*For the Life of Laetitia*
by Merle Hodge

As the first in her family to go to secondary school, 12-year-old Lacey struggles with a variety of problems, including a cruel teacher and a difficult home life with her father and stepmother.

☐*Words by Heart*
by Ouida Sebestyen

In 1910, a young black girl struggles to fulfill her papa's dream of a better future for their family in the southwestern town where they are the only blacks.

☐*Hazel Rye*
by Vera and Bill Cleaver

An 11-year-old girl with no appreciation for land and growing things finds her values beginning to change when she agrees to let an impoverished family live in a small house she owns, in exchange for working in the surrounding orange grove.

☐*Maizon at Blue Hill*
by Jacqueline Woodson

After winning a scholarship to an academically challenging boarding school, Maizon finds herself one of only five blacks there and wonders if she will ever fit in.
Sequel to *Last Summer with Maizon*

☐*The Moves Make the Man*
by Bruce Brooks
1985 Newbery Honor Book

A black boy and an emotionally troubled white boy in North Carolina form a precarious friendship.

Pet Dogs
Sounder

☐*Strider*
by Beverly Cleary

In a series of diary entries, Leigh tells how he comes to terms with his parents' divorce, acquires joint custody of an abandoned dog, and joins the track team at school.
Sequel to *Dear Mr. Henshaw*

☐*Cricket and the Crackerbox Kid*
by Alane Ferguson

Pampered, 11-year-old rich kid Cricket thinks she has finally found a friend in Dominic, who lives in low-income housing, until they quarrel over ownership of a dog, and their classroom becomes a courtroom to decide who is right.

☐*Jim Ugly*
by Sid Fleischman

The adventures of 12-year-old Jake and Jim Ugly, his father's part-mongrel, part-wolf dog, as they travel through the Old West trying to find out what really happened to Jake's actor father.

☐*Shiloh*
by Phyllis Reynolds Naylor
1992 Newbery Medal

When he finds a lost beagle in the hills behind his home, Marty tries to hide it from his family and the dog's real owner, a mean-spirited man known to mistreat his dogs.

☐*Tuck Triumphant*
by Theodore Taylor

Fourteen-year-old Helen, her blind dog Friar Tuck, and her family face some dramatic challenges when they discover that the Korean boy they have adopted is deaf.
Sequel to *The Trouble with Tuck*

Teachers Who Take an Interest
Sounder

☐ *Stargone John*
by Ellen Kindt McKenzie

Six-year-old John, emotionally withdrawn and resistant to traditional teaching methods, experiences ridicule and punishment at his one-room schoolhouse, until an old retired teacher reaches out from her blindness to share with him the world of reading and writing.

☐ *The Bears' House*
by Marilyn Sachs

Fran Ellen is ostracized by her class because she sucks her thumb and smells bad, but her dreadful home life is a secret she tries to keep from them all.

☐ *The Miracle Worker*
by William Gibson

The play tells the inspiring story of the blind and deaf Helen Keller and her teacher, Annie Sullivan.

☐ *Bridge to Terabithia*
by Katherine Paterson
1978 Newbery Medal

The life of a 10-year-old boy in rural Virginia expands when he becomes friends with a newcomer who subsequently meets an untimely death trying to reach their hideaway, Terabithia, during a storm.

☐ *Gruel and Unusual Punishment*
by Jim Arter

Undaunted by his second stint in the seventh grade, Arnold continues to specialize in antisocial behavior, but becomes uncomfortably aware that the teacher he calls Apeface has taken a special interest in his case.

Steal Away

Jennifer Armstrong

Learning About a Grandparent's Past
The Night Journey
Three Names
Toning the Sweep
The Eyes of the Amaryllis
A Dig in Time

Telling Stories from the Family's Past
Front Porch Stories at the One-Room School
The Winter Room
Sourland

Leaving Home After the Death of a Parent
The Journey of the Shadow Bairns
Up a Road Slowly
Onion Tears
True Grit
The Secret Garden
Thicker Than Water

Black and White Friends
The Friendship
The Cay
Maizon at Blue Hill
Maniac Magee
Everywhere

Dual Voices
Morning Girl
Thicker Than Water

Steal Away

Jennifer Armstrong

Dangerous Journeys
Grab Hands and Run
The Bandit of Mok Hill
The Goats
Save Queen of Sheba
The Flight of the Doves

Whites Helping Blacks Escape from Slavery
The Adventures of Huckleberry Finn
Brady
A Gathering of Days
The Slave Dancer
Jump Ship to Freedom

Seeing Yourself from Another's Point of View
The Light in the Forest
North to Freedom
The Winchesters
Arthur for the Very First Time
All About Sam

Runaways
Come to the Edge
From the Mixed-Up Files of Mrs. Basil E. Frankweiler
Slake's Limbo
The Dulcimer Boy
Bless the Beasts and Children
Rite of Passage

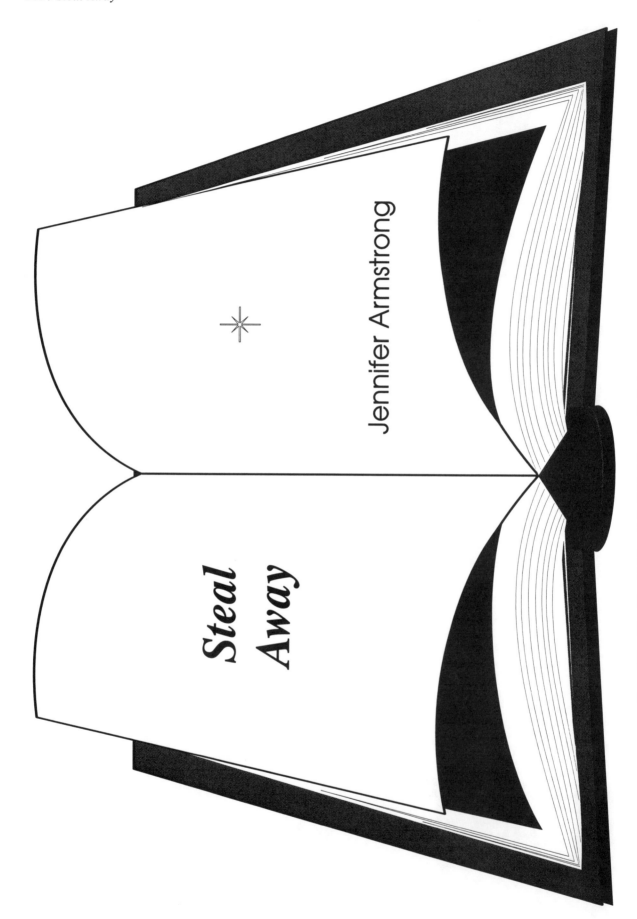

Jennifer Armstrong

*Steal
Away*

**Whites
Helping Blacks
Escape from Slavery**

*The Adventures
of Huckleberry Finn*

Brady

A Gathering of Days

The Slave Dancer

Jump Ship to Freedom

**Learning About a
Grandparent's Past**

The Night Journey

Three Names

Toning the Sweep

*The Eyes
of the Amaryllis*

A Dig in Time

Dual Voices

Morning Girl

Thicker Than Water

**Telling Stories from
the Family's Past**

*Front Porch Stories at the
One-Room School*

The Winter Room

Sourland

**Seeing Yourself from
Another's
Point of View**

The Light in the Forest

North to Freedom

The Winchesters

*Arthur for the Very
First Time*

All About Sam

**Leaving Home After
the Death of a Parent**

*The Journey of the
Shadow Bairns*

Up a Road Slowly

Onion Tears

True Grit

The Secret Garden

Thicker Than Water

**Dangerous
Journeys**

Grab Hands and Run

The Bandit of Mok Hill

The Goats

Save Queen of Sheba

The Flight of the Doves

**Black and
White Friends**

The Friendship

The Cay

Maizon at Blue Hill

Maniac Magee

Everywhere

Runaways

Come to the Edge

*From the Mixed-Up Files
of Mrs. Basil E.
Frankweiler*

Slake's Limbo

The Dulcimer Boy

*Bless the Beasts and
Children*

Rite of Passage

Telling Stories from the Family's Past
Steal Away

☐ *Front Porch Stories at the One-Room School*
by Eleanora E. Tate

A father tells his daughter and niece some wild stories about his own childhood.

☐ *The Winter Room*
by Gary Paulsen

1990 Newbery Honor Book

A young boy growing up on a northern Minnesota farm describes the scenes around him and recounts his old Norwegian uncle's tales of an almost mythological logging past.

☐ *Sourland*
by William H. Armstrong

For Anson Stone and his three motherless children, the quiet black man who enters their lives as teacher and friend fills a lonely void but also brings home a tragic reality.

Sequel to *Sounder*

Dual Voices
Steal Away

☐ *Morning Girl*
by Michael Dorris

Morning Girl, who loves the day, and her younger brother Star Boy, who loves the night, take turns describing their life on an island in pre-Colombian America; in Morning Girl's last narrative, she witnesses the arrival of the first Europeans in her world.

☐ *Thicker Than Water*
by Penelope Farmer

Both Will and his cousin Becky have some adjusting to do when he comes to live with her family after his mother's death, especially when the ghost of a child coal miner begins his insistent haunting of Will.

Learning About a Grandparent's Past
Steal Away

☐ *The Night Journey*
by Kathryn Lasky

Rache ignores her parents' wishes and persuades her great-grandmother to relate the story of her escape from czarist Russia.

☐ *Three Names*
by Patricia MacLachlan

Great-grandfather reminisces about going to school on the prairie with his dog Three Names.

☐ *Toning the Sweep*
by Angela Johnson

On a visit to her grandmother Ola, who is dying of cancer in her house in the desert, 14-year-old Emmie hears many stories about the past and her family history and comes to a better understanding of relatives both dead and living.

☐ *The Eyes of the Amaryllis*
by Natalie Babbitt

When 11-year-old Jenny goes to stay with her widowed grandmother, who lives by the seaside waiting for a sign from her drowned husband, she learns a great deal about the nature of love and the ways of the sea.

☐ *A Dig in Time*
by Peni R. Griffin

While spending the summer with their grandmother in San Antonio, 12-year-old Nan and her younger brother find artifacts buried in the yard, and discover how to use them to travel back through time to significant moments in their family's history.

Whites Helping Blacks Escape from Slavery
Steal Away

☐ *The Adventures of Huckleberry Finn*
by Mark Twain

A 19th-century boy from a Mississippi River town recounts his adventures as he travels down the river with a runaway slave on a raft, encountering a family involved in a feud, two scoundrels pretending to be royalty, and Tom Sawyer's aunt (who mistakes him for Tom).

☐ *Brady*
by Jean Fritz

A young Pennsylvania boy takes part in the pre-Civil War antislavery activities.

☐ *A Gathering of Days*
by Joan W. Blos

1980 Newbery Honor Book

The journal of a 14-year-old girl, kept the last year she lived on the family farm, records daily events in her small New Hampshire town, her father's remarriage, and the death of her best friend.

☐ *The Slave Dancer*
by Paula Fox

1974 Newbery Medal

Kidnapped by the crew of an Africa-bound ship, a 13-year-old boy discovers to his horror that he is on a slaver and his job is to play music for the exercise periods of the human cargo.

☐ *Jump Ship to Freedom*
by James Lincoln Collier and Christopher Collier

In 1787 a 14-year-old slave, anxious to buy freedom for himself and his mother, escapes from his dishonest master and tries to find help in cashing the soldier's notes received by his father for fighting in the Revolution.

Black and White Friends
Steal Away

☐ *The Friendship*
by Mildred Taylor

Four children witness a confrontation between an elderly black man and a white storekeeper in rural Mississippi in the 1930s.

☐ *The Cay*
by Theodore Taylor

When the freighter on which they are traveling is torpedoed by a German submarine during World War II, a white boy, blinded by a blow on the head, and an old black man are stranded on a tiny Caribbean island, where the boy acquires a new kind of vision, courage, and love from his old companion.

Prequel/sequel: *Timothy of the Cay*

☐ *Maizon at Blue Hill*
by Jacqueline Woodson

After winning a scholarship to an academically challenging boarding school, Maizon finds herself one of only five blacks there and wonders if she will ever fit in.

Sequel to *Last Summer with Maizon*

☐ *Maniac Magee*
by Jerry Spinelli
1991 Newbery Medal

After his parents die, Jeffrey Lionel Magee's life becomes legendary, as he accomplishes athletic and other feats that awe his contemporaries.

☐ *Everywhere*
by Bruce Brooks

Afraid that his grandfather will die after suffering a heart attack, a nine-year-old boy agrees to join 10-year-old Dooley in performing a ritual called soul switching.

Dangerous Journeys
Steal Away

☐ *Grab Hands and Run*
by Frances Temple

After his father disappears, 12-year-old Felipe, his mother, and his younger sister set out on a difficult and dangerous journey, trying to make their way from their home in El Salvador to Canada.

☐ *The Bandit of Mok Hill*
by Evelyn Sibley Lampman

Twelve-year-old Angel Palma leaves his life among the street orphans of early San Francisco to travel to the gold fields with an eccentric singing teacher, and looks for an old friend who has become a renowned bandit.

☐ *The Goats*
by Brock Cole

Stripped and marooned on a small island by their fellow campers, a boy and a girl form an uneasy bond that grows into a deep friendship when they decide to run away and disappear without a trace.

☐ *Save Queen of Sheba*
by Louise Moeri

After miraculously surviving a Sioux Indian raid on the trail to Oregon, a brother and sister set out with few provisions to find the rest of the settlers.

☐ *The Flight of the Doves*
by Walter Macken

A 12-year-old English boy and his seven-year-old sister run away from their abusive stepfather and set out to reach their grandmother in western Ireland, despite the publicity about their flight and a police search for them.

Leaving Home After the Death of a Parent
Steal Away

☐ *The Journey of the Shadow Bairns*
by Margaret J. Anderson

When her parents die, leaving only a little money and a ticket to Canada, a Scottish girl decides she and her four-year-old brother will relocate.

☐ *Up a Road Slowly*
by Irene Hunt

After the death of her mother, Julie is sent to live with a maiden aunt and ne'er-do-well uncle, and grows up under her aunt's stern but loving care.

☐ *Onion Tears*
by Diana Kidd

A Vietnamese girl tries to come to terms with her grief over the loss of her family and her new life with the Australian family with whom she lives.

☐ *True Grit*
by Charles Portis

Fourteen-year-old Mattie Ross convinces one-eyed Marshall Rooster Cogburn to help her capture the gang of outlaws who murdered her father.

☐ *The Secret Garden*
by Frances Hodgson Burnett

A boy who has lived as a spoiled invalid regains his health when he and his orphaned cousin restore a once lovely garden.

☐ *Thicker Than Water*
by Penelope Farmer

Both Will and his cousin Becky have some adjusting to do when he comes to live with her family after his mother's death, especially when the ghost of a child coal miner begins his insistent haunting of Will.

Seeing Yourself from Another's Point of View
Steal Away

☐ *The Light in the Forest*
by Conrad Richter

After being raised as an Indian for 11 years following his capture at the age of four, John Butler is forcibly returned to his white parents but continues to long for the freedom of Indian life.

☐ *North to Freedom*
by Anne Holm

Having escaped from an Eastern European concentration camp where he has spent his life, a 12-year-old boy struggles to cope with an entirely strange world as he flees northward to freedom in Denmark.

☐ *The Winchesters*
by James Lincoln Collier

Fourteen-year-old Chris, a poor relation of the wealthy Winchesters, must choose whether to be on the side of management or labor when his classmates' parents go on strike at the Winchester mill in response to a wage cut.

☐ *Arthur for the Very First Time*
by Patricia MacLachlan

Arthur spends a summer with his unconventional aunt and uncle and begins to look at life, his family, and himself differently.

☐ *All About Sam*
by Lois Lowry

The adventures of Sam, Anastasia Krupnik's younger brother, from his first day as a newborn through his mischievous times as a toddler.

Runaways

Steal Away

☐ *Come to the Edge*
by Julia Cunningham

After he is befriended by a sign painter, a confused runaway finds trust and a purpose for living.

☐ *From the Mixed-Up Files of Mrs. Basil E. Frankweiler*
by E. L. Konigsburg
1968 Newbery Medal

Two suburban children run away from their Connecticut home and go to New York's Metropolitan Museum of Art, where their ingenuity enables them to live in luxury.

☐ *Slake's Limbo*
by Felice Holman

Thirteen-year-old Aremis Slake, hounded by his fears and misfortunes, flees into New York City's subway tunnels, never again, he believes, to emerge.

☐ *The Dulcimer Boy*
by Tor Seidler

Twin brothers are abandoned on their uncle's doorstep in turn-of-the-century New England with nothing but a silver-stringed dulcimer.

☐ *Bless the Beasts and Children*
by Glendon Swarthout

While at Box Canyon Boys Camp, a group of disturbed boys searches for a way to improve their lives.

☐ *Rite of Passage*
by Richard Wright
PG language

When 15-year-old Johnny Gibbs is told that he is really a foster child, he runs off into the streets of Harlem and meets up with a gang that wants him to participate in a mugging.

Where the Red Fern Grows

Wilson Rawls

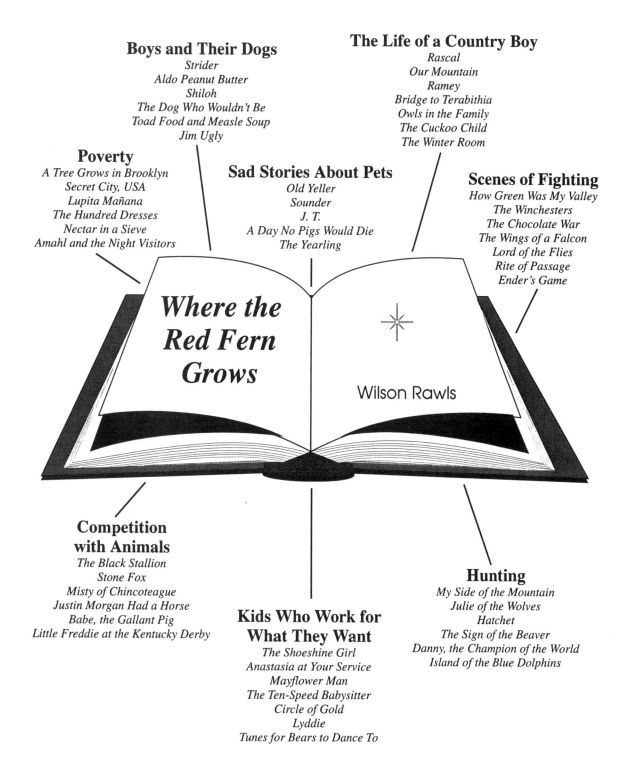

Boys and Their Dogs
Strider
Aldo Peanut Butter
Shiloh
The Dog Who Wouldn't Be
Toad Food and Measle Soup
Jim Ugly

The Life of a Country Boy
Rascal
Our Mountain
Ramey
Bridge to Terabithia
Owls in the Family
The Cuckoo Child
The Winter Room

Poverty
A Tree Grows in Brooklyn
Secret City, USA
Lupita Mañana
The Hundred Dresses
Nectar in a Sieve
Amahl and the Night Visitors

Sad Stories About Pets
Old Yeller
Sounder
J. T.
A Day No Pigs Would Die
The Yearling

Scenes of Fighting
How Green Was My Valley
The Winchesters
The Chocolate War
The Wings of a Falcon
Lord of the Flies
Rite of Passage
Ender's Game

Where the Red Fern Grows

Wilson Rawls

Competition with Animals
The Black Stallion
Stone Fox
Misty of Chincoteague
Justin Morgan Had a Horse
Babe, the Gallant Pig
Little Freddie at the Kentucky Derby

Kids Who Work for What They Want
The Shoeshine Girl
Anastasia at Your Service
Mayflower Man
The Ten-Speed Babysitter
Circle of Gold
Lyddie
Tunes for Bears to Dance To

Hunting
My Side of the Mountain
Julie of the Wolves
Hatchet
The Sign of the Beaver
Danny, the Champion of the World
Island of the Blue Dolphins

Wilson Rawls

*Where the
Red Fern
Grows*

Competition with Animals

The Black Stallion

Stone Fox

Misty of Chincoteague

Justin Morgan Had a Horse

Babe, the Gallant Pig

Little Freddie at the Kentucky Derby

Scenes of Fighting

How Green Was My Valley

The Winchesters

The Chocolate War

The Wings of a Falcon

Lord of the Flies

Rite of Passage

Ender's Game

Kids Who Work for What They Want

The Shoeshine Girl

Anastasia at Your Service

Mayflower Man

The Ten-Speed Babysitter

Circle of Gold

Lyddie

Tunes for Bears to Dance To

Poverty

A Tree Grows in Brooklyn

Secret City, USA

Lupita Mañana

The Hundred Dresses

Nectar in a Sieve

Amahl and the Night Visitors

Sad Stories About Pets

Old Yeller

Sounder

J. T.

A Day No Pigs Would Die

The Yearling

Hunting

My Side of the Mountain

Julie of the Wolves

Hatchet

The Sign of the Beaver

Danny, the Champion of the World

Island of the Blue Dolphins

Boys and Their Dogs

Strider

Aldo Peanut Butter

Shiloh

The Dog Who Wouldn't Be

Toad Food and Measle Soup

Jim Ugly

The Life of a Country Boy

Rascal

Our Mountain

Ramey

Bridge to Terabithia

Owls in the Family

The Cuckoo Child

The Winter Room

Competition with Animals
Where the Red Fern Grows

☐ *The Black Stallion*
by Walter Farley

A boy is pulled to a desert island by a wild black stallion he has freed during a shipwreck at sea, then is rescued by a southbound freighter. The boy befriends the horse, trains him by night, and rides him in a match race.

Many sequels

☐ *Stone Fox*
by John R. Gardiner

Little Willie hopes to pay the back taxes on his grandfather's farm with the purse from a dogsled race he enters.

☐ *Misty of Chincoteague*
by Marguerite Henry

1948 Newbery Honor Book

Two children's determination to own a Chincoteague pony is greatly increased when the Phantom and her colt are among those rounded up for the yearly auction.

☐ *Justin Morgan Had a Horse*
by Marguerite Henry

1946 Newbery Honor Book

An unusual work horse raised in Vermont and known originally as Little Bub becomes the sire of a famous American breed and takes the name of his owner, Justin Morgan.

Many sequels

☐ *Babe, the Gallant Pig*
by Dick King-Smith

A piglet destined for eventual butchering arrives at the farmyard, is adopted by an old sheepdog, and discovers a special secret to success.

☐ *Little Freddie at the Kentucky Derby*
by Kathryn Cocquyt

Follows a young colt named Little Freddie from his foal days on a racing farm until he wins the Kentucky Derby.

Scenes of Fighting
Where the Red Fern Grows

☐ *How Green Was My Valley*
by Richard Llewellyn

A boy grows up in a Welsh coal mining town.

☐ *The Winchesters*
by James Lincoln Collier

Fourteen-year-old Chris, a poor relation of the wealthy Winchesters, must choose whether to be on the side of management or labor when his classmates' parents go on strike at the Winchester mill.

☐ *The Chocolate War*
by Robert Cormier

PG language

A high school freshman discovers the devastating consequences of arousing the wrath of the school bullies.

Sequel: *Beyond the Chocolate War*

☐ *The Wings of a Falcon*
by Cynthia Voigt

Fourteen-year-old Oriel and his friend Griff flee the slavery of Damall's Island and seek a new life on the mainland, where they face raiding Wolfers, rival armies, and other dangers.

☐ *Lord of the Flies*
by William Golding

Stranded on an island, a group of young boys reverts to savagery as they struggle to survive.

☐ *Rite of Passage*
by Richard Wright

PG language

When 15-year-old Johnny Gibbs is told that he is really a foster child, he runs off into the streets of Harlem and meets up with a gang that wants him to participate in a mugging.

☐ *Ender's Game*
by Orson Scott Card

Ender may be the military genius Earth needs in its war against aliens.

Kids Who Work for What They Want
Where the Red Fern Grows

☐ *The Shoeshine Girl*
by Clyde Robert Bulla

Determined to earn some money, 10-year-old Sarah Ida gets a job at a shoeshine stand.

☐ *Anastasia at Your Service*
by Lois Lowry

Twelve-year-old Anastasia has a series of disastrous experiences when, expecting to get a job as a lady's companion, she is hired instead to be a maid.

☐ *Mayflower Man*
by Jean Adair Shriver

When his grandmother dies and the farm 13-year-old Caleb has lived on all his life is sold, he knows he wants the house for his own again.

☐ *The Ten-Speed Babysitter*
by Alison Cragin Herzig and Jane Lawrence Mali

Tony's summer job baby-sitting is filled with surprises when his employer jets off to the Caribbean and leaves him in charge of a toddler.

☐ *Circle of Gold*
by Candy Dawson Boyd

Mattie is determined to get her mother a beautiful gold pin for Mother's Day.

☐ *Lyddie*
by Katherine Paterson

Impoverished farm girl Lyddie is determined to gain her independence by becoming a factory worker.

☐ *Tunes for Bears to Dance To*
by Robert Cormier

When Henry is manipulated into betraying his friend, he comes to know true evil.

Poverty
Where the Red Fern Grows

☐ *A Tree Grows in Brooklyn*
by Betty Smith

Young Francie Nolan experiences the problems of growing up in a Brooklyn, New York, slum.

☐ *Secret City, USA*
by Felice Holman

Benno and his friends in the ghetto turn an abandoned house into a shelter for the homeless.

☐ *Lupita Mañana*
by Patricia Beatty

To help her poverty-stricken family, 13-year-old Lupita enters California as an illegal alien and starts to work while constantly on the watch for "la migra."

☐ *The Hundred Dresses*
by Eleanor Estes

1945 Newbery Honor Book

In winning a medal she is no longer there to receive, a tight-lipped girl teaches her classmates a lesson.

☐ *Nectar in a Sieve*
by Kamala Markandaya

The story of a peasant woman in a primitive village in India whose whole life was a gallant and persistent battle to care for those she loved.

☐ *Amahl and the Night Visitors*
by Giancarlo Menotti

Relates how a crippled young shepherd comes to accompany the three kings on their way to pay homage to the newborn Jesus.

The Life of a Country Boy
Where the Red Fern Grows

☐ *Rascal*
by Sterling North
1964 Newbery Honor Book

The author recalls his carefree life in a small midwestern town at the close of World War I and his adventures with his pet raccoon, Rascal.

☐ *Our Mountain*
by Ellen Harvey Showell

Two brothers living in the mountains of West Virginia describe their family, home, and favorite pastimes.

☐ *Ramey*
by Jack Farris

A boy grows up with his father, a backwoods preacher.

☐ *Bridge to Terabithia*
by Katherine Paterson
1978 Newbery Medal

The life of a 10-year-old boy in rural Virginia expands when he becomes friends with a newcomer who subsequently meets an untimely death trying to reach their hideaway, Terabithia, during a storm.

☐ *Owls in the Family*
by Farley Mowat

A young boy decides to raise two owlets as pets.

☐ *The Cuckoo Child*
by Dick King-Smith

With the unknowing help of his pet geese, eight-year-old Jack Daw decides to raise an ostrich on his family farm.

☐ *The Winter Room*
by Gary Paulsen
1990 Newbery Honor Book

A boy growing up on a farm describes the scenes around him and recounts his old uncle's tales of an almost mythological logging past.

Boys and Their Dogs
Where the Red Fern Grows

☐ *Strider*
by Beverly Cleary

Leigh tells how he comes to terms with his parents' divorce and acquires joint custody of an abandoned dog.
Sequel to *Dear Mr. Henshaw*

☐ *Aldo Peanut Butter*
by Johanna Hurwitz

Peanut and Butter, two dogs Aldo gets for his 11th birthday, create chaos inside the house while his parents are out of town.

☐ *Shiloh*
by Phyllis Reynolds Naylor
1992 Newbery Medal

When he finds a lost beagle, Marty tries to hide it from his family and the dog's real owner, a mean-spirited man known to mistreat his dogs.

☐ *The Dog Who Wouldn't Be*
by Farley Mowat

Relates the author's happy boyhood experiences in Canada with his dog Mutt and two owls named Weeps and Wol.

☐ *Toad Food and Measle Soup*
by Christine McDonnell

The adventures of Leo, in which he finds a lost dog, surprises the class on book report day, and survives his mother's experiments with vegetarian cooking.

☐ *Jim Ugly*
by Sid Fleischman

The adventures of 12-year-old Jake and Jim Ugly, his father's part-mongrel, part-wolf dog, as they travel through the Old West trying to find out what really happened to Jake's actor father.

Hunting
Where the Red Fern Grows

☐ *My Side of the Mountain*
by Jean Craighead George

Young Sam Gribley leaves New York City and spends a year living by himself in a remote area of the Catskill Mountains.
Sequel: *On the Far Side of the Mountain*

☐ *Julie of the Wolves*
by Jean Craighead George
1973 Newbery Medal

While running away from home and an unwanted marriage, a 13-year-old Eskimo girl becomes lost on the North Slope of Alaska and is befriended by a wolf pack.

☐ *Hatchet*
by Gary Paulsen
1988 Newbery Honor Book

After a plane crash, 13-year-old Brian spends 54 days in the wilderness, learning to survive with only the aid of a hatchet.

☐ *The Sign of the Beaver*
by Elizabeth George Speare
1984 Newbery Honor Book

Left alone to guard the family's wilderness home in 18th-century Maine, a boy is hard-pressed to survive until local Indians teach him their skills.

☐ *Danny, the Champion of the World*
by Roald Dahl

Danny describes his relationship with his father, a poacher, and the special adventure they share together.

☐ *Island of the Blue Dolphins*
by Scott O'Dell
1961 Newbery Medal

Records the courage and self-reliance of an Indian girl who lived alone for 18 years on an isolated island off the California coast when her tribe emigrated and she was left behind.

Sad Stories About Pets
Where the Red Fern Grows

☐ *Old Yeller*
by Fred Gipson
1957 Newbery Honor Book

In the late 1860s, a big yellow dog and a 14-year-old boy form a close, loving relationship.

☐ *Sounder*
by William H. Armstrong
1970 Newbery Medal

When his sharecropper father is jailed for stealing food for his family, a young black boy grows in courage and understanding with the help of the dog Sounder and learns to read and write.
Sequel: *Sourland*

☐ *J. T.*
by Jane Wagner

J. T. discovers there is more satisfaction in caring for an injured cat than in listening to a stolen transistor radio.

☐ *A Day No Pigs Would Die*
by Robert Newton Peck

To a 13-year-old farm boy whose father slaughters pigs for a living, maturity comes early as he learns to do what's got to be done.

☐ *The Yearling*
by Marjorie Kinnan Rawlings

A young boy living in the Florida backwoods is forced to decide the fate of a fawn he has lovingly raised as a pet.

Words by Heart

Ouida Sebestyen

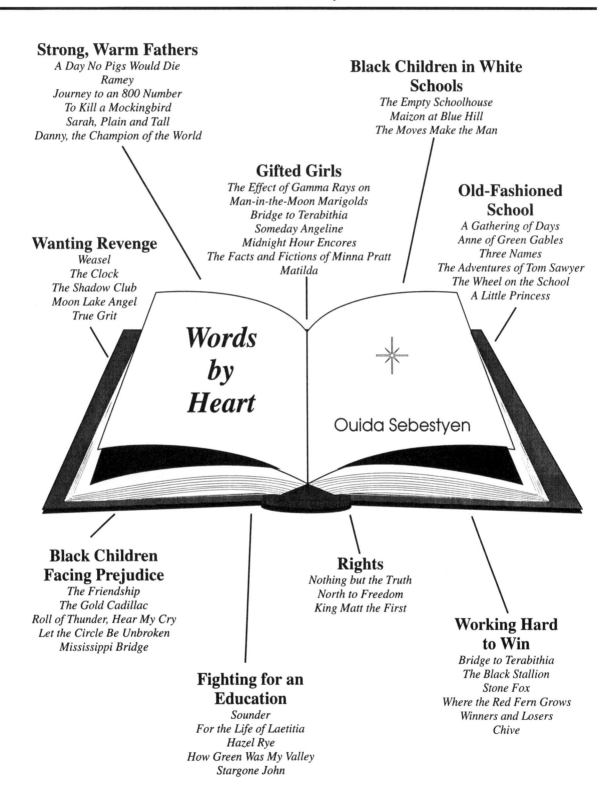

Strong, Warm Fathers
A Day No Pigs Would Die
Ramey
Journey to an 800 Number
To Kill a Mockingbird
Sarah, Plain and Tall
Danny, the Champion of the World

Black Children in White Schools
The Empty Schoolhouse
Maizon at Blue Hill
The Moves Make the Man

Gifted Girls
The Effect of Gamma Rays on Man-in-the-Moon Marigolds
Bridge to Terabithia
Someday Angeline
Midnight Hour Encores
The Facts and Fictions of Minna Pratt
Matilda

Old-Fashioned School
A Gathering of Days
Anne of Green Gables
Three Names
The Adventures of Tom Sawyer
The Wheel on the School
A Little Princess

Wanting Revenge
Weasel
The Clock
The Shadow Club
Moon Lake Angel
True Grit

Words by Heart

Ouida Sebestyen

Black Children Facing Prejudice
The Friendship
The Gold Cadillac
Roll of Thunder, Hear My Cry
Let the Circle Be Unbroken
Mississippi Bridge

Rights
Nothing but the Truth
North to Freedom
King Matt the First

Working Hard to Win
Bridge to Terabithia
The Black Stallion
Stone Fox
Where the Red Fern Grows
Winners and Losers
Chive

Fighting for an Education
Sounder
For the Life of Laetitia
Hazel Rye
How Green Was My Valley
Stargone John

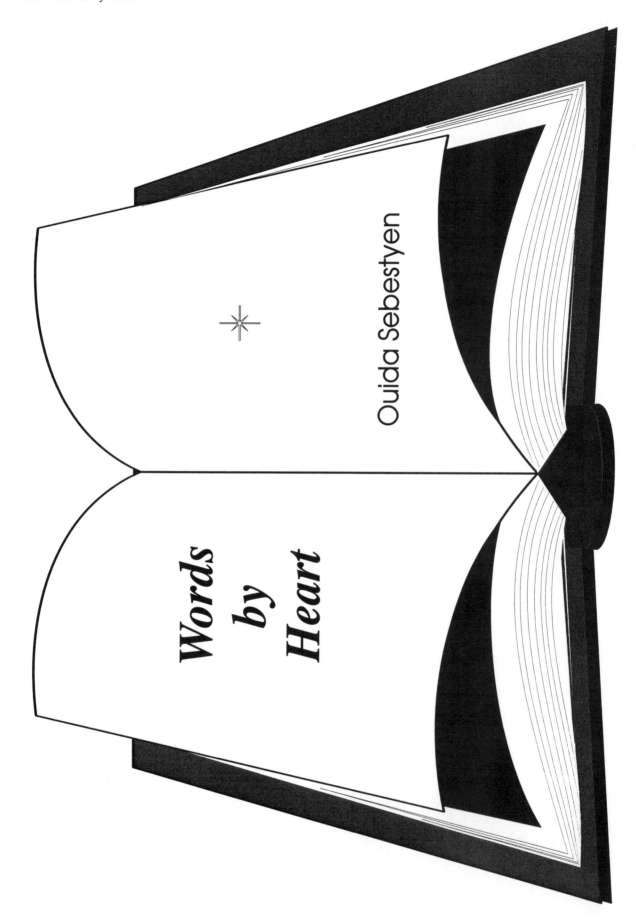

Words
by
Heart

Ouida Sebestyen

Working Hard to Win

Bridge to Terabithia

The Black Stallion

Stone Fox

Where the Red Fern Grows

Winners and Losers

Chive

Strong, Warm Fathers

A Day No Pigs Would Die

Ramey

Journey to an 800 Number

To Kill a Mockingbird

Sarah, Plain and Tall

Danny, the Champion of the World

Black Children in White Schools

The Empty Schoolhouse

Maizon at Blue Hill

The Moves Make the Man

Rights

Nothing but the Truth

North to Freedom

King Matt the First

Black Children Facing Prejudice

The Friendship

The Gold Cadillac

Roll of Thunder, Hear My Cry

Let the Circle Be Unbroken

Mississippi Bridge

Fighting for an Education

Sounder

For the Life of Laetitia

Hazel Rye

How Green Was My Valley

Stargone John

Old-Fashioned School

A Gathering of Days

Anne of Green Gables

Three Names

The Adventures of Tom Sawyer

The Wheel on the School

A Little Princess

Wanting Revenge

Weasel

The Clock

The Shadow Club

Moon Lake Angel

True Grit

Gifted Girls

The Effect of Gamma Rays on Man-in-the-Moon Marigolds

Bridge to Terabithia

Someday Angeline

Midnight Hour Encores

The Facts and Fictions of Minna Pratt

Matilda

Working Hard to Win
Words by Heart

Bridge to Terabithia
by Katherine Paterson
1978 Newbery Medal

The life of a 10-year-old boy in rural Virginia expands when he becomes friends with a newcomer.

The Black Stallion
by Walter Farley

A boy is pulled to a desert island by a wild black stallion he has freed during a shipwreck at sea, then is rescued by a southbound freighter. The boy befriends the horse, trains him by night, and rides him in a match race.
Many sequels

Stone Fox
by John R. Gardiner

Little Willie hopes to pay the back taxes on his grandfather's farm with the purse from a dogsled race he enters.

Where the Red Fern Grows
by Wilson Rawls

The adventures of a 10-year-old boy and the two dogs he bought with money he had earned.

Winners and Losers
by Stephen Hoffius

When a heart condition threatens to curtail his friend Daryl's track career, Curt finds himself taking Daryl's place as lead contender for the conference championship and as the new obsession of Daryl's driven father.

Chive
by Shelley A. Barre

Eleven-year-old Chive, homeless because his parents have lost their farm and are looking for work in the city, strikes up an unusual friendship with 11-year-old Terry and competes with him in a skateboard competition.

Strong, Warm Fathers
Words by Heart

A Day No Pigs Would Die
by Robert Newton Peck

To a 13-year-old Vermont farm boy whose father slaughters pigs for a living, maturity comes early as he learns to do what's got to be done, especially regarding his pet pig, who cannot produce a litter.

Ramey
by Jack Farris

A boy grows up with his father, a backwoods preacher.

Journey to an 800 Number
by E. L. Konigsburg

Bo learns about kindness, love, loyalty, appearances, and pretense from the unusual characters he meets when he is sent to live with his father after his mother decides to remarry.

To Kill a Mockingbird
by Harper Lee

Eight-year-old Scout and her brother are thrust into an adult world of racial bigotry and hatred when their father chooses to defend a black man charged with raping a white girl.

Sarah, Plain and Tall
by Patricia MacLachlan
1986 Newbery Medal

When their father invites a mail-order bride to come live with them, Caleb and Anna are captivated by their new mother and hope that she will stay.

Danny, the Champion of the World
by Roald Dahl

Danny describes his relationship with his father, a poacher, and the special adventure they share together.

Black Children in White Schools
Words by Heart

The Empty Schoolhouse
by Natalie Savage Carlson

Older sister Emma tells the story of the year when Lullah goes to school with the white children.

Maizon at Blue Hill
by Jacqueline Woodson

After winning a scholarship to an academically challenging boarding school, Maizon finds herself one of only five blacks there and wonders if she will ever fit in.
Sequel to *Last Summer with Maizon*

The Moves Make the Man
by Bruce Brooks
1985 Newbery Honor Book

A black boy and an emotionally troubled white boy in North Carolina form a precarious friendship.

Rights
Words by Heart

Nothing but the Truth
by Avi
1992 Newbery Honor Book

A ninth-grader's suspension for singing "The Star Spangled Banner" during homeroom becomes a national news story.

North to Freedom
by Anne Holm

Having escaped from an Eastern European concentration camp where he has spent his life, a 12-year-old boy struggles to cope with an entirely strange world as he flees northward to freedom in Denmark.

King Matt the First
by Janusz Korczak

A child king introduces reforms to give children the same rights as adults.

Black Children Facing Prejudice
Words by Heart

The Friendship
by Mildred Taylor

Four children witness a confrontation between an elderly black man and a white storekeeper in rural Mississippi in the 1930s.

The Gold Cadillac
by Mildred Taylor

Two black girls living in the North are proud of their family's beautiful new Cadillac until they take it on a visit to the South and encounter racial prejudice for the first time.

Roll of Thunder, Hear My Cry
by Mildred Taylor
1977 Newbery Medal

A black family living in the South during the 1930s is faced with prejudice and discrimination that their children don't understand.

Let the Circle Be Unbroken
by Mildred Taylor

Four black children growing up in rural Mississippi during the Depression experience racial antagonism and hard times, but learn from their parents the pride and self-respect they need to survive.

Mississippi Bridge
by Mildred Taylor

During a heavy rainstorm in 1930s rural Mississippi, a 10-year-old white boy sees a bus driver order all the black passengers off a crowded bus to make room for late-arriving white passengers and then sees the bus set off across a bridge over the raging Rosa Lee Creek.

Fighting for an Education
Words by Heart

Sounder
by William H. Armstrong
1970 Newbery Medal

When his sharecropper father is jailed for stealing food for his family, a young black boy grows in courage and understanding with the help of the dog Sounder and learns to read and write.

Sequel: *Sourland*

For the Life of Laetitia
by Merle Hodge

As the first in her family to go to secondary school, 12-year-old Lacey struggles with a variety of problems, including a cruel teacher and a difficult home life with her father and stepmother.

Hazel Rye
by Vera and Bill Cleaver

An 11-year-old girl with no appreciation for land and growing things finds her values beginning to change when she agrees to let an impoverished family live in a small house she owns, in exchange for working in the surrounding orange grove.

How Green Was My Valley
by Richard Llewellyn

A boy faces hardship growing up in a Welsh mining town.

Stargone John
by Ellen Kindt McKenzie

Six-year-old John, emotionally withdrawn and resistant to traditional teaching methods, experiences ridicule and punishment at his one-room schoolhouse, until an old retired teacher reaches out from her blindness to share with him the world of reading and writing.

Old-Fashioned School
Words by Heart

A Gathering of Days
by Joan W. Blos
1980 Newbery Medal

The journal of a 14-year-old girl records daily events in her small town, her father's remarriage, and the death of her best friend.

Anne of Green Gables
by L. M. Montgomery

Anne, an 11-year-old orphan, is sent by mistake to live with a lonely, middle-aged brother and sister on a Prince Edward Island farm and proceeds to make an indelible impression on everyone around her.
Many sequels

Three Names
by Patricia MacLachlan

Great-grandfather reminisces about going to school on the prairie with his dog Three Names.

The Adventures of Tom Sawyer
by Mark Twain

The adventures of a mischievous boy growing up in a Mississippi River town in the early 19th century, who impresses his friends and horrifies adults by associating with the son of the town drunk, attending his own funeral, witnessing a murder, and getting lost in a cave.

The Wheel on the School
by Meindert DeJong
1955 Newbery Medal

The children in a small Dutch town try to bring the storks back to nest on their roofs.

A Little Princess
by Frances Hodgson Burnett

Sara Crewe, a pupil at Miss Minchin's London school, is left in poverty when her father dies.

Wanting Revenge
Words by Heart

Weasel
by Cynthia DeFelice

Alone in the frontier wilderness in the winter of 1839 while his father is recovering from an injury, 11-year-old Nathan runs afoul of the renegade killer known as Weasel and makes a surprising discovery about the concept of revenge.

The Clock
by James Lincoln Collier and Christopher Collier

In 1810 in Connecticut, trapped in a grueling job in the local textile mill to help pay her father's debts, 15-year-old Annie becomes the victim of the cruel overseer and plots revenge against him.

The Shadow Club
by Neal Shusterman

A high school boy and his friends decide to form a club of second-bests and play anonymous tricks on each other's archrivals, but when the harmless pranks become life-threatening, no one in the club will admit responsibility.

Moon Lake Angel
by Vera and Bill Cleaver

Kitty, whose mother does not want to deal with a child, stays with Aunt Petal and eventually learns to accept her mother's weaknesses.

True Grit
by Charles Portis

Fourteen-year-old Mattie Ross convinces one-eyed Marshall Rooster Cogburn to help her capture the gang of outlaws who murdered her father.

Gifted Girls
Words by Heart

☐ *The Effect of Gamma Rays on Man-in-the-Moon Marigolds*
by Paul Zindel

A two-act play depicting an embittered mother who vents her frustrations upon her two daughters.

☐ *Bridge to Terabithia*
by Katherine Paterson

1978 Newbery Medal

The life of a 10-year-old boy in rural Virginia expands when he becomes friends with a newcomer who subsequently meets an untimely death trying to reach their hideaway, Terabithia, during a storm.

☐ *Someday Angeline*
by Louis Sachar

As an eight-year-old genius in the sixth grade, Angeline is not too popular, but she tries to adjust to being different.

☐ *Midnight Hour Encores*
by Bruce Brooks

A 16-year-old cellist and musical prodigy travels cross-country with her father, a product of the 1960s, to meet her mother, who abandoned her as a baby.

☐ *The Facts and Fictions of Minna Pratt*
by Patricia MacLachlan

An 11-year-old cellist learns about life from her eccentric family, her first boyfriend, and Mozart.

☐ *Matilda*
by Roald Dahl

Matilda applies her untapped mental powers to rid the school of the evil, child-hating headmistress, Miss Trunchbull, and to restore her nice teacher, Miss Honey, to financial security.

Author Index

Note: page numbers refer to bookmarks.

Title Index

Note: page numbers in *italic* refer to titles in the center of a book web. Page numbers in **bold** refer to titles found on book webs. All other page numbers refer to titles found on bookmarks.

Topic Index

Note: page numbers refer to book webs.

028.1   Berman, Matt.
BER
         What else should I
         read?

                              30417
$24.50   05/18/1998

DATE			